Dr Jessica Taylor is a working-class feminist, *Sunday Times* bestselling author and chartered psychologist with a PhD in Forensic Psychology from University of Birmingham. She is the founder and CEO of VictimFocus, an organisation which works internationally to change, challenge and influence the way women and girls are portrayed and treated by professionals. In 2019, she was awarded a Fellowship of Royal Society of Arts for her contribution to feminism and psychology.

T0385394

By the same author

Books

Why Women Are Blamed For Everything: Exposing the Culture of Victim-Blaming (2020)

Woman in Progress: The Reflective Journal for Women and Girls Subjected to Abuse and Trauma (2020)

The Reflective Journal for Researchers and Academics (2020)

The Reflective Journal for Practitioners Working in Trauma and Abuse (2019)

The Little Orange Book: Learning About Abuse From the Voice of a Child (2018, with C. Paterson-Young)

Reports

Portrayals and Prevention Campaigns: Sexual Violence in the Media (Taylor, J., VictimFocus, 2020)

Critical perspectives of child sexual exploitation practice and approaches (Eaton, J., VictimFocus, 2019)

'Logically, I know I am not to blame, but I still feel to blame': Exploring and measuring victim blaming and self-blame of women subjected to sexual violence and abuse (Eaton, J., University of Birmingham, 2019)

The Human Rights of Girls Subjected to Child Sexual Exploitation in the UK (Eaton, J., VictimFocus, 2019)

After CSE Films: Supporting children and families without traumatic imagery (Eaton, J., VictimFocus, 2019)

Sexual Exploitation and Mental Health, Research in Practice for Adults (Eaton, J., Dartington Press, 2018)

Can I tell you what it feels like? Exploring the harm caused by CSE films (Eaton, J., VictimFocus, 2018)

Working effectively to address child sexual exploitation: An evidence scope, Research in Practice (Eaton, J. & Holmes, D., Dartington Press, 2017)

SEXY BUT PSYCHO

*How the Patriarchy Uses Women's
Trauma Against Them*

DR JESSICA TAYLOR

CONSTABLE

CONSTABLE

First published in hardback in Great Britain in 2022 by Constable
This paperback edition published in 2023 by Constable

3 5 7 9 10 8 6 4

Copyright © VictimFocus and Dr Jessica Taylor, 2022
Diagrams by Liane Payne

The moral right of the author has been asserted.

A CIP catalogue record for this book
is available from the British Library.

ISBN: 978-1-47213-551-3

Typeset in Sabon by Hewer Text UK Ltd, Edinburgh
Printed and bound in Great Britain by Clays Ltd, Elcograf, S.p.A.

Papers used by Constable are from well-managed
forests and other responsible sources.

Constable
An imprint of
Little, Brown Book Group
Carmelite House
50 Victoria Embankment
London EC4Y 0DZ

The authorised representative
in the EEA is
Hachette Ireland
8 Castlecourt Centre
Dublin 15, D15 XTP3, Ireland
(email: info@hbgi.ie)

An Hachette UK Company
www.hachette.co.uk

www.littlebrown.co.uk

For Jaimi, the woman who has encouraged me, loved me, and held my hand through everything this book threw at me.

This book is dedicated to the thousands of women and girls who have messaged me, written to me, called me, and met with me over the past twelve years to tell me of their experiences of being labelled, discriminated against, and diagnosed with psychiatric disorders. Every single woman or girl was abused or harmed by someone or something, and yet, they were told that their trauma and distress was part of a mental illness that needed to be treated or cured.

I am exceptionally privileged to have learned so much from so many of you; your experiences have shaped my priorities and my passion going forward. I will not stand down, or stand aside, whilst I know that so many of you are still being told that there is something wrong with you.

Thank you for trusting me with your lives, your stories, your innermost thoughts, and your fears.

I hope this book goes some way to challenging and changing the way women and girls are treated and portrayed.

Contents

With thanks and utmost respect to the women who I have written about in this book, who have lost their lives, been pathologised, discriminated against, sectioned, and medicated for being women

Anushka

Valerie

Megan

Brianna

Natalie

Diana

Naomi

Hannah

Jade

Helen

Alice

Danielle

Rachel

Noa Pothoven

Lucy Dawson

Aurelia Brouwers

Maya

Keira

Nicky

Zoe

Emilia

Eleanor Riese

Britney Spears

Demi Lovato

Lindsay Lohan

Miley Cyrus

Ariana Grande

Selena Gomez

Amy Winehouse

Whitney Houston

Kate Spade

Carrie Fisher

Anna Nicole Smith

Peaches Geldof

Bobbi Kristina Brown

Tina Turner

With thanks and respect to the professionals who spoke to me on and off the record about the systemic pathologisation of women and girls

Rose

Lauren

Nora

Shona

Dr Alexis Palfreyman

Selina

Thalia

Tom

Keir

Masuma

Leah

Claire

Kieran Sturgess

Rooshan Alam

Marianne

Penny

Maryam

Bethan

Matthew Morris

Kellie Anne Ziemba

Emma Mitchell

Note from the author: All names have been changed except where I explicitly state otherwise.

Foreword

Psychiatry is the patriarchy with a prescription pad, and a pen full of ink.

Mark my words, there are only a handful of people on this earth who truly understand psychiatry, psychology and mental health to be what they really are, tools of female oppression – despite there being millions of women and girls impacted by their power of pathologisation.

By the end of this book, I will have changed the way you see women and girls' mental health forever.

*   *   *

This book has been burning away inside my brain for years.

Getting it all out, writing it down, and sharing it with the world is a mixture of relief and fear.

Relief because, I know as those years have passed, I've noticed more and more professionals have come to question the pathologisation and labelling of women and girls, which has been reassuring, to know that I'm not alone.

Fear, because alongside a growing critical movement, there is a grow-ing pro-disorder movement which has been deliberately constructed to encourage and support the diagnosis and pathologisation of women and girls. Every single time I've tried to speak out about it, I've been ridiculed, harassed, silenced and threatened. A woman questioning systemic pathologisation is like a red rag to a bull for so many people.

This book won't make for comfortable reading for anyone, though. But the question I am going to pose is:

Why are we deliberately pathologising, sectioning, labelling and medicating women and girls around the world?

It is now commonplace for women and girls who report rape, abuse, distress, or trauma of some sort to be quickly diagnosed with a range of psychiatric disorders, medicated and then discredited. This practice is not specific to the UK, and women from all over the world write to me every day to ask me for help. The emails are heartbreakingly similar – so similar that they could have been written by the same woman over and over again.

They are the types of stories and experiences I am going to share with you in this book, and explain how women and girls are being convinced that they are mentally ill – and why this is so intrinsically linked to objectification, sexualisation and misogyny.

I have several reasons for writing this book, and causing the debate that will no doubt follow. I have been both the woman who is pathologised, and the professional working with women who are pathologised. The only position I have never taken up is of the professional who pathologises women and girls. This is something I will be eternally grateful for, although I am unsure as to why I was never sucked into the misogynistic culture of my fields and my studies.

Throughout my education at school and university – and throughout my socialisation as a woman in the world – I have been sold the same lies and misinformation about women's mental health as everyone else has. But for some reason, I wasn't buying it.

Maybe it was because of an incident in 2009.

It was a sunny, early morning on the day two police officers knocked at my front door. They had woken me up with a phone call thirty minutes earlier, to tell me that they were coming over and needed to speak to me. I had been waiting months for this day.

The day we finally got the court date for the trial of the man who had raped, abused and terrified me for five years.

As a teenager, I had become pregnant by him twice. The first time had resulted in a miscarriage after he pushed me down a flight of stairs. The second time (only a couple of months later) resulted in me having a baby when I was seventeen years old. The case had been horrendous, and I had been ignored for months at a time. Every time I tried to get in touch with my police officer, he told me that they were just waiting for the trial date to be set. I found out later that he had written on my notes that I was a 'tattle tale'.

A 'tattle tale' for ringing the police when I was being beaten up, threatened and abused.

A 'tattle tale' on the day he kicked my front door in and said he was going to kill me.

A 'tattle tale' for ringing 999 as I lay on the floor with a dislocated shoulder and torn neck, frantically clinging on to my baby as I was thrown across a dining table.

I had been waiting for fourteen months for a trial date, and I was often treated like a nuisance by the officers in the case. Throughout those long and frightening months of waiting, I had been stalked, harassed, threatened, beaten up, my social media had been hacked and I lived in fear of my life every single day. I moved forty miles away from where I grew up, in an effort to stay safe and undetected. I had a one-year-old child from the rapist and I was trying to protect my child with everything I had as an eighteen-year-old woman, which wasn't much more than sheer determination.

The police officer in my case was stood at the door with a woman I had never seen before. I assumed it was good news and we were finally going to trial. They sat on the little faux leather two-seater and the male officer quickly said what he had come to say:

The case had been dropped. The bail conditions had been dropped.

At that time, they were two of the most terrifying things I had heard come out of someone's mouth for a long time. Not only had the entire case of thirteen charges been dropped, but they had removed all bail conditions that were barely protecting me as it was.

I, of course, burst into tears.

The officers then did something rather peculiar, and something that will stay with me for the rest of my life.

They reached into their bag and pulled out a leaflet on mental disorders and medication. A purple trifold leaflet about personality disorders and bipolar disorder. The woman whom I'd never met smiled pitifully at me, and started to explain gently to me that the police thought I was mentally ill, and would benefit from medication.

I was a feisty, inquisitive eighteen-year-old and I instantly challenged them on why and how they thought I was mentally ill, especially as one of them hadn't seen me for fourteen months, and the other hadn't seen me before in her whole life.

They explained that they felt I had become 'obsessed' with the trial and the case, and that I was ringing the police too often to report harassment and death threats from the perpetrator. They said that they had apparently met the perpetrator every month as part of his bail conditions and he 'seemed a good guy', and that it was clearly me with the issues.

I told them that I had kept all the forty-seven text messages detailing the death threats, and that I had managed to record some voicemails he had left me. I told them about the men he had sent to my house to attack me, and the way I had hidden under the table with my baby when they came banging on all of the windows and doors to get in.

They suggested that maybe those things didn't happen, and I needed help. They wouldn't look at the text messages or listen to the voice-mails. They had lost interest in me, and had started to regard me as a mentally ill teenage girl.

It was one of those moments in life when you question whether you are awake, and whether any of this is really happening to you.

I had gone from desperately waiting for a trial date to being told that there would be no trial, and that instead, the police (whom I had met only two or three times) felt that I was mentally ill.

I stood up, still crying, and calmly told them to get out. I said no other words. I pointed at my front door, and glared at them both.

I never did go to a doctor, or get medication, or get a diagnosis. I threw the leaflet in the bin. I instead used music, I read books, I learned about abuse and trauma, I accessed anonymous counselling helplines and vital women's services. I wrote journals and poetry, and tried to process what had happened to me.

I consider myself exceptionally lucky not to have been dragged down a medical route with my trauma, and every time I get a letter or email from a woman who has been through this, I realise how easy it would have been for that to have happened to me, too.

I won't pretend that I didn't struggle to do all of that on my own. I did. I developed physiological responses to trauma which took me years to figure out. I had panic attacks that would cause me to collapse sometimes up to eight times per day. I was often in hospital. No one knew what was 'wrong' with me and I was often treated as some kind of attention seeker, or a hysterical woman who kept pretending to faint in the middle of Poundland, or whilst she was making ReadyBrek for her toddler.

It took me several years to understand that trauma presents itself physically, and not just psychologically. I was probably twenty-five years old by the time I had everything under control. The panic attacks were few and far between by then; I would have a few per year. The nightmares had stopped. I had read an enormous amount of literature on understanding my body and my brain.

I had been working in forensic services and women's services since I was nineteen years old and I had started to notice that my experience of being pathologised, ignored, minimised and reframed as mentally ill or exaggerating physical illnesses was very common indeed.

The first job I had was in magistrates' courts at nineteen, and every week, I watched women and girls give evidence in domestic abuse trials against men who assaulted, abused and controlled them. You could almost script the trials, sometimes. The questioning of the women and girls was always along the same lines. A lot of victim blaming and character assassination and then the final blow, comments or accusations about her mental health, sometimes with old medical records, counselling records or lists of medication.

I was present for the case of a sixteen-year-old girl who had been badly beaten up by a twenty-two-year-old man. He had broken into her house after they had split up. He pinned her to the floor and head-butted her eleven times in the face. This was not the first time he had beaten or raped her, but it was the first time that the girl had ever told anyone.

As she stood in the courtroom, being watched by him and his family, the defence barrister started talking about her 'history of mental illness'. She looked confused. I put my head in my hands.

Not this again.

The defence barrister asked the girl if she had ever had help from mental health services as a child. She hesitated, clearly not under-standing what a 'mental health service' was. The defence barrister proceeded to explain to her that they had evidence that she had accessed mental health services at twelve years old when her dad left. He said that she had developed an eating disorder and started to cut her arms and legs.

She stared at him, but agreed that this was true. He then used this to argue that his client was in fact innocent, because she probably head-butted a wall or caused all of the injuries to herself, as she 'clearly had mental health issues'.

Her jaw dropped. Her eyes filled up with tears. She turned bright red. She couldn't answer his questions.

I sat there, willing the magistrates to intervene. But nothing came.

Instead, the defence barrister continued to push her and upset her about her dad leaving, her eating habits and the self-harm. None of this had anything to do with what this man had done to her four years later.

I watched as a sixteen-year-old girl was painted as a mentally ill teenager who had caused significant injuries to her own head because four years ago, she had attended two sessions at CAMHS because of self-harm when her dad left.

It was clearly, and obviously, total bollocks. Everyone in that room knew it was bollocks.

And yet, I went on to see this process repeated hundreds of times, in hundreds of different cases. Like Groundhog Day.

She's unreliable. She self-harms. She's autistic. She's manipulative. She's bipolar. She's secretive. She's borderline. She's crazy. She's malicious. She's obsessive. She's promiscuous. She's delusional.

In some cases, there were no historical mental health records to use, so instead, defence teams sought to suggest or imply undiagnosed mental health issues or psychiatric diagnoses. In many cases, defence teams in criminal courts, or solicitors in family courts, requested psychiatric assessments of women and girls in order to discredit them.

No matter what field I worked in after that, the story was always the same. I worked in rape centres, counselling services, child trafficking services and victim services. Women and girls were being pathologised everywhere.

A new day, a new woman or girl was positioned as a crazy, jealous, psychotic, paranoid, delusional ex with a vendetta and a personality disorder.

It was soul-destroying. It still is.

Only this week, I spoke to a woman who was diagnosed with a delusional disorder because she reported to social care that her child keeps saying she is being sexually abused. Instead of taking the disclosures seriously, professionals have suggested that Mum is delusional and is making these disclosures up. The woman even recorded her four-year-old daughter talking about the sexual abuse, to prove that she wasn't delusional, but when she showed it to them, professionals changed their approach and instead told her that she could have coached her daughter to say those things, because she was delusional.

The issue with being perceived as delusional is that everything you do or say can be put down to delusions.

Say you were abused by your husband? Delusional. Report that your ex tried to break into the house last night? Imagining it. Compiled proof that you're being stalked online by a guy from uni? Obsessive. Reported your ex for rape? Malicious. Prove that your kid is saying that they have been sexually abused? Coached them.

Again, this is common. And I often read or hear these cases filled with the dread of knowing that they will have been real disclosures and that those girls will grow up one day and ask why no one protected them. They may even grow up to think that what was done to them was normal, or that their mothers made it all up.

Many years after my own incident of being pathologised in 2009 had passed, I was a successful twenty-seven-year-old researcher at a top university in the final year of my PhD. I felt a million miles away from my beginnings, and yet I was shoved right back into my 'hysterical woman' box when I tried to report harassment and bullying.

A man who disagreed with my academic work and feminist campaigning had become scarily obsessed with me online, and after reporting him to his employer and the police several times, emails started to be sent to my university department which sought to have me disciplined or even stopped from completing my PhD. I had a feeling that this was all connected, but no one would help me to join the dots. The emails became more serious and I was invited to meetings about my 'well-being'.

As a high-performing PhD student with an additional paid research position and lecturing duties, I didn't expect anyone to actually take the emails about me seriously, especially as they were clearly malicious, and I had a great relationship with everyone in my team. I wasn't worried.

However, in one meeting, I was introduced to a woman I had never met before, a clinical psychologist from my department. I was assured that it was just for a 'chat'. But I was quickly questioned about my mental health, my childhood and my background. I was instantly defensive and recognised what was happening – as it had happened when I was a teenager.

I only found out later that the emails being sent about me by strangers who disagreed with my work had suggested that I had an undiagnosed personality disorder, and required treatment. The academics and professionals involved had used my own childhood that they had read about on the internet to distance diagnose me as mentally ill, and then used my feminist work to 'prove' I was emotionally unstable.

Even as an academic and professional, one of the most impactful and damaging things other academics and professionals could do to me as a young woman was to reframe me as mentally ill and therefore too unstable to complete a PhD. No matter what I said, it was taken as evidence that they were right.

When I made formal complaints, I was labelled a 'conspiracy theorist' and laughed at. During the investigation, one male academic listened to me explain these experiences whilst not being able to conceal his laughter. He said to me, 'This is all very grand isn't it? This conspiracy theory that these academics are working together, to target you?'

Thankfully, after some serious investigative work and sheer determination, six months later I was vindicated when I won an appeal process for discrimination and bullying. I had used law and legislation that I had researched, to learn about accessing data and emails about myself, and had used this to get access to the emails that academics and professionals were sending to each other about me. I presented the tribunal with over 110 pages of evidence, that I was right all along.

I was awarded damages and an official apology.

When I got the email to say that I had won, I burst into tears in a café.

I spent months reflecting on the power of calling a woman mentally ill. No one had any proof, and yet it had been taken so seriously. One day I was a capable PhD student and experienced professional and the next, I was framed as an unstable, unpredictable disordered young woman from a council estate who should be kicked off her doctoral programme for being too outspoken. One of the emails said that to allow a woman like me (I was repeatedly described as attention seeking, mentally ill and from a council estate) to become a psychologist would bring the entire discipline into disrepute.

It was a kick in the teeth and a rude wake-up call.

The simplest and quickest way to harm and silence women is to use psychiatry against them.

I had never really considered this before. Even I had laughed at the 'crazy ex-girlfriend' stereotype. Even I had believed the 'bunny boiler' stories of crazed women. Even I had used words like 'psycho' and 'crazy' and 'hysterical' and 'mental' about women.

As the years have pushed on, I've worked with thousands of women and girls – many of whom have been labelled, pathologised and told that they are mentally ill. I've worked hard to protect them from poor and oppressive practice, and to teach professionals about the ways psychiatry and mental health systems are being used to harm women and girls.

More widely (and especially in the media and in fashion), I've noticed a pattern which is moving us towards the glorification, sexualisation and sensationalisation of women being 'psycho'. Stand this against the backdrop of women and girls being objectified and dehumanised since birth, with entire industries marketing to them as if their only worth is to be sexy and desirable – and we have created a dangerous new trend in which women and girls are being seen as sexy, but psycho.

In some cases, women are even being encouraged to call themselves 'psychos' and take on the identity of the 'crazy ex'. There are thousands of blogs and videos on the internet talking about the way women are hot but crazy, beautiful but manipulative, sexy but psycho.

That's why I titled this book the way I did.

Sometimes it strikes me that we are saying to women and girls:

Look sexy. Be pretty. Act feminine. Be desirable. Be sexually available. Be fun. Be flirty. Be nice.

But do not speak. Do not have an opinion. Do not have ambition. Do not challenge norms. Do not talk about your traumas. Do not disclose abuse. Do not report wrongdoing.

Because if and when you do, you will be labelled as the crazy, psychotic lying witch you always were underneath the sex appeal.

You can either be sexy, or psycho.

Or sexy, but psycho.

But it would appear from historical records, academic research and real-life stories of women, that women and girls are, ultimately, 'psycho'. Especially when they disclose or report male violence.

It's almost as if women and girls who report abuse are seen as sex objects who deserve it and asked for it, and then instantly discredited as psychopathic or mentally ill when they talk about it. And then reframed as sexy, because they are psycho. And so the cycle continues.

Let me show you that this is no coincidence.

Introduction

One day in 2017, I opened my emails to find a message from a nineteen-year-old woman who wrote to me to ask for help.

Dear Jess

I am writing to you in case you can help me. I was trafficked and exploited when I was younger. My case was in the papers. When I was young, the workers referred me to a psychiatrist and I was given more and more drugs until I couldn't even get out of bed. I've worked really hard and had loads of therapy, but no one believes me that I'm getting better. I have an adult social worker now and she won't let me get my own flat or go to college. There's a course I really want to do but she said it wasn't a good idea. I applied anyway but she wrote to the college and told them not to accept me because of my mental illness. The college won't let me study there now and I don't know what she told them. I feel stuck like I'll never be allowed to get a job or study or have my own place to live. I'm stuck in a refuge and they are saying I'm not capable of living on my own because I have borderline personality disorder. When I tell them that I don't think I do, they just say I'm denying it and give me more prescriptions. What do I do? I want to go to college.

Danielle*

I remember having to reread the email several times. Here was an intelligent, articulate and determined young woman, who was being denied access to education because professionals believed that she was 'too mentally ill' to study at college or live on her own. Instead, they had kept her in a busy refuge for women and children escaping male violence, despite her own trauma being caused by male violence.

I spent some weeks talking to Danielle and exploring why the professionals around her were so obstructive. It appeared that she required very little support in her day-to-day life, and only saw her social worker once a month for around an hour. She only saw a psychiatrist to update medication and prescriptions. She was already living independently, and the staff at the refuge often counted on her to support new women and children arriving there. She told me that sometimes, it was chaotic and scary in the refuge, but professionals had no interest in helping her to leave. I learned that she had been given more and more sedatives and antipsychotics that were making her feel very unwell. When she complained about side effects, she was advised that they were a small price to pay for the medication which was merely 'managing' her personality disorders and mental illnesses. Disorders and illness, she was told, would be with her for life.

At this point, it is important that I make something clear about my views and conclusions about Danielle and her experiences.

In my opinion, Danielle was not mentally ill. She was traumatised by years of child sex trafficking and several criminal trials. Her trauma was natural and justified.

She was being medicated against her best interests, against her will and despite significant side effects. She was being denied access to safe housing and education. Her history of being subjected to male violence and her trauma was clearly being used to pathologise and label her as unstable. She saw no future for herself, and had no idea how to gain independence.

Danielle's experiences are not at all rare. As you read through this book, you will encounter many stories about women and girls who have been medicated, sectioned, discredited, abused, harmed, injured and controlled using psychiatric terms and mental health diagnoses that have been positioned as helpful and positive.

Before we get into some of the complex arguments and discussions in this book, it is important to explain my language, and define some key terms.

I have chosen in my writing, my broader work and in my personal life never to refer to women and girls as 'mentally ill' or 'disordered' or 'abnormal'. I also choose not to use broad terms such as 'survivors' or 'victims' when referring to women and girls who have been subjected to male violence, nor do I ever use the term 'experienced' when talking about abuse, violence and crime. These choices are deliberate and purposeful.

I do not believe that women and girls who begin to behave, think or feel differently after they have been subjected to male violence are ill, disordered, problematic or abnormal at all. Instead, I would argue that it is completely natural and normal to be distressed, traumatised and changed by these crimes against them.

Whilst many feminists use the term 'survivor', research conducted with women in the last ten years has consistently shown that they dislike the term as much as they dislike the term 'victim'. This is interesting, not only because 'survivor' suggests that the women have moved on, survived the abuse and trauma and have come out the other side, but it has a strong connection with the concepts discussed in this book of medicalisation, illness and 'cures'. Instead, women often tell us that when we call them a 'survivor', they feel that it must mean that the traumas no longer impact them; and when we call them a 'victim', they feel that it must mean that they will always feel this way.

I choose to position an offender in a sentence or description of abuse, rape and violence wherever I can. This means that I actively avoid the term 'experienced' and I choose not to say or write things like 'she experienced a rape' or 'she experienced domestic violence'. This is an important shift in language, because women and girls are not capable of 'experiencing' rape or violence unless someone subjects them to it. No woman or girl can accidentally or passively experience a rape, for example, there has to be a man who makes a choice to rape, and subject her to that act for his own gratification.

Finally, on this point of language, I have chosen to write this second book in the most accessible way possible. Where I can, I will define terms, arguments and expressions clearly and give examples of what I mean. I will use a numbered reference system which means you can check the references easily, without it breaking up the text.

Key terms

Medical model
The 'medical model' is shorthand for a theory of mental health which suggests that mental illnesses, diseases and disorders should be identified, treated and managed in the same way as physical injuries, illnesses, diseases and disorders. The medical model tends to assume that mental health issues are caused by biological and neurological issues in the brain. It is more heavily used in psychiatry, but is now prominent in psychology and some areas of psychotherapy too.

Social model
The 'social model' is shorthand for a theory of mental health which suggests that humans are impacted by their context, environment and experiences. Instead of suggesting that behaviours, feelings and thoughts are mental illnesses or disorders, the social model encourages us to look

at the factors surrounding the person to consider what might be causing their distress. The social model usually does not support psychiatric diagnosis, but can sometimes be used to argue that social factors are 'causing' mental illness. It is not commonly used in psychiatry. It is more common in psychology and psychotherapy.

Biopsychosocial model

The 'biopsychosocial model' is an interdisciplinary approach to understanding mental health by looking at the way biological factors in the medical model, socio-environmental factors in the social model and other psychological factors intersect.

Psychiatry, psychology and psychotherapy

These three terms are often mixed up, or used as synonyms, despite being three different areas of study and practice.

Psychiatrists are qualified medical doctors who specialise in psychiatry, defined broadly as 'the medical speciality dedicated to the diagnoses, prevention and treatment of mental disorders in humans'. They can diagnose and prescribe medication and treatments.

Psychologists are doctors in their fields (usually by PhD or professional doctorates such as a Doctorate in Clinical or Forensic Psychology). Psychologists do a broad range of jobs in many different settings. In some cases, they can diagnose mental health issues and disorders, but they cannot prescribe medication. They work across a varied spectrum of approaches, theories and methods which range from roles that are very similar to psychiatry, right through to psychological approaches which reject psychiatric theories and treatments.

Psychotherapists are specially trained talking therapists and counsellors who provide a varied range of therapies and approaches to talking about distress and life experiences. They cannot and should not diagnose, suggest or work towards diagnosis. They cannot prescribe medication.

It is most important to note that psychiatry has the largest influence over the other two disciplines. Psychology has slowly morphed more and more into medicalisation and diagnosis, with psychology students regularly being taught modules on psychopathology, mental disorders, 'abnormal psychology', personality disorders and diagnostic psychometrics. Having taught at undergraduate, masters and doctoral level in this field, I am always surprised how accepted the medical model is by student psychologists who have seemingly never been taught or have never considered critical or opposing perspectives of mental health, illness and disorder. For some students, the first time they have ever engaged in critical materials or teaching around mental health has been at doctoral-level study.

Psychotherapy and counselling practice generally resisted the medical model, in favour of humanistic and integrative approaches to human distress. However, current training courses and education for counsellors and psychotherapists now include psychiatric concepts, diagnosis and identifying disorders. For example, it is now common for psychotherapists and counsellors to be offered courses such as 'Managing borderline patients', which not only frames counsellors and psychotherapists as 'managing' difficult people, but positions their clients as 'patients' of some sort of medical disorder.

Mental illness and mental health

The evolving language around mental health is an interesting topic that I will discuss in depth throughout this book. However, as a brief introduction, the best way to understand it is as a slow-moving process (below).

Possessed/cursed/evil/demonic

|

Insane/crazy/mad/sick

|

Mental illness

|

Mental disorder

|

Mental health issues

|

Mental health

As can be seen from the diagram above, the language around mental illness has become more and more professional, and less and less offensive.

However, to focus specifically on the language around mental illness and mental health, it is important to note that all professional and academic literature and guidance (such as the Diagnostic and Statistical Manual of Mental Disorders and the International Classification of Diseases) still consider all mental health issues to be illnesses, disorders and diseases. Despite public campaigns and communications moving the language towards mental 'health' and deliberately cutting out the words 'illness', 'disorder' or 'problem' so it is not perceived as offensive, this change in language is only skin deep. Underneath the public campaigns about ending stigma is an entire field which works on the belief that humans who do not behave, think or feel in a certain way have some sort of disorder or syndrome which needs to be treated or managed. 'Ending stigma' is just lip service in a system which relies on stigmatising people and then medicating them. Stigma is central. Stigma is what keeps the whole system alive. Changing the language from 'mental illness' to 'mental health' was therefore nothing more than a marketing strategy. The theories and practices have barely changed, and millions of people are still being diagnosed with, and treated for, mental disorders.

At the beginning of the diagram, you can see that the origins of the language around mental illness came from religious beliefs. This is something to keep in mind throughout the reading of this book, as these roots have never truly been addressed or resolved. People of all ages who didn't conform, or behaved in a way that was deemed strange, would be accused of being possessed, cursed or evil. Looking back now, this would have included people with undiscovered or misunderstood illnesses, injuries, diseases, difficulties, disabilities and differences. When we look at it from our modern perspective, we can assume therefore that it would be fairly easy to be accused of possession or evil.

The church remained solidly in control of 'mental illness' for centuries, until scientists and physicians started to have more influence. Whilst this could have been positive, even their perspectives and theories were influenced by magic, religion, good and evil. The church was heavily involved in the foundation of asylums and hospitals, and language started to move towards these differences being illnesses, sickness of the mind, insanity and madness. Most of these terms are still prevalent today. Whilst people might call someone 'sick' or 'sick in the head' as an offensive term these days, we never really moved away from the conceptualisation of 'illness' and 'disease' when talking about mental health. In fact, the concept of mental illness has endured for decades.

As the diagram moves on, you can see that we started to reframe mental illness as mental disorders, which is, again, another term that has stuck with us, and is still used in modern psychology, psychiatry and mental health services. You might be surprised to hear that, as we talk of disorders of the mind now without even realising that we are doing it. We rarely even use the word 'disorder' anymore.

What is interesting about this process in the diagram is that the next two terms – 'mental health issues' and then 'mental health' – have been used widely in public campaigns to obscure the medical terms of 'disorder' and 'illness'.

Well-meaning professionals and activists talk about how we should change our language from focusing on 'mental illness' to 'mental health', as if that would be enough to cause the paradigm change we need to stop pathologising and stigmatising people who behave or think differently to ourselves. The reality is less progressive – that whilst the public have been encouraged to call it 'mental health', the medical and support professions have never moved from seeing people as disordered, problematic, chaotic people with mental illnesses.

A disorder is defined as a 'state of confusion', and medically, a disorder is defined as 'a condition characterised by lack of normal functioning of physical or mental processes'.

Whilst I do not support or use this term in my own work, theory or practice, it is unfortunately the term for what psychiatry and psychology currently consider to be 'abnormalities' or 'syndromes' in behaviour, thought and emotion. The 'D' in many mental health issues stands for disorder, for example, personality disorder (PD), eating disorder (ED), post-traumatic stress disorder (PTSD), generalised anxiety disorder (GAD), bipolar disorder (BD) and so on. This is important to note, as whilst we are encouraged to believe that mental health is an accepted and normal issue in today's society, these issues are still being classified and named as psychiatric disorders of abnormal functioning.

They cannot possibly be simultaneously normal, natural and accepted whilst also being categorised as disorders and mental illnesses of the mind which require treatment and supervision.

DSM (Diagnostic and Statistical Manual of Mental Disorders)

The DSM is the official manual for professionals to identify and diagnose people with mental disorders (as suggested in the title). It was originally developed and published in 1952. The DSM is released every ten to fifteen years. The fifth manual (entitled DSM-V) was published in 2013, and so the next DSM (DSM-VI) will be published between 2023 and 2028. The DSM plays a central role in classifying, categorising and diagnosing people with mental disorders, and is often referred to as the 'Bible' of mental health.

Trauma-informed approaches

An approach to understanding mental distress and mental health which considers that a change in behaviour, thought or emotion arises from past or current trauma. Within this context, trauma can be variable and dynamic. Whilst trauma used to be considered to be a one-off, life-threatening event, it is now accepted to encompass any event or set of events that cause deep distress, disturbance, fear, harm or injury.

Deficit-based approaches

An approach to social issues, mental health, abuse and oppression which uses the negative events, experiences and so-called 'deficits' in a person's life to predict their risk level, future or present behaviours, thoughts or circumstances. This is an approach that I strongly oppose, and prefer to teach others not to use the negative events in someone's life to judge, assess or predict their future.

Strength-based approaches

The opposite to deficit-based approaches, the strength-based way of working in social issues, mental health, abuse and oppression focuses on the strengths, skills, talents and wisdom of the person instead of defining them by their 'deficits'. There is a current push towards strength-based approaches in many fields including social care, policing and mental health practice.

Patriarchy

Systems (both private and public) that are controlled and led by men, including social control, politics, authority, norms, narratives and privilege. Up to the present day, the world has always been a patriarchy, as have most institutions including religion, education, law, politics, entertainment, media, finance and so on.

Misogyny

The systemic hatred, contempt and oppression of females. Misogyny has been demonstrated to be a global issue, and has been for millennia.

Pathologisation

To characterise a behaviour, thought or feeling as medically or psychologically abnormal. This includes the practice of seeing those behaviours or thoughts as medical symptoms as an indicator of a disease or disorder of the mind.

This book is an important opportunity to make several key arguments about the way women and girls are sexualised, objectified and pathologised.

The first argument I will make is that women and girls have been systematically and deliberately pathologised, medicated, sectioned and isolated from society for centuries; and that this is still influencing mental health practice to this day.

The second argument I will make is that our most powerful institutions including education, media, criminal justice, civil law and healthcare provision contribute to, or support pathologisation and regularly spread misinformation and misogyny about the mental lives of women and girls.

The third argument I will make is that pathologisation is another tool of the patriarchy and is heavily entwined with gender role stereotypes, objectification, sexualisation and dehumanisation of women and girls in order to discredit and minimise the disclosures, experiences and ideas of women.

The fourth argument I will make is that feminism is not compatible with psychiatry, and to understand trauma-informed approaches and social models of mental health is to understand that narratives, diagnoses and treatments arising from psychiatry are not supportive of women's rights or women's liberation.

I am acutely aware that the arguments I will present in this book will be challenging, controversial and new to many readers. I know that whenever I discuss these topics publicly, they invoke mixed responses and feelings in thousands of people. There is good reason for this, of course. Narratives, theories and beliefs about mental health are central to the lives of many. National statistics suggest that one in four people in the UK will experience a 'mental health disorder' each year (Mind, 2021) and one in five people in the UK are diagnosed with depression or anxiety.

I am also aware that people have come to expect a 'balanced' argument or for authors like me to be 'even-handed'. 'Objective', even. As other critical authors who have come before me have quite rightly said, this topic does not need more objectivity, more 'even-handedness' and more books written as if the mental health system is six of one and half a dozen of the other. John Read and Jacqui Dillon argued in 2014 that what we need more of is not writing that is 'balanced' about psychiatry and mental health, but writing that seeks to balance out the centuries of harmful and abusive practices of psychiatry and mental health. Therefore, *Sexy but Psycho* is written from that perspective. I seek to present counterarguments, real stories and challenging evidence about psychiatry to show that it has always been openly misogynistic, and that society has always sought to position women as sex objects who are psychotic, inferior, dangerous and unreliable.

CHAPTER 1

Mental illness: the myths we live by

Dear Dr Jess

I am really sorry to bother you. Are you saying that mental health issues are not a chemical imbalance in the brain? When I gave birth to my daughter, my husband left me and I was diagnosed with postnatal depression. Professionals told me to get antidepressants and told me that my depression was caused by an imbalance in my brain that the medication would rebalance. I never did get them from the chemist, and instead I went to support groups and had therapy to talk about everything – even stuff I didn't know was affecting me from years before he left me. I thought that because I never took the medication, I must still have a chemical imbalance in my brain, and it was still there all these years later. Is this not the case? It never did make sense to me.

Regards

Rachel*

Every day, I wake up to new emails from women around the world. What strikes me about these emails is how many women are slowly coming to their own awakening that their instincts were right all along, and that their psychiatric diagnoses and years of labelling were harmful and wrong. Sometimes, they start to question the myths they have believed, and the misinformation they were given when they were told that they would need medication for the rest of their lives, or that there was a chemical imbalance in their brain that needed lifelong management.

Letters and emails from women like Rachel are often sent to me in the midst of a transformative lightbulb moment. The moment when the woman questions the very foundations of the theory and logic behind her diagnosis and treatment. And as Rachel dissects her own understanding here, so too will this chapter, which explores the most common mental illness myths.

What is mental illness?

Mental illness, mental disorder, mental health issue or the catch-all, shiny, positive broadchurch term 'mental health' – there are lots of names for what is generally considered to be some sort of problematic, distressing or non-conforming way of thinking, behaving or feeling. Mental illness has been examined, theorised and studied for centuries and yet we have made little progress.

Child psychiatrist Dr Sami Timimi argued in his book *Insane Medicine* in 2021 that when compared to medicine, psychiatry has made virtually no progress in the last hundred years. Whilst medicine has developed an incredible understanding and body of advancements such as antibiotics, tissue cultures, DNA, cancer diagnosis, keyhole surgery, MRI machines, ultrasound scanning, dialysis, the defibrillator, heart transplants and bionic limbs – psychiatry has yet to even settle on a definition of mental health, mental illness, diagnosis and treatment, or prove how most of their medicines work in the brain.

We still don't agree on what causes these differences in behaviour, thinking and feeling. We don't know how best to help people. We don't know as much about the brain as we often claim. We don't yet know what consciousness is, how thought arises in the brain, how to test for or monitor mental illnesses – or whether they even exist.

This might be the first time you have ever read something which suggests that we don't know a great deal about the causes of mental illness, and that what we have instead is a range of contested theories and hypotheses. There is little consensus, and there is a lot of misinformation and myth.

To enable us to discuss these myths, it is first important to understand the current arguments, central theories and proposed explanations for mental illness.

What are the arguments surrounding mental illness?

In the present day, the key questions surrounding mental illness appear to be:

- ◆ Does mental illness really exist as an illness, disease or disorder of the brain, or is it a change in behaviours, thoughts and feelings due to circumstances, experiences or environmental factors impacting the person?
- ◆ If mental illness does exist as an illness or disorder, where does it originate from? Is it chemical, structural, genetic, or caused by something else inside the brain or body?
- ◆ If mental illness does exist and it is caused by something inside the brain or body, how do we diagnose it and how do we treat it? If it doesn't exist and it isn't caused by something inside the body or brain, are our diagnoses useless and are the treatments unethical?
- ◆ How do power structures, cultures, stereotypes, social norms, gender roles, belief systems, oppression and religion influence the concepts of mental illness – and can there ever

be an objective, scientific way of categorising people as 'mentally well' and 'mentally ill', without these influences?

It would be completely understandable for anyone to think that we already knew the answers to these questions; especially considering how aggressive the public campaigns and marketing of mental health (and mental health treatments) has been in the last decade. When we take things back to the drawing board, and suggest that we actually do not know the answers to many of these questions, it does cause discomfort and confusion.

The reality is blurrier than anyone would like to admit, and psychiatry is arguably more politics and social constructions than science. Most people believe that mental health issues, psychiatric disorders and personality disorders are scientific, rigorous, proven classifications of illnesses but are blissfully unaware of how unscientific the process of inventing and agreeing new disorders and treatments actually is.

In 1952, the 'bible of psychiatry' was first published – the DSM. The aim of the DSM was to provide a manual for doctors and psychiatrists to recognise and diagnose people with mental disorders. Whilst we don't use that term in public anymore, it is still in the title of the DSM to this day, and we must never lose sight of the fact that everything contained within the DSM is perceived to be a mental disorder (regardless of how many times we say 'mental health' instead).

The DSM is, and always has been decided by an elite group of middle-class white male psychiatrists who sit around a table and decide what is normal and what is abnormal. That's pretty much the entire process in one sentence. It is widely thought that this is a flawed, biased and political voting process whereby the psychiatrists often vote in and trade diagnoses with each other, 'You can put your new found disorder in there, if I can have mine in there . . .'

This is not facetious or exaggerated. The process of DSM development and inclusion is conducted using a vote within a select group of psychiatrists. I agree with Dr James Davies, when he describes this process as a cumulative voting process framed as an evidence-based classification (Davies, 2017).

Between 1950 and 1973, there was significant criticism of the DSM and psychiatric diagnostic criteria in general, with studies showing that psychiatrists using the DSM often did not agree on the correct diagnosis for a patient. In 1974, the third DSM (DSM-III) was published with the aim of creating more standardised, robust criteria for the diagnosis of mental disorders. The goal was to structure them and publish them to look like illnesses with 'symptoms' and 'tests' and 'recommended treatments' and 'medications'.

The authors of the DSM-III claimed that they had created a scientific and objective manual which was 'ideology free' – a pretty outlandish claim for a discipline that had made a living from centuries of racism, homophobia, classism and misogyny. Despite the large claims, studies showed that the new DSM was just as unreliable as the others, but it had a major difference: it positioned itself as a medical manual which referred to medication, drugs and dosages. It sounded more scientific, and it was treated as more scientific.

Every revision of the DSM has increased the numbers of mental disorders exponentially.

DSM Version	Year	Number of mental disorders
DSM-I	1952	128
DSM-II	1968	193
DSM-III	1980	228
DSM-III-R	1987	253
DSM-IV	1994	383
DSM-IV-TR	2000	383
DSM-V	2013	541

Every publication, the DSM earns the American Psychiatric Association hundreds of millions of dollars in revenue, and thousands more people are diagnosed with new mental disorders and illnesses.

The DSM editions have always contained problematic and ridiculous psychiatric disorders which stereotyped and pathologised marginalised groups in our societies – including Black people, gay people, women and people with disabilities. In 2013, psychiatrists added caffeine withdrawal as a psychiatric disorder along with disinhibited social engagement (children who approach new adults and chat to them with no caution), hoarding, internet gaming disorder, gambling disorder, grief disorder and premenstrual mood changes in women, which was added as a treatable psychiatric disorder (again).

Psychiatry is therefore much less precise and objective than people assume. Further than this though, and much more fundamentally, there is still considerable debate about what mental health actually is, and whether these hundreds of disorders exist at all.

What are the key theories of mental illness?
There are three main competing theories of mental health. Outside of those three, there are many other alternative and competing theories of why our behaviour, feelings and emotions can change so much during our lifetimes. What is also important to note is that psychiatry is predominantly a white, western upper-middle-class profession that takes very little notice of other explanations, cultures, religions, ethnicities, traditions, norms or social environments. Therefore, whilst there are hundreds of different cultural responses to distress and trauma, they are largely ignored in mainstream literature, teaching and professional training about mental health.

For example, in Zimbabwe there is thought to be a mental health issue in the Shona People known as 'kufungisisa', which means that you overthink excessively, ruminate on things and become anxious. In Haiti, there is an illness called 'maladi moun' which means 'sent sickness'. This is a form of mental suffering which has been sent by someone else on purpose, via their jealousy, resentment or hatred of you.

The cultural specificity of mental health has always intrigued me. I have spent years wondering why we as white, western, English speaking professionals think we have got it all figured out, whilst ridiculing and discrediting the research, wisdom and medicine of other cultures. We hear of mental health issues such as kufungisia and maladi moun, and might think that they are impossible, or based on magical thinking, whilst believing that our mental health issues are correct.

Conversely, we also tend to pathologise behaviours and responses that are considered normal, respected and rational in other cultures. In several cultures and countries around the world, it is seen as perfectly natural to cry and wail loudly at the funeral of loved ones who are publicly mourned, but in white western communities, funerals are a silent, solemn affair where emotion is masked with alcohol and embarrassment.

If someone fell to their knees and wailed for hours at a white, western funeral, it would undoubtedly be looked upon as some sort of disrespectful outburst, emotional breakdown or depressive episode. We tend to expect people to be upset at a funeral, but not too upset. Not too loud. Not too obvious. To remain 'dignified' at all times. These are all cultural expectations of how we are allowed to express deep emotion. These norms and narratives create boundaries that you cannot cross. Mental health and the expression of emotion is much more than a scientific set of categories – and arguably has more to do with culture and social norms than anything else.

Look at the way British white people ask each other disingenuous questions every single day and then lie to each other about the answer.

'Hey, how are you?'
'Good, you?'
'Not bad mate, can't grumble!'
'Good.'

None of that conversation is real, because it is based on a cultural norm of greetings, phrases and non-disclosure. Asking each other how we are has become small talk that must never be answered with honesty. Both of these people could be struggling with huge issues in their lives but would still answer, 'Good, you?' to which the other would say the exact same thing. Other cultures perceive this exchange to be dishonest, fake or rude – whilst British people often do not know what to do when someone answers 'how are you?' honestly.

'Hey, how are you?'
'Shattered actually. My mum is really struggling since Dad died, so I've been off work looking after Mum. Work are threatening me with disciplinary action because I keep taking time off. The kids are doing okay I guess, but I think our eldest might be being bullied at school. She doesn't seem to be eating properly. We got behind on the mortgage, but my sister-in-law paid it for us so now we owe her money. My car needs a service, but I can't afford it, and I have had a headache for days.'

We often don't tell the truth when we are asked if we are okay, and we don't express emotion. This is not a psychological issue, but a cultural one which doesn't exist everywhere in the world, no matter how much we frame white as default. We should always keep these differences in mind when discussing theories of mental health and psychiatry, and especially when we consider the oppression and discrimination which has been caused by these systems.

In summer 2021, a young Iranian woman sent me a strongly worded email to express her annoyance and concern that the white, western, psychiatric diagnosis of premenstrual dysphoric disorder (PMDD) had reached her country and community. She told me that before our ideas had reached them, people generally accepted hormonal, physical, emotional, and psychological changes as part of the cycle. However, she said that the concept of PMDD was increasingly being used to harm, isolate, and bully girls and young women. She told me that cultural knowledge of women's fertility, hormones and cycles was being ignored in favour of medicalisation.

The final line of her email said, 'Instead of abolishing the concept of the irrational woman, we are just spreading it to the whole world!'

I read her email whilst standing in my kitchen, and I stopped what I was doing and stared at the screen. She was right, and our arrogance overwhelmed me.

Biological model

The biomedical or biological model of mental illness has dominated for decades, and is the basis of the DSM and all current mental health practice. This model describes and responds to mental illness as 'a set of mental disorders caused by, or linked to brain diseases which require pharmacological treatments to target presumed biological abnormalities' (Deacon, 2013).

Simply put, the biological model (and those who support it, including the NHS, CAMHS, and Mind) argues that mental health illness or issues are a result of brain disorders, diseases and abnormalities which need medication to fix or manage. Whilst you will not hear it described this way on the TV, or by celebrities or influencers, this is what the core of the current narratives comes down to. Some people lean towards 'brain chemistry' explanations and some talk about 'neuroscience' explanations. Some talk about 'hereditary mental illness' and 'genetics'.

This approach places the mental health issues and illnesses securely and exclusively in our brains. It posits that mental illness is 'just like physical illness' (that's probably the bit you have heard in the media).

Like Rachel, millions of people have been led to believe that they have chemical imbalances and disorders which require medication – without any tests, scans or proof. This is, of course, because there is no way of diagnosing or proving these 'imbalances', they are assumptions and theories running wild and free in our everyday lives without due criticism or scrutiny.

Biological model of mental illness (medical model)

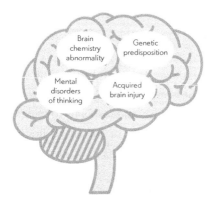

Brain chemistry abnormality

Genetic predisposition

Mental disorders of thinking

Acquired brain injury

Biopsychosocial model

The biopsychosocial model of mental health was developed in part to address some of the gaps of a purely biological, biomedical model of mental health. In 1977, George Engel argued that the biomedical model ignored many other factors that could be contributing to mental illness. There are three domains to explain mental illness:

- Biological factors (genetics, brain chemistry, disease, brain injury)
- Psychological factors (emotions, resilience, interpretation, vulnerabilities)
- Social factors (life trauma and stressors, family and child experiences)

The original arguments were that mental illnesses were made up of complex interplay between these three domains, with many connections between and within them. Unfortunately, it never really did achieve the lofty dreams of offering an alternative to the biological model, and often leans heavily into it. Richard Bentall wrote in 2013 that it would be better named the 'bio-bio-bio model', as those who use it still seem to focus more on the biological 'causes' and 'cures' than the other social contexts or environments that the behaviours or feelings developed within.

The biopsychosocial model of mental illness

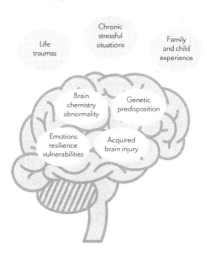

Social model

The social model of mental health locates the cause or root of a so-called mental health issue within the social environment or context of the person, instead of inside the person themselves. The social model opposes all biological models. Rather than suggesting that mental health or illness is in the brain or body of the person, those who subscribe to this model examine the factors around the person. Every and any contextual, social, cultural or environmental factor could be the cause of distress or mental health issues, including accommodation, poverty, oppression, abuse, discrimination, peer and family issues.

Whilst this model doesn't support biological models of mental health, it is often used this way.

For example, it is common for someone to say that someone's childhood experiences 'caused' them to become mentally ill, or develop personality disorders. In this way, the model is being misused somewhat – as the idea is that if we can work to resolve or improve whatever it is that is causing the distress, the distress will lessen.

For example, if a woman is not sleeping, having nightmares and is feeling scared and low because she is homeless and being exploited – it would make sense that a lot of her 'symptoms of mental illness' will improve or completely resolve once she has somewhere safe to live, is no longer being exploited and the trauma from these experiences is being addressed and supported properly.

Thomas Scheff originally argued that people who are diagnosed as mentally ill are 'victims of the status quo', guilty of often unnamed violations of social norms; thus the label 'mental illness' can be used as an instrument of social control. His argument is far removed from the way the social model is often conceptualised now, as it has been absorbed back into the medical model as a legitimate 'cause' of mental illness inside the brain.

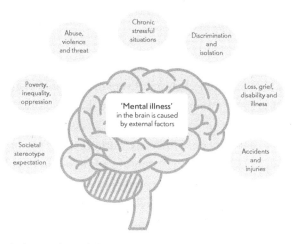

Social model of mental illness

Abuse, violence and threat

Chronic stressful situations

Discrimination and isolation

Poverty, inequality, oppression

'Mental illness' in the brain is caused by external factors

Loss, grief, disability and illness

Societal stereotype expectation

Accidents and injuries

Trauma-informed model

The trauma-informed model of mental health goes further than the social model, but also opposes biological explanations of mental illness and health. It has been talked about for many years, but has become more mainstream in the last few years, and is in grave danger of being misused and misunderstood if not carefully explained and utilised. It has recently become something of a buzzword in public services and academia, without much underpinning knowledge of its activist, anti-psychiatry roots.

The trauma-informed approach to mental health, illness and distress argues that there are undeniable and consistent strong correlations between all so-called 'mental health issues' and human trauma, distress and oppression. Therefore, it is argued that 'disorders', 'illnesses' and 'diseases' are very likely to be natural physical and psychological manifestations of human trauma and distress, in response to events and experiences in our lives – not brain abnormalities or mental illnesses.

On this basis, the trauma-informed model rejects biomedical models, psychiatric theory and diagnosis, labelling and treatment, and instead seeks to work with people as humans who have been subjected to different forms of stress, trauma, oppression, pressure, inequality, injury and abuse (both acute and chronic).

Instead of talking about symptoms and illnesses, we talk about trauma responses and coping mechanisms. Every behaviour, thought, or feeling after distress or trauma can be put into these two categories: they are either a response to what happened, or a way of coping with what happened – and sometimes they are both. It doesn't matter if it is nightmares, binge eating, perfectionism, self-harm, flashbacks, headaches, hearing voices or becoming withdrawn for many years – a truly trauma-informed approach can explain and explore these experiences as either trauma responses or coping mechanisms. They are never categorised as mental disorders, illnesses or syndromes.

For avoidance of doubt, this is the perspective that I choose to work within as a psychologist and activist; and the perspective I choose to write this book (and all my research and books) within as an author.

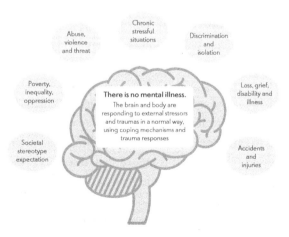

Trauma informed approach to mental health

Abuse, violence and threat

Chronic stressful situations

Discrimination and isolation

Poverty, inequality, oppression

Loss, grief, disability and illness

There is no mental illness.
The brain and body are responding to external stressors and traumas in a normal way, using coping mechanisms and trauma responses

Societal stereotype expectation

Accidents and injuries

When I teach about trauma, I argue that physiological and psychological trauma is always:

Rational – trauma responses are often repackaged as the irrational behaviours, thoughts and feelings of a mentally ill person, and yet, when we look honestly at whatever 'symptom' has brought a person to the doctor's office, we can usually find a rational response to trauma. I worked with a woman who was diagnosed with several mental health issues which surrounded her 'irrational' responses to the breeze. If she felt a breeze, draught or wind on her face, she would experience very distressing trauma responses including flashbacks, chest pains, hallucinations and dizziness.

After years of being medicated and labelled, she had only been speaking to me for two hours when we happened to dig into why the breeze scared her so much. Initially she couldn't tell me why. She said she had no idea why she had such an 'irrational' trigger. She said she had always been told it was part of her mental health issues. I assured her that everything has a root and that all trauma responses had a purpose. Then suddenly she mumbled something about an accident she had decades ago before shaking her head and quickly dismissing it as irrelevant.

I encouraged her to talk about whatever it was, and she told me that she had had a fall from a great height when she was younger and the last thing she remembered before hitting the floor and breaking her spine was the rush of the air on her face. Her trigger was wholly rational. Sometimes, trauma responses and coping mechanisms seem irrational because they are out of context, but generally, patience and compassion will always reveal the root and rational cause.

Normal – when a woman or girl has been through something life-threatening, terrifying, deeply upsetting or violating, isn't it completely normal that it would impact her for many years to come? The study of mental illness was originally (and up until very recently in many universities and books) called 'abnormal psychology'. The question here is why we have ever considered human trauma and distress to be 'abnormal' at all. If a girl is abused and neglected, wouldn't it be completely normal for her to be traumatised by that? Wouldn't her nightmares or fears or anger be totally normal? Wouldn't it be abnormal for her not to be affected?

Psychiatry relies on the framing of normal trauma responses as abnormal or disordered thinking and behaviour. Trauma-informed approaches consider that our 'symptoms' and 'signs' are completely normal responses to distress and trauma, rather than medicalising or pathologising them.

Natural – many of our trauma responses and coping mechanisms are natural physical and psychological responses to something that has deeply affected us. Whether it's a chronic fear of something happening to us through to physiological reactions such as high heart rate, dizziness, headaches or digestive issues, the causes of these responses are natural processes that have a purpose. They do not constitute medical or mental illnesses. Understanding what our body or mind is trying to do to protect us or to cope is of vital importance to a trauma-informed approach.

Proportionate – one of the ways that women have been successfully pathologised by psychiatry and mental health movements is by arguing that their responses to trauma or distress are not justified or proportionate. For example, when I ask why grief is now classified as a psychiatric disorder, people say to me, 'Well, it's normal to grieve for a while and for it to impact you, but when it goes on too long or impacts you too much, that's when it becomes a psychiatric disorder.' I often wonder if those people have ever grieved, because my understanding of grief is that it never really goes away.

It's the same with trauma responses and coping mechanisms. If a woman or girl has been abused or harmed for years, wouldn't it be proportionate for her to struggle with that for many years, maybe even her entire life? Why would we think that there would come a day when she would wake up and it would all be fine? Like nothing ever happened?

Trauma responses are almost always proportionate, in my opinion. Women are oppressed globally, subjected to violence and abuse, harassment and discrimination, gender roles and heteronormative pressures to be the perfect woman for men – and this is without individual events of crisis, trauma, attacks, injuries, rape, trafficking, exploitation, poverty, homelessness, persecution, natural disasters and war.

Being frightened, angry, upset, confused, irritable, tired, frustrated or struggling with negative impacts of all of these stressors – for months, years or entire lifetimes – do not justify a label of a mental disorder. They are all proportionate responses to a very difficult way to live as a woman or girl in a patriarchy.

Explainable – one final thing that I try to make clear when teaching about trauma is that all trauma responses and coping mechanisms are explainable. There are no deep dark secrets, no magical or satanic reasons, no dangerous brain chemistries or hidden genes waiting to be unlocked. If someone has developed a coping mechanism or trauma response, there will always be a reason for it, and often, it's a simple one. Rather than listing 'symptoms' of some obscure underlying psychiatric disorder, or chemical imbalance, exploring and explaining the reasons and causes for a change in behaviour, thinking or feeling (no matter how extreme it may seem) is usually fairly simple.

Myths and misconceptions of mental illness and mental health

One of the ways that psychiatry has continued to reign supreme is by utilising and allowing misinformation and myths of mental illness to become mainstream narratives and explanations of human behaviour. The general public often feel they have a good grasp of the facts, without realising that much of the information they have about mental illness is highly contested, completely debunked or is outright denied as having never been shared at all. It is extremely rare for any authority in psychiatry or psychology to make public statements or retractions about misinformation or myths.

1. Mental health issues are genetic and passed down through families

One of the most common misconceptions or myths in mental health is that mental illnesses are caused by genetic issues or genetic predispositions that have been passed down through families. Despite this being a popular view and something that captured the understanding of the general public, there has never been a single gene proven to be connected to any neurological or psychological issue. What this means then is that there is currently no proof that psychiatric diagnoses or issues result from the mutation of any single gene (Davies, 2013).

When you think about it, this makes a lot of sense considering that the nature/nurture debate has been going on for decades and we have eventually arrived at an understanding that there is no real way of divorcing nature from nurture. In the past there may have been debates on whether nature caused a certain change in humans, or whether it was the social environment. This debate is no longer raging on as we eventually concluded that nature and nurture interact with each other in nuance and complexity. This means that there is no real way of singularly identifying one factor from nature or nurture that causes changes in humans, and this includes genetic explanations of mental illness.

When I speak to professionals, one of the strong beliefs held by psychologists, social workers and therapists is that if there is depression or anxiety in the family, then it is very likely to be passed down from parents to their children and then to their children's children. However, rather than this being proof of a genetic link, it would be more likely that the culture and environment of the family would have impacted those children (and their children's children) and so again we return to the complex debate between nature and nurture.

Other than the genetic theory of mental illness not yet being supported by any robust evidence, it's also deficit-based and reductionist – it is a deficit-based way of thinking and talking about mental illness and mental health. Approaches like this mean that instead of looking at the environment and the context and the culture that humans become distressed within, we look back inside the brain, individualise the issue, and blame a gene. And if the mental illness is indeed genetic, then is the person helpless and defined by their inescapable mental disorder for the rest of their lives?

2. Mental health issues are caused by chemical imbalances in the brain

This idea began to gain attention in the 1950s, but didn't make huge waves until several psychiatrists and researchers suggested the theory that mental illness was caused by differing levels of neurotransmitters in the brain, chiefly norepinephrine, serotonin and dopamine. These were mere theories, without any evidence base, as there was (and still is) no way of testing brain chemical imbalances. The theories came about by analysing data from animal studies and by observing patients with depression. All authors at the time were clear that their ideas were just theories, but that didn't stop the huge uptake of this idea in professional and public life (Davies, 2014). Indeed, it was these animal studies and observations that led to the development of SSRI 'antidepressants' such as Prozac and Zoloft. There are now more than 70 million antidepressant prescriptions in England every year according to NHS data. This topped 50 million in 2013, and by 2017, this figure was 67.5 million. According to the Health and Social Care Information Centre, this is the greatest numeric rise in prescriptions of any drug class.

It's a seductively simple theory – all mental illnesses are caused by a chemical imbalance in the brain that can be rebalanced by drugs. But is any of it true? Has any of it ever been proven?

What is interesting about this key myth is that even the American Psychiatric Association now deny ever supporting this theory. Key psychiatrists around the world reject chemical imbalance theory.

In his book, *Cracked*, James Davies gathered quotes from key psychiatry organisations and individual psychiatrists from Stanford, Harvard, US Congress and the American Psychiatric Association who publicly rejected chemical imbalance theory.

Just some are below:

> '*Many neuroscientists no longer consider the chemical imbalance theory of depression or anxiety to be valid*' – Dr David Burns, Stanford

> '*Chemical imbalance theory is last-century thinking*' – Dr Joseph Coyle, Harvard Medical School

> '*Despite pseudoscientific terms like "chemical imbalance", nobody really knows what causes mental illness. There's no*

blood tests or brain scans' – Dr Darshak Sanghavi, Harvard Medical School

'We do not know the aetiology of really any of the mental disorders at the present time' – Dr Carl Regier, American Psychiatric Association

'We still don't know the relationship between biology and the mental disorders' – Carol Bernstein, American Psychiatric Association

'Patients have been diagnosed with chemical imbalances despite that no tests exist to support such a claim and that there is no real conception of what a correct chemical balance would look like' – Dr David Kaiser, *The Psychiatric Times*

And they are absolutely right to reject this theory of mental health.

There has never been any direct or conclusive proof that antidepressants cure or improve depression by increasing serotonin levels in the brain (Davies, 2013). Further, in randomised controlled medical trials, placebo pills tend to perform the same, if not better than antidepressants, and have done for many years.

Whilst people might say 'I feel better when I take the antidepressants, and therefore, that is proof that the antidepressants cured the chemical imbalance in my brain', this is logically flawed. If I take two paracetamol tablets for my headache and my headache goes away, I still don't know what caused the headache. The headache was certainly not caused by needing some more paracetamol levels in my bloodstream. Maybe I had hit my head. Or stared at my phone screen for hours. Or became stressed about work. Or had a hangover.

The chemical imbalance theory was used heavily in other mental illnesses including 'schizophrenia' and other forms of psychosis which were originally theorised to be caused by excess dopamine in the brain. However, after many years of studies and hundreds of thousands of diagnoses, it was eventually conceded that there was no evidence of dopamine differences between people with and without diagnoses of psychotic disorders, and that even in the tiny handful of studies where dopamine had actually been measured in the spinal fluid of volunteers, results did not support the chemical imbalance theory.

Psychiatrist Daniel Carlat wrote about this finding in 2010 and said,

> ... it is crucial that we realise how much we do not know. In virtually all of the psychiatric disorders – including depression, schizophrenia, bipolar disorder and anxiety disorders – the shadow of our ignorance overwhelms the few dim lights of our knowledge.

More and more people are becoming aware of the fact that the chemical imbalance theory is incorrect. One such lobbying group is called 'Demand Chemical Imbalance Retraction', which lists hundreds of celebrities, politicians and public groups who still support and discuss the debunked theory in the media and to millions of people. Of course, the celebrities have not deliberately chosen to share a debunked myth around mental health, but probably believe it to be correct themselves. However, this means that on a regular basis, millions of young people and adults are still receiving media messages that mental illnesses and psychiatric disorders are caused by chemical imbalances in the brain.

3. Mental health issues are for life – they can only be managed but not cured

In 2012, I started to notice more and more women that I was working with were telling me that they had treatment-resistant depression or other forms of psychiatric diagnosis that they had been told that they would have for the rest of their lives. What concerned me most about this was how subdued women became after being told that there was nothing that could be done for them. Many of the women who I met were accessing a rape centre that I was managing at the time, and had been told by doctors and nurses that their mental health issues could only ever be managed with medication.

In almost every single one of these women, long-term trauma therapy had a positive and long-lasting impact on their well-being and on their mental health. The women attended sessions on a weekly basis to talk through the trauma of being raped, abused, beaten and trafficked and they often made huge progress within a few months.

From a trauma-informed perspective, I would argue that when we are subjected to traumatic experiences those memories will stay with us for the rest of our lives. I often explain to professionals, students and women who write to me that they should never expect themselves to go back to being the person they were before that trauma. This isn't because they are going to be mentally ill or disordered for the rest of their lives, but because every experience they have shapes them and changes them. We are a product of all of our millions of experiences in life. However, trauma is a lifelong journey and it will impact women in different ways throughout the lifespan.

There will be times in a woman's life where the trauma does not impact her on a daily basis (in medical terms, a psychiatrist might say that her mental illness is in remission, or improving) but there will be other times in her life where the trauma is triggered and she re-experiences trauma responses, coping mechanisms, psychological and physiological distress from experiences that may have happened months, years, or decades ago. This is completely normal, but a psychiatrist may call this a 'relapse'.

This medicalisation and the use of medical terms of 'remission' and 'relapse' mean that women feel that they can never escape the psychiatric diagnosis they have been given – and they will be disordered for the rest of their lives.

4. Mental health issues are rare

This particular myth is important to address. Every year we see a newspaper article or a headline on the television that talks about the prevalence of mental health issues and psychiatric diagnosis in the general public. This is usually met with shock or concern that one in three, or one in four of us will experience mental health issues in our lifespan. What this reveals is a deep belief that mental health issues are actually and should be very rare.

Partially, this has to do with the medicalisation of everyday situations, common experiences of distress and natural emotions. From a trauma-informed perspective, I would expect every single person to go through something traumatic or distressing each year. Whilst that might sound terrifying, if we consider that within one year a person could possibly experience a bereavement, an illness, an injury, a relationship breakdown, an assault, abuse, a stressful job, redundancy, a house move, financial difficulties, discrimination or endless other possibilities – it makes sense that millions of people would find themselves naturally traumatised or distressed. This would mean that distress, trauma and the physical and physiological responses to those experiences are probably a universal experience – and not a rarity. And if it is not a rarity, it is not an abnormality. If it is not an abnormality, it is not a disorder. If it is not a disorder, it should not be treated or medicated.

Arguably, if something is so common that everyone will experience it, why are we describing it as an abnormality or disorder at all?

Neuromyths and present-day issues

It is important to understand that there has been considerable unrest in the disciplines of psychology and psychiatry, since they are often criticised as not being 'real sciences'. In the 1970s, there was a concerted effort to improve the empiricism and reputation of psychology towards being as rigorous, as serious and as 'scientific' as biology, chemistry and physics. The science of the human mind, of thought and of behaviour, has never quite cut the mustard.

The introduction of MRI and fMRI machines to psychological research was seen by some as the answer to this issue – finally, psychologists and psychiatrists could scan brains and explore brain activity like never before. Finally, they thought they had quantifiable data, verifiable answers and scientific method. This desperate grapple to be considered 'a real science' led to many universities cutting their budgets in child psychology, social psychology and forensic psychology in order to afford MRI machines and to fund neuropsychology departments. In some universities in the UK, there are no longer other departments of psychology, as they were closed to focus purely on neuropsychology.

The reason that this is important for our conversation about the pathologisation of women and girls who report abuse is that the huge popularity of neuropsychology and the scanning of brains has seeped into so many different disciplines that it is now frequently used against women and girls who have been raped, trafficked and exploited. Several serious myths and misconceptions, particularly about teenage girls, influence policy, practice and the education of social workers, teachers, therapists, youth workers and psychologists.

I have spent the last five years attempting to correct and debunk some of the most harmful neuromyths that are being used frequently in children's social services.

Teenage girls are addicted to risk taking

One of the most common neuromyths in children's social services (especially in teams who work with girls who are sexually exploited and trafficked) is that the reason they continue to be exploited and trafficked is because they are going through an adolescent development phase in which they are addicted to risk taking and dopamine release.

Despite there being absolutely no evidence that teenage girls are addicted to sexual risk taking due to brain chemical imbalances, many social workers have been taught that this is the reason that teenage girls cannot see the risks that they are taking. Of course, teenage girls who are being raped and exploited are not the ones taking the risks, and neuromyths are therefore contributing to significant victim blaming of girls who have been raped and abused.

This assumption is made partially due to a hatred of teenagers, and specifically teenage girls. There is a strong social and cultural belief that teenagers are problematic, unpredictable, unreliable, and take unnecessary risks that put them in danger. What adults believe sets them apart from teenagers is that their brains are more developed, that their decision making is better, that they are more rational than teenagers, and that they take fewer risks. Thousands of British social workers have been taught that this is the case. They are often taught that teenagers who are being abused make poor decisions and choices, are irrational, and take more risks around their sexual behaviours than adults.

This victim-blaming myth comes from misused and overgeneralised findings from neuroscience. Risk taking is individual. Some children do take risks, some children don't. Some adults take risks, some adults don't. Some risk taking is excellent and positive. Some risk taking is a learning experience. If, indeed, the reason teenagers are sexually exploited is because their teenage brains are so addicted to risk taking then why do adults still get sexually exploited all over the world? If we were to believe that adolescent brains were categorically different from adults (which neuroscience research has disproven, Moshman (2011)) then surely abuse and exploitation statistics would drop dramatically at biological maturation. Surely once the child becomes a mature adult their risk taking would reduce or end. The reality is that the teenage brain is incredibly similar to the adult brain; it is the child brain which has the most differences from the adult brain.

Neuroscientist David Moshman wrote a book called *Adolescent Rationality and Development* in 2011, in which he set about debunking some of the most harmful neuromyths about adolescence. Some of the key myths that David debunked included the belief that adolescence are less rational than adults and make worse decisions than them. He also challenged neuromyths that would appear to be common sense. For example, he challenged the myth that the brain is immature because teenage girls are not fully grown, and that their brain and their abilities will mature with age and puberty.

He also addressed the myth that teenagers are more impulsive than their adult counterparts. Again though, the neuroscience research does not support this myth. Adolescents tend to be just as impulsive as adults and in any case, impulsivity is an individual difference. Some adolescents are impulsive, just as some adults are impulsive.

Moshman (2011) goes on to say that young children are distinct from adults in terms of neuroscience and neuropsychological development, but adolescents are not. Maturity, decision making, risk taking and rationality tend to evolve in varied ways from the age of ten or eleven onwards, and in empirical studies, many fourteen-year-old children function beyond the level of many forty-year-old adults. Whilst research often ascribes impulsivity, irrational behaviour, poor decision making and risky behaviours to young people, Moshman argues that there are no differences in the cognitive functions between adolescents and adults.

All of this misinformation about neuroscience is relevant to the pathologisation of women and girls. In 2018, I was at a conference about the sexual exploitation of teenage girls and young women in a top university. I was giving a keynote speech about the psychology of victim blaming, but before my speech there was one other speaker who gave a presentation about the neuroscience of trauma in teenage girls who have been sexually exploited and abused.

I was shocked and disappointed to hear the professional speaker (who was not a neuroscientist) say that the brain controls how teenage girls react to a rape or sexual assault and that the reason they freeze during a sexual assault and don't try to fight back is because their 'brain isn't mature enough to process what is happening to them'.

Some researchers state the increased dopamine release to subcortical reward centres encourages attraction to new and risky experiences. This so-called 'sensation-seeking behaviour' is strongly associated with the initiation of a wide range of adolescent risk behaviours such as use of drugs and sex (Romer, 2010). They argue that this impulsivity may lead young people to engage in activities that present serious risk. Some even argue that adolescent emotional responses are affected by a period of change in a part of the brain which governs emotional responses. They argue that teenagers rely more on their primitive limbic system and that they 'lack a more mature cortex that can override the limbic response' (CWIG, 2009). This, it is argued by some, makes them 'more prone to engage in dangerous risk-taking behaviour and not sufficiently able to interpret their emotions' (Brown and Ward, 2013).

The first thing that came to mind when the speaker blamed immature teenage girls' brains for not fighting off a trafficker or rapist was that if this statement is true, why do we know that 70 per cent (Moller et al., 2017) of all adult women who are subjected to sexual assault or rape also freeze? If the freeze response is due to a lack of mature processing in teenage girls, why do adults also respond with a freeze response to danger and violence?

The speaker went on to say that there were automatic brain processes in teenage girls that stopped them from fighting back, and that when girls grew up and became wiser, their brains would become more mature and they would be able to fight off the rapist or abuser. This statement, and statements like this, reveal an interesting bias that we have as adults: that we are better than and wiser than adolescents (and that teenage girls bring sexual violence upon themselves by being immature risk-takers). Our practice and theory positions adolescent girls as a subgroup of humans who are irrational, risky, poor decision-makers, naïve and immature; whilst we position adulthood as the ultimate neurological goal.

I wish I could say that this speech was a one-off, but in the last five years, I have come across more and more neuromyths in practice with traumatised women and girls. One professional told me that teenage girls have a chip inside their brain that sex offenders use to control them. When I asked her where she had learned that, she told me the name of a national training company for social workers. In 2021, I was asked to review training materials for a criminal justice agency who were concerned about the dodgy psychiatric and neuroscience sessions pertaining to women who had been raped and abused. I was shocked to see materials which included myths about the brain, memory, psychiatry, trauma and disorders.

The only thing that should be clear at the end of this chapter is that we're actually not very clear about mental illness at all. In fact, we know very little. A lot of what is shared about psychiatric diagnosis, mental health and neuroscience is guesswork, oppression or myth.

CHAPTER 2

Sexism, homophobia and racism in psychiatry

Dear Jess,

I hope you don't mind me asking this but I read your blog the other day and it got me thinking about my diagnosis and my sexuality. When I was doing all those assessments and talking to the doctor, they kept asking me about my sexuality. I told them that I didn't really know. I thought maybe I was bisexual. I had had some relationships with men and some with women. I thought I might be bisexual but then I also thought maybe I could be lesbian as I don't think I'm attracted to men at all really. I found out much later that they had used these conversations as proof that I had borderline personality disorder and 'identity issues'. I felt really betrayed as I thought they were confidential chats.

I wondered if you had ever heard of this before? Isn't that homophobia?

Thanks

Hannah*

To truly understand the criticisms of modern-day mental health and psychiatry movements, we have to go back hundreds of years and explore the way that mental illness has always been used to marginalise, oppress, harm, control and murder groups of people by those in authority. This may come as a surprise to readers who don't know the history of mental illness and disorder, but as I will demonstrate in this chapter, our understanding and application of psychiatry has been problematic for as long as we have attempted to explain differences in thinking, feeling and behaving.

Looking backwards is often helpful in understanding how we arrived at where we are now. This could be politically, socially or scientifically. Thought and understanding changes constantly, but often builds upon knowledge or practice that has gone before it. Psychiatry has a legacy of harmful, oppressive and lethal treatments and assumptions which still have significant influence on modern-day thinking about mental health.

Treatments and beliefs

- Trepanation – this was a form of neurosurgery which drilled into the cranial bones of the skull in order to create a hole which would allow the evil to escape.
- Hysteria therapy – a specific set of 'treatments' for women which included marriage, torture, being exposed to foul smells, forced pregnancy, and womb extractions.
- Phrenology – the eighteenth-century theory that separate areas of the brain controlled specific functions or thoughts such as 'destructiveness' and 'agreeableness'.
- Mesmerism – the eighteenth-century theory and practice that madness could be cured by ingesting large amounts of iron and then moving it through the body using magnets.
- Rotational therapy – the nineteenth-century theory and practice of spinning patients to such a rate that they experienced g-force (they didn't know this yet, however) and would become subdued and 'calm'. Doctors claimed that it cured madness.

- Organ and tooth extractions – the twentieth-century theory and practice that mental health issues were caused by toxins or infections in the body that had travelled to the brain to cause insanity and madness. This resulted in doctors extracting teeth, tonsils, spleens and, of course, women's uteri. Doctors claimed that it cured madness in 80 per cent of cases, but in actual fact it killed at least 45 per cent of all patients (Stetka & Watson, 2016).
- Hydrotherapy – the twentieth-century practice of forcing patients in mental asylums in the USA to have extremely hot or extremely cold baths or showers for days on end, which they claimed could cure insomnia, suicide ideation, depression and aggression.
- Malaria therapy – the twentieth-century practice of deliberately injecting patients in asylums with malaria to induce fevers and convulsions which were believed to then cure the patient of madness. This therapy earned Dr Julius Wagner-Juaregg a Nobel Prize and this practice continued into the 1930s (Stetka & Watson, 2016).
- Insulin shock therapy – the twentieth-century practice of deliberately injecting 'schizophrenia' patients with insulin so they fell into a coma and became calmer and more cooperative (unconscious). This practice continued well into the 1950s despite having a mortality rate of around 10 per cent (Stetka & Watson, 2016).
- Chemically induced seizure therapy – the twentieth-century practice of injecting chemicals and the blood of epileptic patients into patients with 'schizophrenia' to induce seizures. The seizures were thought to cure schizophrenia. This practice continued into the 1950s and is credited as beginning the tradition of electroconvulsive therapy, which induces seizures using electricity instead of blood or chemicals.

- ◆ Frontal lobotomies – the infamous nineteenth- and twentieth-century practice of psychosurgery which severed the connections in the prefrontal cortex of the brain in order to cure psychoses such as delusions, obsessive behaviours and hallucinations. Between 60 to 70 per cent of all frontal lobotomies were performed on women (Jenell Johnson, 2014).
- ◆ Electroconvulsive therapy – the twentieth-century theory and practice that inducing seizures by electric shocks to the brain in mentally ill patients could reduce their symptoms or cure them. Despite the belief that electroconvulsive therapy was banned or confined to the history books decades ago, the practice still endures to this day, and is delivered by the NHS and many other national health services around the world to both children and adults with psychiatric diagnoses.

To those who have little knowledge about the history and foundations of psychiatry, that list might read like something from an 18-rated horror movie. And yet, hundreds of thousands of women were subjected to these harmful – often fatal – treatments for thinking, feeling or behaving differently.

This is an important point; that simply thinking, feeling or behaving differently (and in some cases, even just looking different) could be enough for a ruling class or someone in authority to diagnose an individual or group with mental illnesses and subsequently suggest that they need treatments, cures, imprisonment or isolation from the rest of society. For this chapter, we will focus on the way white people in power were able to position being Black as a mental illness, the way men in power were able to position being female as a mental illness and the way heterosexual men were able to position homosexuality as a mental illness.

In all three examples, a dominant group were able to reframe a protected characteristic (ethnicity, sex and sexuality) as a disorder, illness or syndrome which required significant intervention. In all cases, this led to the abuse and deaths of people who were simply oppressed by the ruling class. Despite there often being no evidence of any disordered thinking, behaviour, or emotion, it was easy to claim that marginalised groups had mental illnesses which required intervention and control.

As with all other issues of madness, the most powerful thing about being framed or diagnosed as mentally ill, is that the more you protest, the more this is taken as 'evidence' that you are indeed mentally ill. This was (and still is) key to controlling groups of women who are routinely diagnosed as having mental disorders, issues and illnesses. Many women reading this book will know that their criticisms and protests against diagnosis, medication and treatment they did not agree with were often met with the accusation that their mental health issues were so severe, and worsening, that they were 'in denial about' or 'refusing to accept' their reality – as a mentally ill woman in need of medical intervention.

Every woman I spoke to as part of my research for this book had stories to that effect. Some were direct extreme examples in which their criticism of their doctors had led to them being sectioned or forcibly medicated or sedated, but for others, the disagreement with their diagnosis or treatment had led to a much longer, slow-burning impact of being discredited, questioned and undermined for decades.

Crucially, this led to women (and as I will show here, several other oppressed groups) having no way out of the mental health system, or to escape the label of mental illness and madness.

Being Black as a mental illness

Whilst it is no longer spoken about, the history of psychiatry, psychology and the theories of mental health are steeped in violent racism. Black women and men were frequently captured and locked up in insane asylums, where they were tortured and experimented on for decades.

Dr Benjamin Rush, who is often cited as the 'Father' of psychiatry, held the belief that Black skin was an illness, a disorder of the skin caused by leprosy. He also suggested that enslaved Black people were insane and had an irrational obsession with wishing they were white, and believed that the only way they would achieve this was by marrying and having children with white people. To this end, he argued strongly against any kind of interracial marriage or partnerships, as he believed that Black people would spread their mental illnesses into the white population.

His understudy, Dr Samuel Cartwright, was the man who developed the psychiatric disorder 'drapetomania', meaning a mental illness which caused enslaved Black people to want to escape from slave owners, plantations and oppressors. Yes, you read that correctly. White men in power created a psychiatric disorder of oppressed people trying to escape oppression. They reframed it as a form of madness, and diagnosed Black people with it. Further than this, white medical researchers and psychiatrists developed the concept of 'dysaethesia aethiopia' which they described as a depressed, lethargic, dullness of enslaved Black people. Rather than considering that enslaving and torturing Black people would result in them being traumatised, Dr Samuel Cartwright recommended that all mental illnesses in Black people could be cured by prolonged, severe whipping.

When Black men and women were eventually emancipated, psychiatrists further diagnosed them with psychoses, arguing that freeing Black people from slavery harmed their mental health and caused them to become even more insane because slavery was 'the natural state of Black people who needed hard labour and control to function in society' (Segrest, 2020).

These choices are just some of the key white supremacist foundations of the myth that there is a higher prevalence of mental illness and psychiatric disorders among Black communities – as pro-slave politicians and physicians often argued that Black people in slavery were 'insane or idiotic', and that Black people freed from slavery were psychotic and dangerous.

Black people were described and treated as 'savages', 'primitive', 'undeveloped', 'uncivilised' and in need of control by white psychiatrists and psychologists. They were segregated in mental health facilities, and kept outside or in separate workhouses and farming blocks – away from the white patients. It was believed that the presence of Black people would harm the 'healing' of white people in the asylums, who were generally treated significantly better than the Black people, who were much more likely to starve and die in psychiatric asylums (Segrest, 2020).

The twentieth century brought more danger and more psychiatric oppression for Black people, who were faced with the growing belief from eugenics that they should be sterilised and stopped from procreating. The belief was that only people from 'good stock' should be able to pass down their genes and have families, which came with the assumption that Black people (and Black genes) were not from 'good stock'. The legal sterilisation of Black women surged between the 1920s and 1970s, with some countries and US states seeking to sterilise as many Black women as possible, usually by diagnosing them with psychiatric disorders first. By the 1970s in North Carolina for example, 85 per cent of all legally sterilised people were Black women who had been declared 'mentally defective' in order to stop them from having their own children (Umeh, 2019).

As if this sustained racist attack on Black people was not robust enough, between 1930 and 1970, they were also the primary victims of frontal lobotomy experiments and surgeries which caused incisions or removals of parts of the frontal lobes of the brain to 'treat' psychiatric disorders. Records show that this surgery was also carried out on Black children as young as five years old (Umeh, 2019).

And as the development of psychiatric disorders continued, the racist diagnosis and treatment of Black people deepened, with schizophrenia becoming well known as the 'Black man's disorder' by the 1970s. The term 'aggressive' was added to the diagnostic criteria of schizophrenia and antipsychotics were directly marketed to Black people who were felt to be 'out of control' (Smith, 2020). Psychiatrists described Black men as angry, aggressive and disenfranchised, whilst completely ignoring the oppression, segregation and persecution of Black people in deliberate poverty in a racist society. They chose to pathologise and recast Black men as violent, unpredictable criminals with mental illnesses and then medicate them heavily with antipsychotics – or lock them away in asylums and prisons for the rest of their lives. Today, 90 per cent of all psychiatric care beds in the USA are in prisons, which are disproportionately populated by Black men (Segrest, 2020).

The legacy of schizophrenia cannot be understated. Black people who protested in civil rights movements and anti-racism demonstrations were often diagnosed with 'protest psychosis' – especially when they were linked to, or in support of, Black Power, Black Panther movements and Nation of Islam between 1960 and 1990. Black schizophrenia was named as the cause of 'urban violence', and in the 1960s and 1970s, the white mainstream media developed powerful stereotypes of crazed Black schizophrenic murderers who were on the loose, searching for white victims to kill because of their 'delusional anti-whiteness' (defined and published by the *Archives of General Psychiatry* in 1968). This stereotype continued for several decades, is still prevalent now, and has influenced everything from Jim Crow Laws and the mass incarceration of Black people to the more recent pro-police brutality narratives during Black Lives Matter protests. Black people who try to push back against oppression are still routinely positioned as dangerous, obsessive, mentally ill, anti-white extremists – which many people do not realise is linked to the original racist diagnoses of Black people.

Being female as a mental illness

Being female was literally classified as a mental disorder for centuries. Women had always been described by philosophers, scientists and physicians as defective, deformed, mutated versions of men. This is where the 'male as default' thinking comes from, which plagues science to this day. Women were described as problematic, with a range of mental and physical disorders that men couldn't (or wouldn't) decipher.

By the eighteenth century, one of the most common psychiatric diagnoses used to control, imprison, and violate women was that of hysteria.

The word and concept of hysteria is thought to originate from the Ancient Greek physician Hippocrates, who wrote that the uterus was a problematic organ. Hysteria was described as a female disease, caused by women's wombs detaching from their usual position and floating around the body, causing havoc in the brain, heart and other organs – hence the term 'wandering womb syndrome'. Hysterical women were described as responding in disproportionately emotional ways to life and daily events – hence the modern term 'hysterical'.

Hysteria was complete nonsense of course, but as 'doctors' of that era had no scientific training and were steeped in racism and misogyny whilst holding significant local and national authority, no one sought to question the validity of an entire reproductive organ detaching itself and then moving around the female body, causing insanity and emotional unrest.

Until 1980, this was still considered to be a legitimate medical and psychiatric condition – listed in the DSM – which could be cured by medication, treatment and therapy (and pre-1970, women were told to use dildos, have sex with men, become pregnant or have womb extractions as a cure for their hysteria). An interesting mix of cures, you may notice, especially for the time period.

Whilst women were still being demonised for female masturbation, and female pleasure was nowhere on the patriarchy's priority list, women were being diagnosed as insane and hysterical and then advised by doctors to use a dildo or to have sex with their husbands to relieve their illness. This was not for female pleasure or fulfilment, though, especially as doctors in the eighteenth to twentieth centuries did not believe that women could experience sexual desire or sexual pleasure (unless they were a witch of course; in that case, they should be burned alive).

Doctors invented vibrators and dildos as a medical treatment for hysterical and insane women – whilst natural female masturbation was described as 'self-abuse' and used to diagnose women with further psychiatric disorders. At the same time, doctors would prescribe marriage to single women who were diagnosed as mentally ill, as women were seen to need the control and authority of a man to keep them in line. Once her life was on track as a submissive wife and mother, she would be well again.

In the nineteenth century and early twentieth century, women were being committed to asylums for anything that men found remotely offensive, from novel reading to imaginary female troubles. According to the historical records from the West Virginia Hospital for the Insane (1899), women were treated with a range of dangerous procedures for 'insanity symptoms' such as studying, not having enough sex with their husbands, not smiling enough, being interested in politics, masturbating and overusing their limited female mental powers.

Women were the main recipients of almost all of the most dangerous and fatal psychiatric treatments, including electroconvulsive therapy, frontal lobotomies and insulin therapies. Right through to the end of the 1960s, women with a range of psychiatric diagnoses were prescribed forced womb extractions and forced sterilisations in psychiatric hospitals. It is hard to ignore the centuries of misogyny which underpin psychiatry, and the ways in which any women who did not conform to the expected standards set by men were quickly positioned as mentally ill and in need of treatment or isolation from society.

In 2017, Helena Bonham Carter starred as Eleanor Riese in the film *55 Steps*. It told the true story of Eleanor's life and death at the hands of the psychiatric systems in the USA between 1970 and 1991. When she was twenty-five years old, she was diagnosed with schizophrenia and heavily medicated using forced injections which caused her serious physical symptoms and illnesses. At the time, she had no right to refuse antipsychotic medication, sedatives or any other forced treatments. She was often restrained by several men, pinned to the floor, and injected with drugs that she had no knowledge of and had never consented to.

When challenged, doctors would say that patients in psychiatric hospitals were so delusional and disordered that they could not make informed decisions about their care, and therefore, their consent was not required. Eleanor was persistent though, and contacted human rights lawyers who were interested in taking on cases of the most vulnerable and oppressed people.

In 1989, and after a prolonged and controversial set of hearings and appeals, the courts ruled that people in psychiatric care should be given the right to refuse treatment, and should be given full information about the medication and treatment they are being given. However, Eleanor already suffered significant bladder and kidney damage from prolonged lithium injections and other powerful antipsychotic drugs, and she died from a kidney infection in 1991, at the age of just forty-seven.

Being gay as a mental illness

Before homosexuality was considered a mental illness, it was first considered to be a form of demonic possession.

The history of homosexuality as a mental illness is predominantly concerned with the persecution of white gay men, many of whom were diagnosed as 'sexually deviant' or 'mentally disordered' and according to Carr & Spandler (2019) were either criminalised under sodomy laws (if they were working class), or sent for psychiatric treatment (reserved for the middle- and upper-class men).

The history of lesbian and bisexual women is the same as much of female history – sparse, fragmented and undocumented. Researchers often struggle to find any writings or evidence about the experiences of lesbian women when they were referred or self-referred into psychiatric services. What little has been found was discussed by Carr & Spandler in 2019, when they reported that lesbian and bisexual women were unlikely to be criminalised, but were very likely to be found in psychiatric services where psychiatrists, psychologists and therapists either felt that there was nothing they could do for female homosexuals, or that they needed therapy and medication to 'overcome their homosexual tendencies'.

In their research, they found examples such as:

◆ Women being given aversion therapy using electric shock or chemical emetics being given to same-sex attracted women (Crumpsall Hospital in north Manchester between 1962 and 1967).
◆ Women being given aversion therapy to cure their lesbianism who reported feeling terrible for months afterwards, and whilst it did reduce their sexual attraction to women, it never caused sexual attraction to men.
◆ Women dying by suicide after being given aversion therapy to 'cure' lesbianism.
◆ Women being given experimental LSD therapy to 'overcome homosexuality' (London, Leicester and Newcastle hospitals in the 1950s and 1960s).
◆ Putting women into insulin comas to cure their sexuality in a UK hospital in the 1950s.
◆ Conducting psychosurgery (e.g. frontal lobotomies) on women to cure their homosexuality.

There is, therefore, a conversation to be had about the ways in which lesbianism in a heteronormative patriarchy comes to be seen as nothing more than insanity, or illness. The possibility of a woman not needing or wanting a man, and instead loving or desiring women was (and always has been) so unthinkable, that where the church argued that it was evidence of demonic possession and witchcraft, modern medicine argued that it must mean that the thinking and behaviour of the woman is disordered, damaged or corrupted.

Being poor as a mental illness

I think often about the classism and wealth divide in mental health and psychiatry. What is the difference between eccentricity and creative genius – and mental disorders? How can a wealthy, middle-class person display the exact same behaviours as a poor, working-class person and still avoid being sectioned, or having their children removed from their care? The answer appears to be money and social status.

For decades, there has been an apparent relationship between being poor, being of lower social class, and mental health diagnoses. The most obvious reasons for why that might be, have been successfully obscured by classism.

Being poor is not just an experience of having less wealth than other humans; it instead comes attached to assumptions, narratives, expectations and stereotypes of who you are, what you are capable of and what you are worth in society. It makes sense then, that a class of people is created – an entire group of millions of people who are all assumed to think, act and look the same: poor.

To be clear, the assumptions have been developing throughout history, and as the social class system became embedded:

Poor people were slovenly, lazy and unkempt
Poor people were poor because they didn't work hard enough

Poor people were unclean and unhealthy
Poor people were uneducated and stupid
Poor people were sly, manipulative and criminal
Poor people couldn't take care of their children properly
Poor people behaved and thought differently/less rationally than
those with higher social status and wealth

Back in 1895, French aristocrat Gustave Le Bon wrote extensively on 'crowd behaviour' amongst other theories and beliefs he had about human behaviour (which included white supremacy and male superiority). His theories of 'herd mentality' and 'crowd behaviour' are widely taught in university and college psychology courses, despite them being mainly based on his views that poor and working-class people were stupid, easy to control and primitive in nature.

He theorised that poor people behaved in uncivilised ways in crowds because a crowd removed their identity, and turned them into aggressive, primitive thinkers that turned into a 'group mind' which could in turn, be manipulated and controlled by governments and mass media.

Not surprisingly, from a man who had created entire diagrams of ethnic hierarchies, intelligence hierarches and theories which positioned women as intellectually inferior, he did not consider that people of higher social class could be caught by 'group mind' or 'social contagion', as this was only specific to people of lower social classes.

As a terrifying but interesting aside, it is widely taught at undergraduate and postgraduate social psychology that Gustave Le Bon's work on controlling the working classes, and the concept of 'social contagion' and 'crowd behaviour' was avidly read and utilised by both Adolf Hitler and Benito Mussolini.

By the early 1900s, researchers had become more interested in stereo-types, and what children understood about poverty, class and wealth. In studies before 1950, children as young as five years old would report to researchers that wealth was desirable, and poverty was undesirable (Woods et al., 2005). Further, children and adults were being primed with stereotypes of 'poor people' and 'rich people' – in which, of course, poor people were lazy, dishonest, ignorant, incompetent and disinterested in self-improvement or education (Bullock, 1995).

Present day hangovers of these beliefs in mental health practice and theory

It would be easier, and a lot more comfortable for us all, if I could conclude this chapter by reporting that psychiatry, psychology and mental health services had made huge advancements and improve-ments in their approaches to and treatment of marginalised groups; however, this is not the case. Being Black, female, lesbian, bisexual, poor or gender non-conforming (or several of these as a woman) is still dangerous when it comes to pathologisation. There are significant and enduring hangovers in modern practice and theory.

When I interviewed Brianna* for this book, we talked for a long time about her experiences of being pathologised, gaslit and demonised by mental health services, but it wasn't until the final ten minutes of the conversation that she reflected that she felt the services she had engaged with were racist. I had absolutely no doubt that she was right, not least because Black women absolutely know when they are being discriminated against or typecast; but also because the evidence has persistently shown that racism is still rife in psychiatry.

Brianna had quickly found herself diagnosed, medicated, sectioned, assessed and monitored for several years after she was raped and exploited whilst at university. Speaking to me as a thirty-five-year-old professional who had worked in banking and the criminal justice system, she told me how exhausted and angry she was when she found that doctors had written about her 'dishevelled hair' in her diagnosis of borderline personality disorder and adjustment disorder. She told me that they had made comments about her natural Afro hair, called her 'aggressive' and 'angry' and had written on her case notes that she was 'African' without ever asking her what her ethnicity was. Brianna is Afro-Caribbean. Not that anyone cared, or even apologised when she corrected them in 2020.

Coincidentally in 2020, a letter signed by 175 psychiatrists was published in the British Medical Journal which called for the Royal College of Psychiatrists (RCP) to urgently and transparently address the systemic, institutional racism and colonialism in historic and modern-day mental health theory and practice. The RCP issued a statement to respond.

In the statement, President of the RCP Dr Adrian James said that he agreed that racism and inequality existed in society, that it also existed in mental health services and the NHS, and that he would develop specific roles and streams of work around equality and inclusion.

However, Dr James would not commit to an independent inquiry into the decades of harm caused by the theories and practice of psychiatry, which was met with further criticism from psychiatrists from minoritized groups. Instead, he stated in a further response that an independent inquiry into systemic racism would 'slow down our work'.

The lead author of the response was Dr Sami Timimi, who replied in the BMJ in July 2020 to express disappointment that the president of the RCP would not support an independent inquiry, or effectively address the concerns of current trainee and qualified psychiatrists who were still seeing and being subjected to racism frequently. Dr Timimi included accounts from trainee and new psychiatrists, including the comment below:

'I am entering into a profession that has used "science" and "facts" to systematically oppress Black people and POC for centuries, with the perhaps naive hope to work against this in my career. However, I and my fellow medical students who are politically active will have a hard time reconciling our anti-racist work and principles with the state of psychiatry at the moment. To work within the guidelines and rules as they are now, for me would mean being complicit in racial violence. It would mean contributing to a system that sections Black people under the Mental Health Act at four times the rate of white people. A system that forces sedation and medication on Black people because they are disproportionately seen as a danger to themselves and others. A system that routinely works with the police in criminalising illness and often fatally detaining Black people and POC. Until the Royal College of Psychiatrists commits to independent examination and works to rid itself of the practices and guidelines that actively militate against Black and POC people in the UK, I cannot choose psychiatry.'

(BMJ, 2020;370:m2657)

The trainee above raises legitimate concerns that would be explored in an independent inquiry, and still need to be urgently addressed.

At the time of writing this book, there had been no further movement on this topic, and whilst the RCP had published other apologies to minoritized groups in which they publicly discuss the unethical and oppressive treatments, sectioning and harm caused by psychiatry, no such statement has been made about Black and other minoritised people.

Being lesbian or bisexual

With pride being celebrated in countries across the world, and companies turning their websites and logos rainbow colours in apparent support of gay pride, it would seem contradictory that women were still being pathologised and diagnosed as mentally ill with reference to their sexuality. At the beginning of this chapter, I presented the email from Hannah in which she asked whether it was homophobic to quote her bisexuality (and later, her realisation that she was lesbian), as a symptom of a personality disorder which required medication and lifelong treatment.

Again, the reality of progress and tolerance is much harder to swallow. Research by Reich & Zanarini (2008) has recently shown that women with borderline personality disorder diagnoses are much more likely to be lesbian or bisexual than heterosexual; and that their sexuality changing or being questioned is often cited as evidence of their changing, unstable 'identity' issues. Unfortunately, the authors concluded that women and girls who have been sexually abused in childhood are likely to 'identify themselves as a homosexual or bisexual, not because it is their sexual orientation, but because they have been abused in childhood by men. In these cases, their choice of partner has less to do with sexual attraction and more to do with attempting to feel safe.'

This assumption is common, and ignores the complexity of sexual attraction and the commonality of male violence. Statistically, many girls will be sexually abused in childhood by men and boys in their lives – but this does not mean that the abuse is a causal factor in their sexual orientation. If it was, and being subjected to male violence caused women and girls to change sexuality, the majority of the female population would be lesbian or bisexual.

The danger here, of course, is that women who are diagnosed with borderline personality disorder will have their sexuality used as evidence of an identity crisis or mental illness instead of their protected right to be attracted to, and to have relationships with, adults of the same sex.

Whilst I know that many professionals and services would fiercely argue that they are not homophobic, I often came across subtle ways that lesbian women (and their children) were pathologised in therapeutic and medical settings. I was privileged to interview twenty-three-year-old Megan in 2020, who was raped as a teenager by a man who was then found not guilty in a court in the UK.

She told me she had always wanted to speak out, but had been dismissed and silenced many times. Although she had suffered from chronic stomach ache and migraines for many years since the trauma, professionals had not only positioned the cause of the physical illnesses as 'anxiety' and refused to give her any tests, but her mum's sexuality had been questioned.

Megan explained to me that after many years of seeking support, she finally managed to access therapy to talk about the rapes she had been subjected to, and the trauma responses she had been experiencing. Instead of validating her traumas or talking about the sexual violence, the counsellor seemed to want to focus on her mum being a lesbian, as if this was a cause or root of her feelings.

Megan told me that the counsellor frequently moved the conversation towards her mum's sexuality, and away from the conversation about being raped as a teenager, and again by her boyfriend a few years later.

This isn't the first time I had been concerned about the over-analysis of lesbian mothers and their children, especially considering that in

2020, I knew of two separate family court cases in which lesbian women who had children from previous abuse or relationships with men were heavily scrutinised in court, which included psychological reports, assessments – and even one instance where the absent father accused the lesbian couple of being witches. This would sound like a parody, or joke, but after accusing the women of being inappropriate parents due to being lesbian, and then requesting extensive assessments of them, the next port of call was to accuse them of witchcraft. This was taken seriously by the judge, who then expected the two feminist lesbian women to defend or explain the accusations as if they were real.

In a courtroom. In 2020.

Yet, in 2017, then-President of the RCP Professor Wendy Burn issued a statement to BuzzFeed about the role of psychiatry in homophobia. In striking contrast to the RCP response to systemic racism, this one was clear, accurate and apologetic.

She wrote that 'there are no words that can repair the damage done to anyone who has ever been deemed mentally ill simply for loving someone of the same sex', and that these treatments were known to be used up to and throughout the 1970s. Professor Burn accepted that the homophobic 'aversion therapy' treatments (that had routinely included showing gay people homoerotic images whilst subjecting them to electroconvulsive therapy, or leaving gay people in serious pain, vomit, faeces or urine for days in order to develop an association between serious negative consequences and homosexual thoughts), were wrong, disproven and debunked.

Whilst this statement was welcomed by many, it is a disappointing reality that several years later, bisexuality and lesbianism in women and girls is still being used as a symptom or marker of personality disorder. Indeed, there are still clear descriptions of symptoms in women and girls with borderline personality disorder which include 'engaging in casual sexual relationships, reporting a greater number of different sexual partners as well as promiscuity, and engaging in homosexual experiences', according to the *Innovations in Clinical Neuroscience Journal, Psychiatry Journal*, and the *Journal of Mental Disorders*.

Being gender non-conforming

One of the most controversial issues around women and gender at present is the psychiatric diagnosis of teenage girls as having 'gender dysphoria' when they do not conform or identify with femininity. Gender dysphoria in girls is described by the NHS as a strong, lasting desire to express their gender identity by changing the way they look or behave. The NHS clearly states that 'gender dysphoria is not a mental illness', but fails to note that gender dysphoria is listed as a psychiatric disorder in DSM-V, which is the diagnostic manual of mental disorders (APA, 2021). It is notable then, that national information denies that gender dysphoria is a psychiatric diagnosis, despite the term 'gender dysphoria' itself being the name of the recognised disorder.

In 2009, seventy children were referred to the Tavistock and Portman Gender Identity Service as they wished to transition. In 2019, 2,590 children were referred into the same service. What is surprising however, is that in 2009, 75 per cent of the children were boys who wanted to present and live as girls – but by 2019, 70 per cent of the children were girls who wanted to present and live as boys.

Arguably, the exponential rise in young girls being diagnosed with psychiatric gender disorders must be viewed through a lens of oppression, misogyny and centuries of theories and beliefs that women and girls are inferior, mentally ill, defective versions of men and boys. This critical argument is often missing from broader discussions of gender and psychiatry.

When girls are growing up in a misogynistic society that frequently sexualises, objectifies, traumatises, patronises, feminises and vilifies them – a trauma-informed perspective would clearly argue that it is rational for girls to wish to escape femininity, and their female bodies. It would make sense that they would feel safer if they presented to the world as non-binary or masculine. Therefore, there is much evidence to suggest that a girl or woman seeking to live as non-binary or masculine does not constitute a psychiatric disorder. It does, however, suggest that girls are traumatised, looking for an escape hatch from the patriarchal norms which govern them, and place great value on non-binary, non-feminine and pro-masculine roles and presentations.

Unfortunately, rather than a growing understanding that psychiatry continues to harm girls and women, the development and utilisation of gender dysphoria as a psychiatric disorder positions any deviation from socially constructed traditional gender roles as a mental illness. Following this thread of logic, psychiatry has then supported the medicalisation of this so-called psychiatric disorder by prescribing puberty blockers, artificial cross-sex hormones and even cosmetic surgery.

The key argument here is that girls wishing to present as androgynous or masculine are certainly experiencing some distress and dysphoria, but to medicalise and diagnose them with a publicly denied psychiatric disorder is only continuing the psychiatric tradition of pathologising women and girls when they do not conform to conservative ideals and gender roles. What is now being pushed as progressive and inclusive looks very much like old-time traditional, medicalising, misogynistic psychiatry.

Rather than supporting women and girls to present and live however they like, without any commitment or connection to traditional gender roles, psychiatry has once again achieved patriarchal power by convincing them, and the rest of the world, that being gender non-conforming is a mental illness in need of treatment. And this time, like many times before it, professionals in power have embraced the medical treatment of teenage girls as positive and sorely needed, rather than exploring why so many girls seek to shed their female and/or feminine identity and expectations.

Classism and social status

A muted conversation in academia and medicine is that of the existence, and impact, of classism. It's not a surprise that institutions which have always been surrounded by, and built upon, elitism, wealth and the education of privileged people, struggle to have meaningful, reflective discussions about it; right up to the present day.

I will always recall the day I had a meeting with a professional social worker back in 2017, when she was talking to me about two of her cases. Both cases were women of similar ages, with children of similar ages. In both cases, the children had disclosed abuse by their fathers, and investigations were under way.

What interested me mostly were the descriptions of each mother, and their coping mechanisms. Both were using alcohol, but only one of them was scrutinised for it.

One mother was unemployed, and the other was a headteacher. The unemployed mother was being scrutinised for every response she had (her confusion, her anger, her sadness, her exhaustion – and her tendency to go out on the weekend with friends, drinking). Her children were safe, being looked after by her parents, but professionals were concerned that she was not a fit mother and had 'mental health issues' and 'problems with alcohol'.

The headteacher, on the other hand, was drinking at least a bottle of red wine every night, would often turn up to work late and hungover, the children would find her asleep on the living-room floor, or on the sofa, and she was clearly struggling to cope with the traumatic disclosures of her children. And yet, the professional I spoke to seemed to think that a bottle of wine at night, to help the busy professional headteacher to relax and 'wind down', was normal, and acceptable. She didn't think that the headteacher had any 'problems with alcohol'.

The most obvious difference between the two women is social class, and social status. The unemployed woman was positioned as problematic, chaotic, mentally ill and alcoholic – whilst the headteacher was seen as a busy woman with an important job who needed a bottle of wine at night to wind down.

This further led my interest to the coping mechanisms of the social workers themselves – versus those of the women they worked with. Over years of teaching and training about vicarious trauma in social workers, it had become obvious that many social workers were drinking to cope with the disclosures, the deaths, the abuse, the neglect and the trauma of their jobs. Some told me that their entire team drank, and would get to their mid-morning break feeling like they needed a gin.

In workshops about vicarious trauma, thirty to fifty social workers would put their hands up when I asked how many of them drank at least a few glasses of wine or spirits at night to cope with their jobs. It was an open secret that they were not coping, and instead, were drinking. Many told me that they couldn't get to sleep without being drunk. Drinking was normalised; and in some teams in the UK, was sensationalised. They bought each other funny gifts, stationery and coffee mugs which said, 'I wish this was gin'.

And yet, the same teams were scrutinising and judging the alcohol use of women who had been abused, raped, trafficked and traumatised as a mental illness, or a dependency in need of treatment and rehabilitation.

In 2021, I spoke to a senior police officer who confirmed that cases of rape of women were being dropped if the woman was known as an 'alcoholic' or there had ever been notes which suggested she drank frequently.

It appears then, that social status and class can change the perception of a response, or an action. If you're poor, drinking alcohol is a dangerous, reckless habit of the mentally ill – but if you're middle class or wealthy, drinking alcohol is a great way to wind down and get to sleep after a busy or stressful day.

The same has always been true for drug use, too. Poor people using drugs are a disgusting scourge on society and a drain on medical and mental health resources, but rich people snorting cocaine and popping pills is a sexy, wealthy, exciting behaviour which features in movies and music videos.

What is the difference between the rich and privileged talking about their mental health, suicidality and drug use as if it's a philosophical learning curve that anyone could go through – and the poor being sectioned, heavily medicated, having their children removed and their opportunities limited for their mental health, suicidality and drug use?

What's the difference between a privileged, middle-class woman saying that she can hear the voices of dead people, being given a popular TV show and a book deal – and the poor woman on a zero-hours contract in a supermarket saying that she hears the voices of dead people, who is sectioned for the next six months for non-consensual treatment of her 'mental illness'?

Do we even notice the class gap in pathologisation anymore?

Being a woman

Today, as I write this, women are still at grave risk in our modern psychiatric and mental health services.

They remain the group most likely to be given electroconvulsive therapy, and the group most likely to be forcibly sedated using injected tranquillisers.

Recent NHS data gathered and presented by Dr John Read has revealed that in 2019, 67 per cent of people being given electroconvulsive therapy were women. In twenty NHS trusts in the UK, ECT was given to women twice as often as men. Further than this, NHS trusts reported that 36 per cent of their patients in 2019 were given ECT without their consent. When asked whether the dangerous treatment was shown to improve women's conditions, the NHS reported that they only collected efficacy data in 16 per cent of trusts – and only 3 per cent of trusts had a procedure to collect any adverse reactions to ECT. The rest of the trusts collected neither efficacy data, nor adverse reaction data.

In June 2021, Dr Chris Harrop and colleagues published an independent audit of NHS Trusts which reported alarming inaccuracies in the information given to patients and their families about electroconvulsive therapy, often minimising the risks involved and exaggerating the potential benefits.

ECT involves passing electricity across patients' brains to cause seizures. It is still being used on about 2,500 patients a year in England, predominantly women over sixty years old. Research suggests that some patients experience a temporary lift in mood, but there is no research evidence it has any long-term benefits, or that it prevents suicide. Between 12 per cent and 55 per cent of patients suffer permanent memory loss.

Freedom of Information Act requests were sent to fifty-one NHS Trusts for a copy of their ECT information leaflet. Thirty-six (71 per cent) provided leaflets. The number of accurate pieces of information contained in them, from a possible twenty-nine, ranged from four to twenty, with a mean of 12.8.

The most commonly omitted information was:

◆ there are different forms of ECT, with different risks of brain damage (mentioned by just fourteen Trusts)
◆ psychological therapy should be tried first (twelve Trusts);
◆ serious cardiovascular side effects (six Trusts);
◆ lack of long-term benefits (six Trusts);
◆ patients' right to take 24 hours to consider giving consent (one Trust);
◆ memory loss is higher in women and older people (zero Trusts).

The number of inaccurate statements averaged 5.8, out of eleven, and ranged from two to nine.

The most common inaccurate statements included:

- ◆ ECT corrects biological deficits (twenty-eight Trusts);
- ◆ exaggerated claims of very low mortality risk (twenty-eight Trusts);
- ◆ minimisation of memory loss (twenty-three Trusts);
- ◆ claims that ECT saves lives (twenty-two Trusts);
- ◆ exaggerated claims of very high improvement rates (nineteen Trusts).

The most recent document provided by the Royal College of Psychiatrists included seven inaccurate statements. The only document not to include any false statements was produced by the mental health charity, Mind.

The audit concluded:

> *Information leaflets about ECT comply neither with National Institute for Health and Clinical Excellence (NICE) recommendations nor the principle of informed consent. Patients are being misled about the risks they are taking and the limited nature of ECT's benefits.*

What is alarming about these new findings is the lack of regulation of ECT, and the lack of regulation of the misinformation being spread about ECT. Despite being one of the most dangerous treatments that the NHS offer, with the least evidence base, it is frequently encouraged by using outdated, inaccurate narratives that most people would believe were confined to history books.

Indeed, it would surprise most people to learn that the NHS delivers ECT to thousands of people per year at all. I only became aware of this after four years of working with women and girls subjected to violence and abuse, when I met a fifteen-year-old girl who was being given regular rounds of ECT in my local NHS trust. It was 2012, I was still only young and had never come across ECT before. Like many others, I assumed it had been banned along with the other torturous and barbaric procedures and treatments in psychiatry. The only knowledge I had of ECT was from horror movies.

Nicky had been referred to the service I was managing after she had been raped by some men on her way home from school. She was one of several girls who had been approached, and the perpetrators had filmed the rapes on their mobile phones. The local police were linking the cases together, as more and more girls came forward to report one strange thing that was common across all the attacks: the perpetrators were two young adult men who raped the girls and then high-fived each other on the videos they were making. The act of high-fiving each other had been reported by several girls, and led police to think it was the same perpetrators.

Nicky had struggled for almost a year with the impact of the rape. Having also been abused in childhood, this was a devastating trauma for her to be subjected to again. Whilst she was accessing our services for counselling, she became interested in an empowerment group I ran on a Thursday for teen girls and young women who wanted to focus on themselves. I noticed that she would often fall asleep at my sessions, or curl up on the sofa and become unresponsive, almost like she was in a totally different dimension to everyone else. She sometimes forgot what she was doing, or why she was with me.

I raised my concerns about her, only to be told by her social worker that she was being given regular rounds of ECT for 'treatment-resistant depression'. I gasped. She had only been raped nine months earlier. How could anyone think that her trauma was resistant to treatment at fifteen years old? I had never even considered that anyone would prescribe electroconvulsive therapy to a child.

Unfortunately, whilst this was the first time I had come across a girl being given ECT after rape or abuse, it was not the last. It remains, to this day, one of the most impactful red flag moments I had about the pathologising of women and girls.

In May 2021, I was given access to further NHS data collected by Kieran Sturgess of the Life Learning Academy, this time, on the use of chemical restraints in the UK in 2020 and 2021.

The NHS defines chemical restraint as:

> *The use of medication which is prescribed, and administered for the purpose of controlling or subduing disturbed/violent behaviour, where it is not prescribed for the treatment of a formally identified physical or mental illness.*

In plain terms, this means that chemical restraints are used to rapidly sedate a person (using forced injections or forced oral medication) even where it is not prescribed or agreed upon.

Keiran Sturgess is from the Mavam Group, which includes a service called 'Your Life Our Help' (YLOH), and are a group of independent services based in Ipswich, Suffolk; offering supported housing and help in people's homes, they are dedicated to offering people help and support. Their aim is to focus on seeing people as people. To get to know them, to hear their stories and to learn about the things that have happened to them. To look beyond the labels that others have applied to them and understand that the main reasons for needing help are to be found within their stories.

Another part of the Mavam Group is the Life Learning Academy, led by Kieran. One of his first tasks for the LLA was to create 'Anti-discriminatory Practice' training. As part of this he was interested in exploring the way that people are treated within the NHS. Following a Freedom of Information Request, he was subsequently referred to NHS Digital, where the NHS routinely collect data regarding the use of chemical and physical restraint within psychiatric hospitals and units.

Kieran found much that he expected to find, in that there is evidence of significant differences in the use of restraint according to ethnicity, age and sex. What was shocking to him and his colleagues, however, was the scale of the difference when it came to gender. In particular the amount of restraint that young woman and girls are receiving.

The research that Kieran has done raises many questions and reveals that there are practices in services that require closer scrutiny. He has exposed that young women and girls, who are likely to already have experienced abuse, trauma and discrimination, are then exposed to further trauma in the name of treatment; and that it appears that young women's and girls' distress is met with violence. What urgently need closer investigation are the mechanisms and structures that make this happen.

The data clearly shows that the NHS conducts thousands of forced chemical restraints on people each month, but that 63 per cent of all of those chemical restraints are on females. Further, when this data is broken down by age, we see that girls under eighteen are being given the most chemical restraints of all sexes and age groups.

NHS Restraint Use October 2020–February 2021

Restraint type	Females	Males
Chemical restraint by injection	3,910 (71%)	1,615 (29%)
Mechanical restraint	473 (86%)	80 (14%)
Chemical restraint of a child under eighteen years old	257 (91%)	26 (9%)

Despite Kieran finding almost equal numbers of males (49.87%) and females (49.95%) in the services, the data analysis showed that girls and women under thirty-four years old receive 64 per cent of all chemical restraints and girls under eighteen years old are given forced chemical restraints more than any other group. Girls under eighteen years old were found to have been chemically restrained an average of five times per month, whereas boys in the same age group were found to be chemically restrained an average of twice per month. Girls under eighteen years old were found to account for 20 per cent of all chemical restraints of females, whereas boys under eighteen years old were found to account for only 3 per cent of all chemical restraints of males.

Simply put, girls under eighteen in NHS mental health facilities are being chemically restrained using forced injections around seven times more than boys under eighteen are. And when we look at women in totality, women and girls receive *52 per cent more* chemical restraints than men and boys.

The question, then, is why?

When the majority of all attacks on NHS staff are committed by men, and the majority of all violent crime is committed by men, why are teenage girls being chemically restrained more than once per week using forced injections of tranquillisers, but the same NHS data shows that men and boys are being physically restrained and placed in seclusion or isolation rooms to calm down?

Could it be that the distress of women and girls is so pathologised that professionals believe it warrants restraining them and then forcibly injecting them for their own good? Or is it that male anger and aggression is so tolerated and normalised that professionals don't see it as abnormal or disordered, and therefore don't seek to tranquillise them?

Or maybe, it is that women and girls making a fuss is so problematic that it's easier to just inject them with chemicals, shut them up and leave them to sleep for days?

Is this progress?

CHAPTER 3

A history of perfect women and crazy women

We and our whole community of canons, recognising that the wickedness of women is greater than all of the other wickedness of the world, and that there is no anger like that of women, and that the poison of asps and dragons is more curable and less dangerous to men than the familiarity of women, have unanimously decreed for the safety of our souls, no less than that of our bodies and goods, that we will on no account receive any more sisters to the increase of our perdition, but will avoid them like poisonous animals.

Pope Innocent III

The ideal, or perfect, woman, has not changed much in hundreds of years. As old as some of the stories and examples from history books will be, it is important that we see how similar they are to present-day cases.

As far back as we can go, women have been classified as the inferior sex. Not just inferior though, because that is too forgiving for the patriarchy. Simply classifying women as inferior and weaker was never going to be powerful enough for men to gain complete control over them – because all it would take would be a demonstration by a handful of women that they were not inferior, and were as capable as men, and the jig would be very much up.

Instead, it was vital that men framed women not only as physically inferior but mentally inferior, too. Most people are aware of this systemic misogyny and the way it stopped girls from participating in education, and stopped women from being able to vote. However, men went much further than simply suggesting that women couldn't get their pretty little brains around mathematics and politics, and deliberately and persistently described and treated women as unreliable, unstable, evil, crazy and dangerous. That way, no matter what they did or said (or attempted, or disclosed, or reported, or invented, or criticised), it could be positioned as a hysterical lie, a malicious accusation, or as the mad ramblings of a crazy old fisherman's wife.

The concept of the 'ideal woman' has barely changed in centuries – and what is probably the most interesting fact about the ideal woman concept is that it is curiously similar around the world, despite there being large differences in cultures, religions, languages, fashion, economies, laws, rights and norms.

The ideal woman has always been the same:

Beautiful
Young
White
Heterosexual
Feminine
Childbearing
Obedient
Dependent
Submissive
Polite
Committed
Faithful
Virginal, or with only one significant sexual life partner

Sexually available to her male partner (but only when he says so, and how he says so)

Any deviation from this strict set of requirements would (and still will) lead to women being ostracised, demonised, pathologised, sexualised or criminalised.

Consider the opposites of the list above, and how hated a woman would be if she contradicted all of the criteria of the ideal woman.

Ideal woman	Crazy woman
– Beautiful	– Ugly
– Young	– Old
– Heterosexual	– Lesbian or bisexual
– Feminine	– Non-feminine or masculine presenting
– White	– Black
– Childbearing	– Infertile
– Obedient	– Disobedient
– Dependent	– Independent
– Submissive	– Powerful
– Polite	– Impolite
– Committed	– Casual
– Faithful	– Unfaithful
– Virginal, or sexually conservative	– Sexually liberated or active
– Sexually chaste	– 'Promiscuous'

Interestingly, all of the attributes from the list on the right have been used to diagnose, section, medicate, abuse and imprison women in the past (and for some, in the present day, too). Many of the attributes on the right were used to describe and then prosecute women for being witches.

Whilst it may seem odd to trace psychiatry back to its supernatural origins, there are undeniable and influential roots in religion, satanism, witches and Catholicism that should never be ignored. In fact, I would suggest that understanding the history of religion, misogyny within the church and the witch trials increases our understanding of modern-day feminism, and modern-day mental health systems exponentially.

Much before witches, the 'perfect woman' was created by Christian priests and theologians in Mary, the mother of Jesus. The story of Mary is an interesting one, as she is invented, reinvented, shifted and changed over the course of several hundred years to make her womanhood utterly unattainable to every other female in the world.

Jack Holland traces this reinvention of Mary in his book *A Brief History of Misogyny: The World's Oldest Prejudice*. He writes that in 431AD, Mary was announced as the mother of Jesus – and the mother of God. A young peasant Jewish girl from Palestine was elevated to the highest possible position in the world – she was the mother of God, and therefore, the mother of the entire universe. However, whilst most people will be familiar with the issue around her 'immaculate conception' and the way the church invented her story to mean that she was a virgin, that her hymen never split and that she was completely 'clean' when she gave birth to Jesus, what most do not know is that for hundreds of years there were also questions about her own conception.

How could this young peasant girl be divine enough to carry Jesus, if she herself was born from sin? If she was born from sex between two humans, she was tainted by lust, and therefore, could never be good enough to birth God. It became an unthinkable scandal that Mary, the perpetual virgin, the mother of Jesus and God, the queen of heaven and birther of the entire universe, could ever have been conceived this way.

What followed was an amazing sleight of hand in which Pope Pius IX officially proclaimed the doctrine of Mary's Immaculate Conception in 1854 – making her the only person other than Jesus to be conceived without sex. Mary, the young peasant girl from Palestine, was born divine, and no further questions were needed. She had never been tainted by lust or sex, and she lived as a perfect woman, died, and then went to heaven.

Holland writes that Mary served as a constant, contradictory and impossible role model for women, as no other women would ever achieve immaculate conception, and all of their children would be tainted by original sin. No other woman would ever be as perfect, passive, obedient or dutiful. No other woman could ever be as sexless, and repress their desire or lust for others.

And yet, women tried.

Between the ninth and thirteenth centuries, women moved to convents to remove themselves from society, to give themselves to God, and to practise all of the obedience, celibacy and passivity that Mary had demonstrated. By the thirteenth century, nunneries were common-place across Europe, with hundreds of thousands of women teaching and learning how to write, read, sew, meditate, pray and work together on beautiful pieces of poetry, art and literature.

This was eventually denounced by Pope Innocent III who prohibited women from becoming leaders or authorities within the church, which was met with misogyny and celebration from men who sought to keep women away from religion and power.

We and our whole community of canons, recognising that the wickedness of women is greater than all of the other wickedness of the world, and that there is no anger like that of women, and that the poison of asps and dragons is more curable and less dangerous to men than the familiarity of women, have unanimously decreed for the safety of our souls, no less than that of our bodies and goods, that we will on no account receive any more sisters to the increase of our perdition, but will avoid them like poisonous animals.

Quoted in Holland (2006)

This decree was to have a lasting and important impact on women for many centuries to come, and was to become the set-up for the belief that women were the most evil, dangerous and wicked creatures of all.

The word 'witch' is thought to come from the sixteenth-century derogatory term 'wicche', which was used to describe women who were evil, ageing, malicious and 'dried up'. Simultaneously, the word 'slut' was developing from its fifteenth-century origins which meant an unkempt, dirty, slovenly woman (Sollee, 2017). As time went on, both terms became intertwined to mean women with low morals, evil intent and loose sexuality – and because morals and religious law were so tied up with female biology and female sexuality, they became intrinsically linked over time.

In 2017, Kristen Sollee wrote an excellent historical account of the links between the categorisation of women as witches and sluts, in which she argues that the mysteries and contentions of female biology have dominated religion and artistic thought for over 200,000 years. Whilst modern mainstream religions chose to ignore or subjugate women, historic and ancient religions often had female gods and female elders. However, as time went on, society rejected the concept of females in power and all major world religions moved towards patriarchal models of power and humanity. This is important, because at around the same time, female power, intellect and non-conformity began to be repositioned as a sin, or as demonic possession.

In some ways, witches are a stereotype of everything that the patriarchy attempts to control, ignore or eradicate in women and girls. Sollee

(2017) writes that everything about the witch flew in the face of patriarchal control – and so, men made them into the most obscene caricatures possible. A message to women, to never be like the witches, or be subjected to trial, hanging, drowning or burning.

> *Don't age. Don't step out of line. Don't read too many books. Don't know too much. Don't question men. Don't learn about the moon or the stars. Don't know about nature. Don't be gay. Don't be unattractive to men. Don't be outspoken. Don't be angry. Don't be independent. Don't be disobedient. Don't be impolite. Don't be powerful. Don't be a slut. Don't be a witch.*
> *Or we'll kill you.*
> *And even if you are none of these things, we can accuse you of them, and the weight of that accusation would be enough to have you killed anyway.*

This is of vital importance. Look at how little has changed in the last five centuries. Replace the word 'witch' with the word 'crazy', and replace reference to 'killing' with new medical terms such as 'sectioned' or 'treated' and what do you have? Traditional psychiatry. Replace the word 'crazy' with the term 'borderline' or 'emotionally unstable', and what do you have? Modern psychiatry.

Therefore, what we can argue is that there has been a clear path from being castigated as a witch, to being labelled as crazy, to the modern-day diagnosis as a woman or girl with a personality disorder. And I am not the first person to argue this. Ussher (2013) wrote that borderline personality disorder is the 'wastebasket of mental health' and is simply the gradual modernisation of the same stereotypes and accusations that would have a woman burned at the stake.

True to the title of this book, witches were often seen as sexy, but psycho. Women who were reported or accused of being witches were often punished and killed due to their sexuality, female masturbation, discussion of female pleasure or their sexual behaviour. The Catholic Church played an instrumental part in this construction of sexual women as witches, and shared posters and leaflets about female pleasure being satanic and devious.

In 1486, a document entitled *The Malleus Maleficarum* was published and shared widely across Europe. The document used the most misogynistic texts from the Bible and from famous classical philosophers to create a doctrine about the hunting and killing of witches (and women in general). It is widely regarded as one of the most misogynistic texts of all time, with entire sections made up of lies and accusations about women's biology, brains, sexuality, sexual pleasure and links to the devil. It accused witches of being able to stop women from becoming pregnant, making them leave their husbands, and being able to make men impotent. The text stated that non-conforming women had been having sex with the devil, which had made them evil and powerful – with incredible knowledge of female biology, reproduction, pregnancy and birth (Somasundaram, 1985).

The accusations of witchcraft had longstanding impacts on medicine, in which only male doctors were trusted. When women demonstrated any competent knowledge of female biology, they were often accused of being a witch and then killed. This meant that women who were learned or experienced in supporting women to give birth or have safe pregnancies became prime suspects of witchcraft: if the pregnancy went well with her advice, witchcraft was blamed and she was killed – and if the pregnancy ended in miscarriage or stillbirth, witchcraft was blamed and she was killed. Because of this, midwives were often seen as some of the most dangerous and evil of all witches, because men in power felt that they knew far too much about birth, death, health, fertility and female biology. Leaflets and rumours were spread by the Catholic Church that midwives received their powers from the devil, and that

God would only work his powers through male doctors, as women were too inferior to receive power and knowledge from God.

Witches were essentially whatever men in power wanted them to be. Sollee (2017) says that men created images of witches to be whatever they needed them to be at the time, to either excuse, explain or confuse women. If a man had been cheating on his wife, he might argue that the young woman he had slept with was a witch who cast a spell upon him. If his crops had died, he might argue that the woman next door was an evil witch who killed all his crops, or salted the earth. If his child was unwell, he might accuse his wife or another female family member of cursing them. Women were scapegoated for anything and everything during the centuries of witch trials.

So, in the seventeenth century, when women started to pass knowledge to each other about natural birth control and abortion of unwanted pregnancies, one of the first accusations made by the church was that birth control, contraceptive methods and abortions were satanic witchcraft. During her research, Sollee found that the early anti-abortion movements in the late 1800s were heavily based on the demonisation of midwives and female doctors, and instead encouraged the public to trust and favour male doctors instead of female midwives, doctors and nurses (an issue that has never really gone away).

In 2020, I interviewed Natalie*, an experienced and qualified nurse from Scotland who had been subjected to rape and domestic abuse by her ex-partner and father of her baby. In order to discredit her, he had repeatedly accused her of being mentally ill during the court cases and this had then been recorded on her personal files.

Natalie's child had a short illness as a toddler which presented as a persistent temperature which did not respond to paracetamol. Having tried everything she knew from her own knowledge, she called an out-of-hours hospital service for advice and was told to give more paracetamol. Natalie argued and said that she had already given it and then listed dosages and times, with the corresponding hourly temperatures. She explained that she was a nurse and that she felt her child needed to be seen by an out-of-hours doctor urgently.

Two days later, she was visited by two child protection social workers who informed her that the call handler had reported her to social care for having 'too much knowledge' about children's health issues and suggested that she might be fabricating the illness of her child due to her own so-called mental health issues.

What interested me most about this example was the way that Natalie's years of experience and qualifications as a registered nurse meant very little when contrasted against the testimony of her ex-husband and rapist who had defended himself by telling every agency he could that she was mentally ill. Years later, and even after he was convicted, she was still being regarded as mentally ill and 'knowing too much', even when utilising her own medical expertise.

After the Renaissance, and after the outlawing of witch trials, women were not suddenly liberated from these stereotypes and stories of evil, dangerous, sexually deviant women. Instead, men looked to 'science' and 'medicine' for reasons as to why women were so inferior and problematic – and as expected, they found what they were looking for, in abundance.

What used to be known as original sin, demonic possession or witchcraft quickly moved to medical explanations of imbalances of four humours in the body, which controlled personality types and caused illness and madness. The four humours were theorised to be choleric (yellow bile), melancholic (black bile), sanguine (blood), and phlegmatic (phlegm).

Beliefs began with Hippocrates and Galen, who both theorised that the humours in the body could determine your moods, personality and character. We could think of it as the earliest form of personality psychology – which is now dominated by trait theory.

Humour/Fluid	Location	Character
Phlegm	Lungs	Calm
Yellow bile	Spleen	Irritable
Black bile	Gall bladder	Depressed
Blood	Liver	Optimistic

Too much black bile would be reported to be the cause of depression. Too much yellow bile would be reported as the cause of aggression and violence. This would be the beginning of the medicalisation of mental health, trauma and distress. Hippocrates wrote of women who were incoherent, scared, depressed, nervous, and relied heavily on humours to explain their experiences. Their complex mental and social lives were reduced to four fluids in the body, an archaic idea which we seem to be moving back to with every step back towards reductionism, genes and biological theories of 'mental illness'.

Women were considerably impacted by the move towards medicalisation of distress and emotion, especially as there was virtually no science about the female body or reproductive system, which remained shrouded in mystery for centuries. Reams of laughable and harmful diagnoses and treatments were based on humoral, and then later medical, explanations of women's suffering and distress which led to everything from being bled until they died to holding frogs to remove evil from their bodies.

Whilst medicine was moving forward, mental illness was still entwined with magic, religion, spirituality and myth – and so was the stereotype of the ideal, perfect woman. As time has progressed, the concept of the perfect woman has hardly changed at all, and women who step outside of this narrow expectation are regularly positioned as crazy, obsessed, psychotic, promiscuous or disordered.

As of today, being female is widely reported as correlating with almost every mental disorder in the DSM-V. Women are more likely to be diagnosed with depression, anxiety and somatic disorders. They are also more likely to be diagnosed with borderline personality disorder, general anxiety disorder, panic disorder, phobias, suicide ideation and attempts, postpartum depression and psychosis, eating disorders and PTSD (*The Lancet*, 2016; WHO, 2019; *Psychology Today*, 2019).

Women are also much more likely to be diagnosed with multiple psychiatric disorders at one time (Anxiety and Depression Association of America, 2019).

It is as if no one has ever been able to join the dots – why have we not considered that women are living in a patriarchy which oppresses, objectifies, sexualises, controls, humiliates and discriminates against them on a daily basis? Why are we ignoring the most obvious explanation – that women and girls exist in an environment which causes them serious harm?

And why have we reframed the global, common and collective trauma of women and girls as hundreds of man-made, misogynistic psychiatric disorders which reside inside the brains of mentally disordered women and girls?

Who could possibly benefit from that, I ponder.

CHAPTER 4

Reframing women's trauma as mental illness

As a girl becomes a woman and moves through her life, the chances of her being subjected to trauma are very high. Most adult women can recall a time when they were sexually harassed on the way to school, bullied, sexually assaulted or raped, threatened, witnessed domestic abuse or suffered the loss of someone they loved – trauma is often prevalent in the lives of the majority of women and girls.

Not only do they suffer these individual traumas, but they exist as women in a patriarchy – a world which has positioned them as 'less than' since they were born. Less intelligent, less capable, less confident, less successful, less important. When and if they do step outside of their assignment of 'less than', they are often punished by society and their support network. This is why girls who are too confident, too opinionated, too successful and too intelligent are so often framed as problematic or disruptive.

'Tall poppy syndrome', a woman once told me. The cultural phenomenon of cutting down and eliminating anyone who is deemed too intelligent, successful or non-conforming. In Japan, the same concept is described as, 'the nail that sticks up gets hammered down'.

To understand the female experience in a patriarchy, we must acknowledge that women and girls are subjected to distress, discrimination and trauma throughout their lives. Whether it's throw-away comments about 'throwing like a girl' or a hobby they like being 'not for girls' or the constant sexual harassment by men out of the passenger window of a van, girls grow up learning how to navigate a world that sexualises and degrades them. All these experiences are traumatic – just as any form of oppression and discrimination is.

It's hard to cope with such treatment on a daily basis, for years, and then for decades. It's hard to live in a world which talks down to you like a stupid child – but ironically, only recognises your adulthood when deciding whether to fuck you or not. And even then, that happens before you are a consenting adult for most girls.

From a trauma-informed and social model perspective, it makes total sense that women and girls go on to develop behaviours, feelings and thoughts that might seem odd, harmful, abnormal or extreme to some. What might be considered a disorder or mental health issue seems pretty rational and normal when we consider what women and girls are up against.

This is why it is so important that we do not reframe women's traumas as mental illnesses, personality disorders and forms of psychoses. In my view, knowing that women and girls exist in a patriarchy where they are likely to be subjected to traumas and violations over and over, and then convincing them that their natural and rational reactions are mental health issues, psychoses and personality disorders is one of the most insulting, insidious and powerful forms of victim blaming of women that has ever been developed and maintained.

Not only does it seek to position all of women and girls' responses as illnesses and disordered thinking, but the systems, media and society do this by grooming women and girls to believe that is in their best interests to believe that they have an incurable mental disorder, rather than validating and listening to their traumas and experiences. It is an amazing sleight of hand.

I know this section will be one of the most controversial in this book, and so I want to give you some real examples to break down and explore whether you really believe that women who have been diagnosed and treated for mental health issues are mentally disordered or unwell in some way.

Postpartum depression

Whilst writing this book, I heard from many women who were given diagnoses of postpartum depression or postpartum psychosis when they were being subjected to domestic abuse, sexual abuse and coercive control. This is particularly important, because we have known for decades that male violence towards and abuse of women increases when they are pregnant.

Statistically, being subjected to domestic abuse during pregnancy is more common than any other pregnancy complication or health issue (UCSF, 2021). Simply put, you are more likely to be beaten and abused whilst pregnant than to have medical issues or complications arising from your own body or the baby.

In 2013, a meta-analysis of sixty-seven studies published by Howard et al. found that women who were subjected to domestic abuse during pregnancy were three times more likely to be diagnosed with PTSD, anxiety, depression, and other mental health disorders.

At first glance, this makes a lot of sense (minus the unnecessary pathologisation, and the insistence that it is somehow a mental disorder to be traumatised by being abused whilst pregnant). However, it would make sense that we would be more likely to see trauma responses and distress in women who had been abused during their pregnancy – and yet, there is still a concerted effort to suggest that they are mentally ill, and their responses are abnormal. Not only abnormal, but dangerous to their baby, who is then seen as the true 'victim' in the situation – not of the domestic abuse, but of a mentally ill mother.

One of the women I spoke to had walked out of one of my speeches in 2019, visibly distressed. The speech I was giving had the same topic as this book: the pathologisation of women and girls who have been subjected to abuse. She was a bright, experienced criminal justice professional sat at the back of the room with her colleague. Suddenly, she stood up, hiding her face, and quickly left the room. I was so relieved to see her an hour later when she came to speak to me personally.

Jenny told me that listening to my speech had 'hit her like a ton of bricks', as she had realised that she had been diagnosed with post-natal depression, medicated, pathologised and ignored instead of anyone responding to the abusive situation she was living in.

When Jenny was twenty-one, she became pregnant by a thirty-year-old man whom she had only been seeing for six months. He wasn't physically violent, but he frequently gaslit and psychologically controlled Jenny. He would often have sex with other women and when they contacted Jenny to tell her that he was cheating on her, he would tell her that she was mentally ill, her mind didn't work properly and that she was delusional. Over time, she began to believe him.

When their baby was born, he was quickly hospitalised with a serious complication and had to undergo surgery. Jenny's partner was nowhere to be seen, and told her that he couldn't visit the hospital or support her because he was dealing with the grief of losing his own dad. Jenny accepted this, but later found out that he was having sex with a woman who later contacted Jenny to tell her the truth.

The abuse continued; Jenny tried to leave several times but struggled immensely. She stopped sleeping and eating, and lost six stone in weight in a matter of weeks, leaving her at seven stone. She told me that she wasn't depressed, she was traumatised by the abuse and the feeling that it was all in her own head. On at least one occasion, he seriously sexually assaulted Jenny to 'see if she had been having sex with other men'.

After four more months of this abuse, Jenny went to her GP and told them everything, including her abusive ex-partner and what he had been doing to her (he had recently left her as a single mother to their six-month-old baby). By this point, her eating and sleeping was seriously impacted, she was physically unwell and she had developed a stutter when she spoke. She described herself as constantly frightened, especially of men. The GP listened, and then diagnosed her with postnatal depression.

Jenny told me how this only escalated the abuse and violence from her ex-partner, who used the diagnosis to confirm his gaslighting narrative that she was mentally ill and unstable. She also reflected on the fact that the diagnosis solidified her own self-blame and doubt, and her belief that everything was in her own head and that her ex must have been right, that she was mentally ill.

She was prescribed citalopram and in her own words, 'that was that'. Even years later when she had her second child, she was assessed and monitored closely by a consultant because of her 'mental illness' and tendency for 'postnatal depression'.

She told me that my speech in 2019 was the first time it had ever become clear to her that she didn't have postnatal depression, and that the sexual and domestic abuse she was subjected to was completely ignored by professionals who, instead, diagnosed and medicated her.

This story is surprisingly common, and Jenny is certainly not alone. It is curious that the doctor would hear her disclose abuse, sexual assaults and deeply traumatic experiences such as her newborn needing major surgery whilst her partner left her alone to sleep with other women – and yet they still positioned the 'problem' as within her own hormones and her own brain. It is no wonder that it reinforced everything she had been told by her abuser – especially as she was then given daily medication to take for many years to come.

BPD/EUPD

By far, one of the most common diagnoses a woman or girl will receive after being subjected to male violence is of borderline or emotionally unstable personality disorder. Anyone working with women and girls in refuges, rape centres, women's services, domestic abuse support services or sexual exploitation services will know that the majority of their caseload will be women or girls with this diagnosis. According to the DSM-V, 75 per cent of all diagnoses of BPD are female.

The NHS describes personality disorders as 'longstanding ingrained distortions of personality that interfere with the ability to make and sustain relationships' (NHS, 2004). This has always seemed far-fetched to me, even before I developed my own knowledge and practice. I couldn't imagine how anyone could have a 'disordered' personality when personality itself was such a contested concept. For decades psychologists and psychiatrists have attempted to classify 'personality types', often by using psychometric measures which can be highly flawed.

Personality is generally theorised as a stable feature of ourselves, that we have throughout our lives. However, even anecdotal evidence would suggest that most people change consistently throughout their lives. Do you have the same personality now as you did ten years ago? Do you expect to have the same personality and character in twenty years' time?

And what about the questions in psychometric evaluations of personality?

Would you answer them in the same way on the day you found out you were being made redundant as the day you woke up to a lovely sunny day off work? Would you answer the same way if your relationship was breaking down versus when you were in the throes of a new and exciting relationship? Would you even answer the questions the same way from one day to the next?

It is likely that 'personality' is flexible, dynamic, nuanced and complicated – and virtually impossible to pin down into categories. But shouldn't that mean that personality disorders are also the same – slippery and impossible to nail down?

One of the things that has always perplexed me about personality and personality disorder is how white, western and elite the discipline has always been, and the way it ignores diverse personalities, norms and characters in different cultures, time periods and languages. What might be considered a 'normal' personality in the UK or USA could be considered to be highly abnormal and disordered somewhere else.

If we took me as an example, I am generally introverted but I am assertive, confident, analytical, logical, critical to the point of cynicism, honest, persistent, fiercely independent and determined. I am committed to a purpose, and I tend to become narrowly focused on my goals or dreams. I don't have many strong emotional connections to people, but the ones I do have are extremely important to me. I have no interest in small talk, frivolous issues or being polite for no reason. I am not very diplomatic and I can come across as cold and disinterested in others. I'm not necessarily a good team player, but I am a strong leader and a natural 'lone-wolf' type. I have a sharp sense of humour. I don't follow rules that I don't feel are ethical or in the best interests of humans. I don't like bureaucracy. I can be quite sceptical about human nature and the state of the world. I don't compromise on my values, no matter what that risks. I am a perfectionist and contrary to what people 'see' of me, I am a very private person who only shows the 'real me' to one or two people.

This is a little window into my 'personality' – which if we were talking in psychological terms, is classified as INTJ by the Myers-Briggs Type Indicator (for now – who knows where I'll be in a few decades). According to the MBTI, I have one of the rarest female personality types in the world. It's described by Myers-Briggs as the personality of someone with a lot of successful and desirable traits. This personality type is apparently much more common in men than women, probably because so many of my 'traits' are attributed to masculinity rather than traditional femininity.

However, this is a specific misogynistic western view in a pro-capitalist society. Would my character be revered or celebrated in other more collectivist cultures? Would I be seen as mentally ill? Would I be outcast, punished or tortured? Would I have been castigated as a witch? Would I be sectioned and medicated? If I moved to another country, would I be perceived as sociopathic? Would I be regarded as emotionally unstable or unavailable? And what if I was Black, how would that change the perception of my personality? What if I presented more masculine? What if I was a man?

Isn't personality (and what constitutes whether it is disordered or not) socially, culturally and historically situated?

Huge questions, I know. But nonetheless, if we are going to diagnose tens of thousands of women and girls with personality disorders which impact them for the rest of their lives – shouldn't we be asking these difficult questions?

I was managing a rape centre back in 2013 when it became apparent to me that almost every woman on our caseload and waiting list had been told that she had borderline personality disorder, within months of disclosing or reporting sexual violence. Many of them were put on a cocktail of different medications and were then subjected to all sorts of maltreatment and discrimination as a 'borderline' patient.

As of 2021, the NHS uses the following questionnaire to diagnose BPD. A diagnosis is generally made where a woman can answer 'yes' to five or more of the questions below.

◆ Do you have an intense fear of being left alone, which causes you to act in ways that, on reflection, seem out of the ordinary or extreme, such as constantly phoning somebody (but not including self-harming or suicidal behaviour)?
◆ Do you have a pattern of intense and unstable relationships with other people that switch between thinking you love that person and they're wonderful to hating that person and thinking they're terrible?
◆ Do you ever feel you do not have a strong sense of your own self and are unclear about your self-image?
◆ Do you engage in impulsive activities in two areas that are potentially damaging, such as unsafe sex, drug misuse,

gambling, drinking, or reckless spending (but not including self-harming or suicidal behaviour)?

◆ Have you made repeated suicide threats or attempts in your past and engaged in self-harming?

◆ Do you have severe mood swings, such as feeling intensely depressed, anxious or irritable, which last from a few hours to a few days?

◆ Do you have long-term feelings of emptiness and loneliness?

◆ Do you have sudden and intense feelings of anger and aggression, and often find it difficult to control your anger?

◆ When you find yourself in stressful situations, do you have feelings of paranoia, or do you feel like you're disconnected from the world or from your own body, thoughts and behaviour?

The questionnaire and diagnostic criteria are so broad that pretty much anyone who is traumatised or distressed could answer 'yes' to five or more of the items. It is very common for women and girls seeking support in rape and abuse services to struggle with most of the items on this list – not because they have a personality disorder, but because they have been violated and traumatised by male violence. Often, this abuse, violence and control took place over a period of months or years.

Unfortunately, borderline personality disorder is one of the most harmful diagnoses a woman can be given, as she will be reframed as a manipulative, deceitful and emotionally unstable person (Timoclea, 2020). This is why women with borderline personality disorders are often 'flagged' to health and emergency services without their knowledge. Many GP surgeries flag a female patient with borderline personality disorder as a high-risk person; as do ambulance services, fire services, police services and social services.

What this means in reality is that women and girls with this diagnosis can be treated as if they are unstable, unreliable or exaggerating when they call emergency services for help.

In 2017, a young woman called Keira* wrote to me to ask whether I knew that emergency services were flagging women and teenage girls as 'borderline' on their internal systems. She told me that she was diagnosed after reporting sexual exploitation and trafficking to police. She was involved in a trial which found several men guilty, but still, she was diagnosed and medicated for a personality disorder.

A couple of years later, she noticed that her doctor would treat her as if she was crazy. He ignored all of her physical complaints about everything from headaches to irregular periods. When she contacted police about a woman who was harassing her, four police officers turned up to her accommodation instead of just one or two officers as standard. When she had children, she was assessed as if she was going to be a grave danger to her babies. When she called an ambulance in an emergency one evening, they sent out a police patrol car with it. When her baby was ill, the hospital referred her to social services. She couldn't understand why she was always treated with belt and braces – until a professional told her that it was standard procedure because she was known to have a personality disorder.

Personality disorders are notoriously difficult to get removed from women's medical records – even if there is substantial evidence that it is an incorrect or harmful diagnosis. It is widely considered that personality disorders are lifelong diagnoses with no cure. Rather curiously then, a ten-year study of hundreds of people with borderline personality disorder found that 85 per cent of them were 'in remission' within ten years with only 12 per cent of them 'relapsing' within the same time period (Gunderson et al. 2011). What is interesting about this is that despite there being clear evidence that their symptoms were temporary, the language and conceptualisation of the personality disorder means that professionals never consider them to be 'cured', but only in 'remission', until such a time that they inevitably 'relapse' due to their disordered personality.

We should stop, and take a moment to consider how significant this medicalising language is. Once diagnosed with a personality disorder, you can only ever be in 'remission' – but never 'cured'. When and if you struggle again, it is seen as evidence that you have 'relapsed'. How does a woman or girl ever escape this diagnosis when the language and theory is so circular?

A trauma-informed view of this phenomenon would simply argue that women are very likely to go through long periods of their lives where their trauma and coping mechanisms do not necessarily interfere with their daily lives, but that being triggered or retraumatised one day is common and likely. None of this suggests the presence of a lifelong personality disorder.

Borderline personality disorder in women has earned its place as the modern-day 'hysteria'. Women and teen girls are the majority of people diagnosed with it, the criteria are as loose as the professional needs or wants them to be, and it results in years of medication, discrimination and treatment.

Ussher (2013) puts it well by saying that the same women who were once burned at the stake for being witches then became the women who were diagnosed as hysterical and locked away in asylums, and are now the women being diagnosed with borderline personality disorders and medicated for the rest of their lives.

Rape trauma

In 2018, I was working closely with a team of UK social workers who sought to make their practice with teenage girls more trauma-informed. They worked in child sexual exploitation, and so the vast majority of their cases were girls aged eleven to seventeen who were being raped, groomed, abused and trafficked by men in their local areas.

One social worker was working with Jayden*, a sixteen-year-old girl who had been violently raped by multiple men in parks and hotels in a nearby town. Initially, the social worker described Jayden as difficult to engage, lazy, school-refusing and disconnected. However, during my training, we discussed issues around the pathologisation of teenage girls and she asked a question about the medicating of teenage girls who had been raped.

Current NICE guidelines are clear in stating that children under eighteen should not be medicated for depression or anxiety – and medical research has shown that antipsychotics cause a range of health conditions in children including significant weight gain, drowsiness and diabetes. This risk is so profound that new guidance was issued in 2003 to warn parents and professionals of the danger of childhood diabetes caused by antipsychotic drugs, and to continually monitor children for signs of diabetes. Despite there being no trials or evidence on efficacy or safety, by 2011 there had been a twofold to fivefold increase in the prescribing of antipsychotics to preschool children (Harrison et al., 2013). Further, the majority of all children prescribed medications have been told to take them for 'disorders' and 'syndromes' that are not approved for medication. Simply put, doctors are increasingly misusing off-label medication to respond to challenging child behaviours, aggression, irritability, low moods and trauma (Harrison et al., 2013).

We discussed the evidence base for medicating children who are traumatised by abuse, neglect and rape. We discussed the way that medication is significantly cheaper as a 'quick fix' than months of support and therapy.

At the end of the session, the social worker reported that Jayden had been increasingly medicated over a period of two years (between fourteen and sixteen years old) since she had reported the rapes to police. The doctors had started her off on 20mg of sertraline per day due to her being anxious (an antidepressant used primarily for adults and children diagnosed with 'obsessive compulsive disorder' and 'major depression') but they had not seen any improvement in her moods or behaviours. Over a period of time, her medication was increased to 200mg per day, at which point the social worker described her as, 'like a zombie who slept twenty hours a day and couldn't hold a conversation'. She had stopped going to school and had not been able to complete her GCSEs. She constantly complained of feeling unwell, having weird symptoms and not being able to think or concentrate. She became reclusive and rarely left her bedroom.

I asked her whether Jayden had been offered any other support or therapy since she was raped, and she told me that there was nothing available for her because she was 'too mentally ill'. The social worker became tearful and anxious in front of me, as she realised that she, and several other professionals, had supported a process which had profoundly medicated and sedated a teenage girl who was suffering from trauma from multiple rapes.

I wish these were one-off examples, but there are many current cases like this in the UK and USA.

In 2020, I worked with another team of child abuse professionals who specialised in working with girls who had been sexually abused and exploited. One of the team was supporting a twelve-year-old girl called Molly who had not been able to sleep since she had been raped by her dad. In this case, the professional had fought the diagnosis and medication of Molly for months, but was ultimately ignored as she was not a doctor. Instead, Molly was given a diagnosis of major depression and sleep disorder, and was given a prescription of melatonin.

Initially, this had not had any impact on her, and she complained of panic attacks, flashbacks and lack of sleep. The prescription of melatonin was then increased significantly, which did cause her to sleep more at night, but also caused the onset of dangerous incidents of sleep walking, night terrors, night sweating and episodes of falling asleep at school and waking up screaming in classrooms. Molly attributed this to the melatonin medication and started to refuse to take it, which triggered a referral to both the mental health teams and the child protection teams who arranged meetings with her and her parents to encourage her to keep taking the medication.

Molly argued back, and said that she had read on the internet that melatonin medication could cause serious side effects and she didn't want to take it anymore; a decision which was supported by the professional I had been working with. Despite this, Molly was told not to believe everything she read on the internet and no one listened to her, or the professional advocating for her. Instead, pressure was put on her parents to make sure she continued to take the medication regardless of side effects. Molly, of course, and even at twelve years old, was absolutely right. It was highly likely that the symptoms she was experiencing were caused by the increased dosage of melatonin coupled with the dismissal of her trauma from her dad raping her.

Recurrent themes in examples like this include the chronic dismissal or ignorance of trauma from abuse, neglect and harm whilst girls and women are heavily medicated until they are as docile, tired and subdued as possible. In almost all cases like these, girls and women are prescribed increasing dosages of medication which ultimately makes them drowsy, confused, scared, low and forgetful. However, they are often then described as 'calmer' and 'able to sleep' or 'more agreeable' and 'easier to work with'.

This bears striking resemblance to the way doctors used to describe women with melancholia as being 'just the type of lady one would like to meet', because they were so quiet and subdued (Ussher, 2013).

It appears then, that instead of addressing the enormous and complex traumas of women and girls subjected to male violence, there is a strong culture of diagnosing them with mental disorders and encouraging them to take daily medication. One of the most damaging impacts of this practice is the subsequent internalisation of self-blame and self-doubt for women and girls who are told that their trauma responses and coping mechanisms are not valid or relevant, instead, they are mentally ill due to some form of 'disorder', or 'imbalance', or 'faulty genes'.

Attachment disorders

As if pathologising women's trauma, their personalities and their responses to having babies in highly stressful circumstances weren't enough, women and girls have also been diagnosed and pathologised with 'attachment disorders' for decades.

Attachment disorders relate broadly to attachment theory; and attachment theory is one of those enduring, famous theories that receives very little scrutiny or critical thinking.

In the 1930s, John Bowlby was working as a psychiatrist (where he was treating 'emotionally disturbed children' with a range of psychiatric treatments) when he began to theorise that the initial and earliest relationships that babies have with their primary caregiver (the mother) would leave a lasting imprint on them for the rest of their lives. This suggestion spurred thousands of studies and several theories of attachment which have dominated developmental psychology, social work, psychotherapy and child development studies for decades.

Bowlby argued that babies would develop one main form of attachment to the person who responded accurately and quickly to their needs, and that this attachment would become their secure base for being able to explore and understand the world, and the rest of their attachments to other people. If this initial attachment was not successful for some reason (a lot of attachment theory blames the mother for this), it is theorised that this lack of secure attachment will result in irreversible developmental consequences such as reduced intelligence and increased aggression. Therefore, the initial attachment that the baby develops is seen as the prototype for all other relationships and attachments for the rest of their lives (Bowlby, 1969).

Eventually, this resulted in a set of theories and models called 'attachment styles'. Researchers suggested that infants would develop an enduring internal working model of their attachments, and then use that to form all further relationships across childhood and into adulthood (and even into their own parenting).

Attachment styles

Secure Attachment	Bowlby (1988) described secure attachment as the capacity to connect well and securely in relationships with others while also having the capacity for autonomous action as situationally appropriate. Secure attachment is characterised by trust, an adaptive response to being abandoned, and the belief that one is worthy of love. Research shows that 50 per cent of children are 'securely attached'. (Moulin et al. 2014)
Avoidant Attachment	Children with avoidant attachment styles tend to avoid interaction with the caregiver, and show no distress during separation. This may be because the parent has ignored attempts to be intimate, and the child may internalise the belief that they cannot depend on this or any other relationship. Research shows that 20 per cent of children are 'insecurely attached – avoidant'. (Moulin et al. 2014)
Ambivalent Attachment	Ambivalent attachment relationships are characterised by a concern that others will not reciprocate one's desire for intimacy. This is caused when an infant learns that their caregiver or parent is unreliable and does not consistently provide responsive care towards their needs. Research shows that 25 per cent of children are 'insecurely attached – ambivalent/anxious'. (Moulin et al. 2014)
Disorganised Attachment	Main and Solomon (1986) discovered that a sizeable proportion of infants actually did not fit into the first three groups of attachment. They categorised these infants as having a disorganised attachment type. Disorganised attachment is classified by children who display sequences of behaviours that lack readily observable goals or intentions, including obviously contradictory attachment behaviours. Research shows that 5 per cent of children are 'insecurely attached – disorganised'. (Moulin et al. 2014)

As an undergraduate, as a professional working with children, and as a PhD student, I was taught that attachment was solid, lifelong and unchangeable. When I was much younger and this was taught to me with authority, I didn't question it at all. It was only through working with thousands of women and girls that I began to question whether the notion of a lifelong prototype attachment was true.

I started to wonder:

What about the girls who had loving, safe, brilliant parents, but who were then raped and abused by their boyfriends in their teens, and who then become terrified of intimacy for decades?

What about the girls who were raped and beaten by their dads, and went on to have loving, stable, happy relationships with partners in the future?

What about the girls who were abused and trafficked by both parents and who went to foster families whom they had safe, happy, secure attachments to?

What about the women I knew who had secure attachments to one partner and anxious attachments to another? What about women who had several attachment types at any one time?

What about women and girls who were, for example, securely attached to mum, avoidant of dad, securely attached to their friends, anxiously attached to partners, and then securely attached to a future lifelong partner?

None of this seemed to make sense to me. Surely, attachment was dynamic, fluid, ever-changing and influenced by our entire lives? Surely 'attachment' would depend on whether you had been groomed or abused, too? Some women and girls present as being very securely attached to an abuser who hurt and scared them frequently – what would the theory say about them?

I got my answer to that question during years of working with those women and girls – they were frequently diagnosed with 'attachment disorders' in childhood or adolescence and told that their disorder would impact them for the rest of their lives.

Attachment disorders are defined by the DSM-V as, 'effects of significant disruptions in attachment, especially disturbed social relatedness, mostly because of abuse, neglect, or prolonged maltreatment during early development. Pathogenic care is the cause of the disorder. The effects of disrupted attachment are the converse of a secure attachment.'

Essentially, the DSM diagnoses insecure attachment as a mental disorder which requires treatment. Whilst the majority of children and teens will be prescribed therapy, many of them will also be given medication which is suggested to 'control the behavioural issues of attachment disorder'.

> *Attachment disorders have so many comorbidities that the presentation can be complex and confusing. Atypical antipsychotic medication and mood stabilizers (used off-label) appear to be the medical treatments of choice for children with attachment disorders and psychiatric comorbidities.*
>
> Alston, J.
> The Psychiatric Times, 2007

Many girls who have been raped, sexually abused by family or sexually exploited and trafficked will be diagnosed with attachment disorders (among many other disorders). This is commonly seen in social work, child protection and other third-sector services which provide support for girls and their families. My work in rape centres, criminal justice and then child trafficking meant that I came across this assertion a lot; all of these thousands of women and girls had disorders of attachment that would impact them forever. Professionals talked about them like they were damaged, and doomed to failed relationships and parenthood.

I met Holly a few years ago when she was working with Deana*. Deana was a fifteen-year-old girl who had recently been placed in semi-secure care after being trafficked for sex by her mum, dad and family friends. Holly was an experienced, exhausted professional who knew that Deana was traumatised, and rejected any suggestion that she was mentally ill or disordered.

Deana was eleven when a group of her family members started to sexually abuse her at family gatherings. They took videos and photographs of the abuse and shared the imagery online with paedophile networks. As she got older, the family members took Deana to hotels on motorways where people from the online networks paid her family to rape and abuse her.

At fifteen years old, Deana was taken into care by the local authority and legal action started against her parents and wider family. In care, Deana trusted no one. When professionals showed her care, attention, and respect, she rejected them and became defensive. She refused to be left alone with any care staff members and she was unable to form a healthy relationship with any of them. At school and in the care home, Deana struggled to maintain friendships or relationships with anyone. If anyone got too close to her, she would push them away or make allegations about them so she could be alone again.

After a few months, staff asked for a referral for Deana to CAMHS who diagnosed her with borderline personality disorder and attachment disorder.

Holly approached me for support and guidance, and spoke eloquently about Deana. She told me that she felt that Deana was naturally reacting to serious trauma, and that none of her behaviours were irrational or disordered. I agreed. Deana was showing some very clear and obvious signs of trauma, and of attempting to protect herself, but none of them were abnormal or disordered. In fact, they were intelligent and rational responses.

She protected herself from future abuse by cutting everyone off. She refused to be suckered into another relationship with an adult who claimed to love her. She pushed people away who told her they cared about her and would keep her safe. She used allegations to keep staff away from her.

What she was doing was genius. She was using every tiny bit of power she had left to protect herself at all costs. She was a fifteen-year-old girl being held in a secure unit away from all of her family and friends, her parents were being prosecuted, she had been raped and sold thousands of times, she was hundreds of miles from her home and school – and now these adults were all telling her that she was special, cared for, loved and safe.

Her instincts were bang on the money. She did the right thing. She used all of the evidence she had gathered about adults who lie to her and then harm her, and was using it to protect herself from further harm. This did not constitute a disorder of any kind – her responses were rational, justified, explainable, normal and natural.

I would go as far as suggesting that medicating Deana and placing her in therapy designed to 'manage' or 'improve' her attachments is abusive in itself. We must ask the question, why would professionals want to break down her final line of self-protection? Why would they want her to unlearn what adults do to groom and abuse her? Why would they want to trample on her instincts and get her to trust them all?

It is obvious that this treatment was never for Deana. It was always for the benefit of professionals and institutions. I saw cases of girls treated like this over and over again, and it made me wonder why we would want to extinguish their responses to trauma like this, and whether this could be categorised as a form of gaslighting. Girls who knew that adults lied to them and made them feel wanted and safe, who then exploited and harmed them – now being told that they had a mental disorder? A mental disorder that stopped them from forming healthy attachments, which needed medication and therapy? That they were told they would need to 'work on'?

Those girls are right not to trust us. I would never want to diminish that instinct. Given the abhorrent history and presence of misogyny in our professions, I would rather that they distrust us, remain critical of us, and protect themselves.

'Trauma causes mental illness' arguments

One of the most common responses I get when teaching, lecturing or writing about these examples is people writing to tell me that I am mistaken, and they know someone who has, or they themselves have, several diagnoses of psychiatric disorders but have 'never been traumatised'. I get this response a lot. People genuinely do believe that they have never been subjected to a single traumatic or stressful experience, that there is nothing (and no one) in their environment harming them and that their mental health issues are down to a freak chemical imbalance in their brain that no one can cure or explain.

In my experience, less than an hour with someone like this will uncover years of struggles, worries, fears, anger, loss, injustice, trauma, distress, discrimination or abuse that they have never linked to their feelings and thoughts. Indeed, it is very common for people to begin accessing therapy or support services feeling sure that they know what is bothering them and how to solve it, only to find out that there is something much more complex and deeper buried within them that has never been addressed or supported.

For some though, they will dismiss most of my arguments and the content of this book by saying that trauma is what causes psychosis, personality disorders and mental health issues – and that the two are not mutually exclusive. Some will argue that the way I separate psychiatric disorders as harmful and trauma as the root cause of behavioural and emotional change is unhelpful or unprofessional. Some may even argue that they are harmful distinctions.

However, as this book demonstrates, you cannot divorce the oppression and abuse of psychiatry from the foundations of the disorders, diagnostic criteria or treatments. The entire tradition and discipline of psychiatry has relied on creating victims and then convincing them that they are mentally ill and in need of months or years of treatment.

The modern message of 'end mental health stigma' is therefore an oxymoron. It is impossible to end 'stigma' against people who are being stigmatised and diagnosed as mentally ill and abnormal by psychiatry. The definition of the word 'stigma' is 'the perception that a certain attribute of a person makes them unacceptably different or abnormal from others, leading to discrimination and prejudice'. Isn't this the entire foundation of psychiatry? Isn't psychiatry just a legitimate way of stigmatising and isolating people who are profoundly different?

We cannot end stigma of a system which relies on stigma.

We cannot normalise conditions which the system says are abnormal and in need of medical treatment.

The process of diagnosing someone with a psychiatric condition from the DSM is to diagnose them with a 'mental disorder' which sets them apart from everyone else as being mentally ill, in need of treatment, supervision, control, medication and assessment. They are diagnosed and therefore they are stigmatised. The only way to end the stigma is to stop making psychiatric diagnoses and focus more on humanistic, person-centred, non-pathologising approaches to supporting humans in distress.

Trauma is trauma. Trauma responses are natural, normal, rational and justified. Trauma performs an important physical, social and psychological function. It does not cause personality disorders. It does not cause psychiatric issues. It does not cause criminality. It does not cause attachment disorders.

The troubling takeover of ACEs

In 1998, researchers Felitti et al., set out to explore whether adverse childhood experiences (ACEs) could predict outcomes in lifestyle, health and death. In a sample of over 9,500 adults, they found that those who were subjected to abuse were more likely to go on to commit crime, die from cancer and diabetes, become teenage mothers, abuse their own children, smoke, binge drink, become unemployed and have chronic illnesses.

Or so the story goes.

I say 'story' because that is what ACEs have become. A story. A legend. A myth. A pack of lies.

In such a short time, the studies and findings have become folklore. Lay press, websites, conferences, speakers, influencers, cowboy trainers and opportunists set themselves up as experts in ACEs, and overnight, there was a whole industry of people who had clearly never read the tentative, population-level suggestions about the links between abuse and physical health outcomes.

The ACEs study was based on thousands of middle-class, predominantly white professionals working for Kaiser-Permanente in America in the 1990s. It was born out of some interesting findings from the 1980s which linked obesity to other health issues, and socioeconomic factors. It was a very specific sample, taken at one point in time. The data analysis was not based on individuals but based on trends and distribution within a large population sample (which is the definition of epidemiological studies). The point of the study was not to predict outcomes, or to make any inferences about individual children or adults. Indeed, the studies have never actually included children in the sample, as their nature required that all participants had to be adults.

The study only contained ten possible adverse experiences, because, as the authors point out, it is not for screening trauma, or for any use with individuals – it was simply a selection of ten possible forms of abuse and neglect, to explore population-level data for any links between childhood harm and later health issues.

The ten adverse experiences were limited and flawed in many ways. They included sexual abuse, physical abuse, verbal abuse, neglect, imprisonment of a parent, divorce of parents, addiction/dependency of a parent, and a family member with 'mental illness'.

For example, the researchers only included sexual abuse if the perpetrator was more than five years older than the victim. They only included domestic abuse where mothers were the victim. They only included impacts within the family home. They held the divorce of parents as being the same as sexual abuse, neglect and the incarceration of parents.

They did not include any social adversities such as poverty, racism, homophobia, sexism, bullying, asylum or refugee status, chronic illness, homelessness, serious injury or accident, displacement, or other forms of crime and inequality.

This is not because their study was poor quality, but because they were looking specifically at only ten items of adversity for their population-level investigation in the health data of adults. Their study was not about inclusive forms of trauma, or about exploring the different ways children could be abused and oppressed. This means that their ACEs questionnaire excluded some of the most common forms of adversity in the world – and cannot be considered a way to measure or explore trauma.

It became increasingly clear that professionals had not read the studies or understood them to be epidemiological, but that professionals and policymakers had also made up several findings which were never reported on.

Most notably, in an ACEs awareness cartoon video made by the Department for Health in Wales. In the video (with almost one million views on social media) there is a repeated assertion that girls subjected to adversity go on to become teenage mothers, and that girls born of teenage mothers become teenage mothers themselves. Not only does the video depict this in a poor, underprivileged family, but in a way which seemingly discounts the obvious: girls who become pregnant under the age of sixteen were raped.

Rather than positioning this as the issue (girls being a victim of male violence), the teenage mothers are centred as the problem of proliferating ACEs – a cycle that can never be broken. Some sort of intergenerational, genetic, deterministic trauma from which they can never escape. As if their pregnancies were the result of a miraculous conception caused by previous childhood trauma.

This isn't the only misinformation in the video, which I critiqued on my YouTube channel in 2020. The video claims that childhood adversity causes irreversible brain changes in children, which make them angry and unable to control their emotions. It suggests strongly that children subjected to 'adversity' go on to be criminals, truants, smokers, binge drinkers, domestic abuse perpetrators and unemployed.

The mother-blaming in the video is truly something to behold.

Throughout the cartoon video entitled 'Adverse Childhood Experiences Wales', a male character tells his story of 'ACEs' in which he is subjected to abuse and neglect as a child, becomes a violent, abusive, truanting teenager who then becomes an obese, smoking, drinking, bald, uneducated, ignorant, unemployed criminal who dies early of heart failure and cancer.

The mother of his children – and his own mother in the video – is positioned as a depressive, incapable woman who needed to learn to cope with domestic abuse, read her son more stories and buy him more toys to fix him. The character tells how the police had to come to his house to 'have a word' with his mother about protecting him better from his abusive dad, and how to 'cope' when it 'all gets too much'.

Misinformation about ACEs has successfully spread across the UK, USA, Australia, New Zealand, Sweden, Canada and other countries for almost a decade.

This is not because of the authors obscuring their findings, or because they jumped to huge conclusions only possible with a pole vault. They did not give misinformation, or encourage this interesting spread of assumptions and pathologisation of those subjected to adverse childhood experiences.

In fact, in July 2020, the original authors of the 1998 ACEs study released a statement in the *American Journal of Preventative Medicine* to set the record straight: their work was being misused to pathologise and predict the outcomes of children and adults who had been subjected to abuse and neglect.

And yet, as I write this, in 2021, the use of ACEs is still enjoying a growing reputation of being evidence-based, trauma-informed, and helpful to women and girls who have been subjected to sexual violence and abuse in childhood.

ACEs 'scores' (out of ten, based on the original, stolen framework from Felitti et al. 1998), are used to give children and adults 'ACE scores' of how much childhood adversity they were subjected to, and then used to predict their outcomes, or change the services they are entitled to. Generally, it is 'known' that a score of over four out of ten is related to poor health and education outcomes, criminality, mental illness and dependency.

Please note that the word *known* is used here to mean that there is a collective assumption of belief among professionals that this is the case, despite there being no evidence for it – and despite the entire premise being a flawed interpretation of a study that was never meant for scoring or individual predictions in the first place.

These scores caused, and are still causing, untold harm to individuals. To groups whose trauma has always been marginalised and minimised, the misuse of ACEs and ACE scores has only compounded their marginalisation, by ignoring oppression, racial trauma and persecution.

Pathologisation of women and girls using ACEs

In 2016, I was sat in a meeting in the north of England, discussing how to make local authority social services more trauma-informed. A manager began to describe a new pilot programme they had developed, to take the ACEs scores of pregnant women who were attending their twelve-week scans. I looked up from my notebook. I wondered where this was going. Were they screening pregnant women for their childhood traumas, to offer them more support? To offer them trauma-informed birthing plans? To make sure they had extra support if they became triggered at medical appointments?

No. No, they were not.

They were screening pregnant women and girls for their ACEs score as part of a new pilot which would place thousands of unborn babies on 'at risk at birth' registers, and begin proceedings and investigations into whether the mother was fit and capable to keep her baby.

Here, the assumption should be clear: women who were abused in childhood are not fit mothers, and their babies are at risk.

I have no poker face, so it was probably clear that I was shocked and appalled at such an intervention. I spent some time explaining why this approach was not trauma-informed, and was in fact, the opposite: pathologising and traumatic. After much persuasion, this pilot was ended, and my contract was unceremoniously cut short

– but as I write this book, I never did find out how many babies were placed on a child protection register, how many babies were removed from new mothers, and I don't know how we could ever find out.

There are many further examples of the way the misuse of ACEs is being used to oppress and pathologise women and girls.

In 2020, I received a message from a twenty-four-year-old woman who told me that she had been raped as a teenager and abused in childhood. A charity support worker had completed an ACEs questionnaire with her when she was seventeen, and her score was eight out of ten. The support worker had then informed her that with an ACEs score of eight, she had a high chance of cancer, diabetes, obesity, suicide, criminality and unemployment.

She told me in the message that she had decided to stop her application to university, and to accept that her life had been ruined by childhood abuse. She was doing well at school, but her ACE score had made her feel like she would be damaged for life.

Now twenty-four, she had messaged me to say that she had watched some of my videos about ACEs being misused and misguided; and said that it had made her realise that she could go to university after all. She had applied as a mature student that day.

Whilst this might sound somewhat of a success story of a trauma-informed approach informing and overcoming a pathologising approach, what struck me was that she spent seven years of her life feeling like she wasn't good enough to access higher education because one misinformed professional thought fit to lecture her about how she was going to die early because of her ACE score.

How could ACEs have gained a reputation for being in the best interests of women and girls, when they were being used to oppress and pathologise them like this?

The answer is annoyingly simple: it's seductive, and it's easier than validating years of trauma.

Professionals have genuinely believed through nothing more than whispers and shared misinformation that they could give women and girls a 'trauma score' out of ten, which could predict their futures and inform the service provision they would need.

It's quick. It's easy. It requires little brain power or compassion. It reduces humans to a score out of ten.

She's a two, she'll be all right.

She's a five, she needs therapy and medication.

She's a seven, better risk-assess her capability to be a mother to her own kids.

She's a nine, how is she even still alive?

In Australia, ACE scores are already being used to assess applications for life insurance and health insurance. Several times a month, I receive emails from Australian women who have been refused vital insurance policies because their ACE score was too high.

I have been warning professionals for several years that this would eventually find its way to the UK, and that insurance underwriters would start to use childhood adversity and trauma to stop women from accessing insurance policies – on the assumption that the 'science' would position them as at higher risk of illnesses, suicide, self-harm and criminality.

In Summer 2021, campaigner, public speaker and Rotherham survivor Sammy Woodhouse tweeted publicly that out of all the main insurance companies in the UK, she could only find one who would offer her life insurance because of her childhood experiences of being trafficked and sexually exploited.

If the pathologisation of women and girls was not enough of a concern for the misuse of ACEs, I noticed in 2019 how more and more criminals were learning to blame their offences on their 'ACEs'. I saw it happening on social media, in the press, and heard it in case discussions with professionals. Probation officers have frequently raised concerns about the use of ACEs in their services, which implores them to look at the ACE score of sex offenders and domestic abuse perpetrators in order to offer them support.

Whilst I would accept that everyone has a human right to support and safety, my concern is more towards the way ACEs are being used as explanations for male violence – men stating that the reason they are abusive and violent is because of their ACEs.

In 2020, I heard from one man (if you can call repeated, abusive emails over a period of days 'heard from') who supported ACEs. He had seen that I had given a speech opposing ACEs and wrote to me to share what he thought of my views. He set up his own training and support company on 'ACEs', and believed that his own ACEs completely explained his previous offending behaviour, his relationship breakdowns and his time in prison. He had no previous experience of this field, and his background was in sales.

When I replied to say that adverse childhood experiences do not cause, or lead to, adults making decisions to abuse, harm and violate another human being, he became predictably angry and sent almost a hundred messages across several social media platforms because I wouldn't reply to him. The truth hurts. Millions of women and girls are raped, abused, trafficked, harmed, violated and discriminated against in childhood, and yet globally, they only make up 1–2 per cent of all violent criminals. Statistically then, this would suggest that there is no such relationship between ACEs and later criminality, unless those who suggest this are only talking about male violence.

Women and girls are significantly more likely to be abused and traumatised in childhood, and so, they should make up the majority of all violent offenders – outnumbering boys and men in every country. And yet, they make up a small fraction of violent offenders. The ACEs folklore about abused children growing up to be violent criminals doesn't stand up to basic maths and logic.

Abusing, violating, harming, oppressing, raping and assaulting people is an active choice – not a predetermined outcome caused by childhood adversity.

The story of ACEs has become the story of a stolen, misused set of questions, now used to give arbitrary adversity scores to humans, to pathologise women and girls, and exonerate violent men and boys.

CHAPTER 5

Using psychiatry against women and girls subjected to male violence

They treated me like I was a nuisance and told me to grow up, respect my parents and stop wasting their time. I was placed on a mixed-sex ward with adult men, and they wouldn't let me wear my pyjamas to breakfast because my pyjamas kept arousing the men. They told me that the men can't control themselves and it would be my fault, which just reinforced everything I thought about my own sexual abuse at home. Eventually, they gave me meds and sent me back home without ever asking me what was happening to me.

This chapter discuss real cases of rape, trafficking and abuse of women and girls who have been pathologised, medicated, sectioned and labelled after they reported male violence. This includes discussions of how this process is twofold: professionals are told that getting them diagnosed 'proves' that the perpetrator psychologically harmed them, but then that diagnosis is used against them to claim that their disclosures are fantasy or malicious. Ultimately, cases are dropped because of the diagnoses that are encouraged as 'good practice'.

Over the years, I have worked with or spoken to hundreds of women who have built the courage to finally talk to someone about the abuse they have been subjected to, only to find themselves in psychiatric wards or on daily medication that makes them feel ill. They have then been called fantasists, delusional, borderline, psychotic, neurotic, attention seekers, pathological liars, obsessive and promiscuous.

This is a common experience for women, and this chapter will discuss several real-life accounts of women I had the privilege of interviewing in 2020 and 2021.

Sectioned for being abused

It might seem a sensationalist claim, that women are being sectioned for being abused, but this is a common experience for many women who are currently, or have historically been sectioned. We must consider the impact of this in a society which regularly frames women as liars who report malicious and false allegations of rape and abuse to police. Despite there being no evidence of women and girls frequently submitting false allegations against men to police, there is nonetheless a considerable and enduring belief that women and girls make up rape and abuse for attention or revenge.

In 2020, I met Diana and interviewed her about her experiences of being pathologised and sectioned. Diana is a thirty-nine-year-old woman living in the UK who is now a teacher, and mother to her own children.

She explained that she grew up in a dysfunctional, abusive family where she was subjected to sexual abuse. Throughout this, she developed many signs of trauma including wetting the bed until she was fourteen years old, not sleeping through the night, chronic headaches every day, eczema and trouble with digestion and bowel movements. She was prescribed many different drugs throughout the 1990s including different types and dosages of antidepressants, sedatives and painkillers which made her feel very unwell.

During my secondary school days I developed an eating disorder and lost a lot of weight. I went down to about six and a half stone. My periods stopped. I counted and restricted calories. I exercised excessively. I used laxatives. Nobody noticed. The medical staff that saw me for routine or other appointments didn't pick up on it or offer me treatment. When I asked for help, when I realised it was out of control and I couldn't stop it, I was told to eat more, do yoga, relax. As if it was my fault that I was stressed and I should just calm down. As if I couldn't cope and this was my fault and my responsibility to remedy. Nobody asked me why I was doing this, nobody listened, nobody asked what was happening to me. I feel massively let down by the medical staff who missed or ignored the signs that I was being abused for years and years. They could have helped. They chose not to. I was really suffering. They just labelled me as being ill and blamed me for not coping better, without actually offering any useful or realistic suggestions as to how I could cope any better, or any support to do so.

Still being abused at home, she tried to disclose but no one believed her. She decided to try to end her life and was 'sectioned without being sectioned' at seventeen years old for trying to kill herself twice.

I was never actually sectioned – rather I was told if I didn't comply to their instructions, or if I tried to leave or if I did anything 'silly' (as in tried to kill myself) that I would be sectioned. And that it was best for me that way. I was basically sectioned, without being sectioned. The same rules applied. I also knew that if I didn't comply, if I 'resisted' or was 'difficult' that ECT was an option – and seeing good people going to those sessions and then returning with less of a brain, disoriented, afraid, child-like, with reduced memory, was enough to persuade me to do anything they asked of me pill-wise, just to avoid that. I just had to wait it out until I got out so I could stop taking them. They didn't help. But to say that was a sign of being a 'bad patient' and that wasn't a label you wanted. ECT was a real threat, often seen by the patients as something handed out to silence or punish or make us easier to manage for the staff, rather than purposefully treat anything. It didn't seem to benefit the patients at all.

Diana was often heavily sedated and told that there were no places for her in children's mental health facilities, so she was being taken to an adult psychiatric facility where she would be for at least six weeks.

It felt like prison. They took away all my A-level study books which were the only things that kept me going. I loved studying. I don't know why they did that. I was only allowed to do art stuff like paint glass bottles. They treated me like I was a nuisance and told me to grow up, respect my parents and stop wasting their time. I was placed on a mixed sex ward with adult men, and they wouldn't let me wear my pyjamas to breakfast because my pyjamas kept arousing the men. They told me that the men can't control themselves and it would be my fault, which just reinforced everything I thought about my own sexual abuse at home. Eventually, they gave me meds and sent me back home without ever asking me what was happening to me. I flushed all of those pills down the toilet when I left the hospital and never took them again. I knew that if I ever told them, they would see it as resistance and section me again.

Diana took some months longer to escape the abuse, but she eventually escaped, continued her education and achieved excellent results in her academic studies.

What is appalling about her experiences is that no one thought to safeguard her or talk to her about what was happening to her, and that no one believed her. Instead, they placed her in a dangerous mixed-sex, adult ward where she was at such high risk of being sexually assaulted by men on the ward that they would isolate her and make her wear more clothing than anyone else. There were also no safeguards when she was discharged to go home, where the abuse picked up just as it had left off.

There were no locks inside the unit other than preventing us from leaving. So anyone could come in to the toilet, the bathroom, the room you were sleeping in, and do or say whatever they wanted; there was no privacy or safety from the other patients. Many of whom really were struggling and didn't feel safe to be around. This was very scary, especially given my past.

Diana went on to struggle with her trauma and her physical health for decades, and we pick up again with her in Chapter 7.

I wanted to learn more about women being sectioned, medicated and diagnosed when they disclosed abuse, so I spoke to Penny, who is an experienced medical professional working in a secure mental health unit. She has been working there for over a decade. She currently works with adults aged eighteen to sixty-five years old in an acute mental health ward, where there are two wards for females, and one mixed-sex ward.

She told me of noticing concerning patterns, not only in the diagnosis of women, but of behaviours of male psychiatrists she works with.

A majority of the females that come into the unit are diagnosed with EUPD. I started to question this, as I noticed a pattern forming – many of the psychiatrists are male who 'prefer to work with females' (code for easier to manipulate and charm) and the women had trauma in common – either traumatic childhoods, rape and assault, or abusive relationships. One of them said once, 'It's easy for me to charm them'. Women are often viewed as inferior beings that can be mollified with some charm and a smile from a nice male doctor and that they 'respect the boundaries male doctors put in for them a lot more'. Women come in with obvious trauma, but we take them and tell them they have a disorder, and their behaviour is abnormal, and that it's something that needs 'correcting'. Female patients are often put on heavy medication as it is seen as 'validating' why they are in hospital, and when the medication doesn't work, it's an endless cycle of increased doses and trying new medications. These medications have severe side effects as a lot of them are heavy antipsychotics, but they are put on them with a saying of, 'might as well try this'.

Her description of sinister male psychiatrists who enjoy charming sectioned women in their wards is nothing new to me. Some of my closest friends work in psychology and psychiatry, and often tell me of situations where they have challenged abusive and manipulative male doctors who seem to enjoy toying with women diagnosed with 'personality disorders'.

We cannot ignore the connection between patriarchy, sexualisation, misogyny and psychiatry. For many women working on these wards, they witness male doctors abusing, controlling, derogating and even flirting with women with diagnoses of personality disorders. Challenging them on their decisions and behaviours is not easy, and is risky. For some women, it will cost them their jobs, their shifts, or their promotions.

Despite this, I know that every professional I interviewed for this book had stepped in at least once, and for many of them, intervening in or challenging poor practice was a daily occurrence. Penny spoke of the perceptions of women who had been sectioned after abuse and rape – and the ways they were seen as attention-seeking women who used the services like a revolving door.

As for how these women are viewed, the dismissal is palpable. People roll their eyes and sigh when we get certain patients admitted, patients we know well, as they repeatedly get admitted when they are in crisis, and the first thing that is discussed is how quickly to get them out. When the female patients with 'EUPD' express emotion or if they engage in risky behaviours such as self-harm, there is more eye rolling and they get referred to as 'typical PDs', or they get called 'difficult', or get told they are attention seeking. Some women come into the unit having been subject to abuse or assault/rape from a spouse or partner and they get brushed off because it's viewed as a waste of time to help them as people will say 'Oh, they will just go back to their partner anyway'.

Penny told me that she had once supported a woman who was being sectioned, and her male partner was behaving strangely. She told me that she picked up an 'odd vibe' between them. As she was being admitted, he asked for her bank card. Penny refused to hand it over and looked at the woman, quickly figuring out that she was being abused, and gaslit.

She waited until he had left, and spoke to her alone, where she disclosed that he was violent and abusive. When Penny raised this as a safeguarding issue with her managers, and the safeguarding teams, she was told that 'it can't be that bad if she stays with him'. Even when she reported that she was trapped in violent abuse, no one would do anything to protect the woman, as they considered her to be a waste of time.

Much of Penny's job, then, revolved around a personality disorder she didn't even believe existed. A label that positioned the women as crazy, stigmatised, difficult, time-wasting troublemakers.

I do not believe in EUPD as a diagnosis. As soon as women are given that label, they are written off. Their emotions now have a massive stigma attached and when they have poor mental health due to a life of abuse (sexual, physical, emotional and psychological) or relationships full of abuse, they are told the fault is with them and instead of validating their trauma, they are 'validated' with mind- and body-altering drugs that is deemed as okay because they are given by a doctor. These women are viewed as hysterical, too emotional, manipulative, troublemakers and timewasters. They are tone policed and have to always speak to doctors nicely or they will be ignored. It is evidenced repeatedly that the medical psychiatry approach to women with 'EUPD' does not work.

It is sobering, and in some ways, reassuring to hear this from a current mental health professional working in a secure, acute ward. These issues are talked about, but are often dismissed as if they are nothing more than conspiracy theories of disgruntled patients and 'quacks' (as I am often called).

There is a strong survivor movement online, made up of men and women who talk about their experiences of psychiatric harm and abuse. I have noticed the way authoritative psychiatrists mock, laugh at, and bully them on Twitter – without seeming to care that we can all see them doing it. Throughout 2020 and 2021, I've watched several male psychiatrists with thousands of followers quote tweet and reply to survivors of psychiatric abuse and harm, to tell them that they are delusional, obsessed, psychotic, anti-science and anti-expert. They often tweet about women and girls with personality disorders and psychosis as if they are parasitic, or deranged.

One woman who has been subjected to this is Fiona French, an activist and campaigner against psychiatric harm. I follow many academics and activists who talk about the pathologisation and medicalisation of vulnerable groups of people, but I have been particularly interested (and appalled) in the way Fiona is regularly attacked by powerful, influential, affluent psychiatry professors and practising psychiatrists when she talks about the damage benzodiazepines have done to her body and brain. I have spoken to her, and watched, as male academics and psychiatrists have publicly mocked her and other women who speak out.

What I have noticed is that these men seem to talk about women who disagree with them (whether in activism or in professional practice) as if they are one of their delusional, problematic, outspoken patients who needs to be nicer to them. Fiona often says that she worries about the female patients of the professors and doctors who attack her online, and wonders how they treat the women and girls they work with on wards. It appears that Fiona has a right to worry, if Penny's account of her own male colleagues is anything to go by.

Penny finished by saying that what women really needed was long-term trauma therapy, and that women on her wards were often shocked when she simply listened to them, and treated them like humans.

Women need more trauma-focused therapists. EUPD should not be a thing as a diagnosis and these women need to be believed. That is the very basic of things that needs to happen. They need professionals to believe them and take them seriously. I'm a trainee counsellor and I would love to work in trauma-focused therapy – for all the women I have met over the course of my time that have changed the way I respond to people and behave, for all the women whose hands have clutched mine because they are so grateful and shocked that I believed them.

Women as fantasists

Sherry was in her early thirties when she told her GP that she was sexually abused as a child; a disclosure which ultimately led to her being sectioned and medicated for several years. In conversations with her, she told me as much as she could remember about the abuse and rapes committed by a male family member. Her memory was fuzzy and complicated, peppered with self-doubt. She told me that she always thought she was taken to a cellar to be raped, but since learned that none of the houses in her family had cellars. Instead, she wondered if she was being taken to a shed or outbuilding. In addition to this, she has clear memories which make no sense to her, such as being raped by Santa Claus, or a man dressed as The Grim Reaper. These disclosures were used frequently to suggest that she was a rape fantasist, and she was often treated by medical professionals as if she was completely delusional. She was accused several times of making the stories up for attention.

However, as the years have passed and as she has tried to piece together what happened, she eventually came to realise that many of the assaults happened at family parties and gatherings – and fancy dress was a huge part of her family traditions. She thinks this could explain why she has such strange memories (and subsequent fears) of fancy dress, Christmas and Halloween.

For Sherry, her disclosures led to years of antipsychotic medication, several experiences of being chemically restrained and many medical appointments in which she was treated as though she was totally delusional. She told me that many professionals had simply sat her down and told her that none of her memories were real, and that she needed to move on. Even when she told professionals that the perpetrator had told her that no one would ever believe her, it was taken as further evidence of paranoia and delusions.

Sherry's experiences remind me of the way hundreds of women who have been subjected to ritual and satanic abuse have been treated since the 1980s. Despite there being thousands of disclosures of religious, ritual and satanic abuse, leading academics have brushed them off as mere fantasies of women and girls for decades. One of the only academics who has written about and explored ritual and satanic abuse from a qualitative and victim-centred approach is Dr Michael Salter.

At the time of writing this book, I was privileged to talk to him and thank him for his work on ritual and satanic abuse; especially as my own discussion of this had been met with the standard ridiculing from other academics with no experience of working with women and girls. Michael had got in touch to offer support, and to reassure me of his trauma-informed work in ritual abuse.

In 2013, I worked with several women who were subjected to ritual and satanic abuse in Wales. Their experiences were some of the worst I had ever heard, and it was around that time that I realised I needed to learn much more about ritual and satanic abuse. One woman in particular was called Amy, and she was in her early twenties when she told me that her parents and local priests had raped and abused her for years, deliberately got her pregnant and then carried out abortions as ritual sacrifices to Satan. She estimated that she had been subjected to at least twelve pregnancies which ranged from eleven to twenty weeks in length. She was also forced to eat faeces and the still-warm flesh of goats and chickens that had been slaughtered in front of her as sacrifices.

One time, they put me in the carcass of a pig. It was absolutely disgusting and I kept being sick. Another time, they sacrificed a baby animal and made me eat some after they had all raped me. My mum and dad were in on it. I think the priests groomed them, too. They thought that I was being given special treatment, or something. And it wasn't just me, there were other little children and other families. It was like a cult.

She was a very frightened and traumatised young woman in need of physical and psychological safety. However, I was met with several professionals who disbelieved her, treated her as a nuisance and were pretty sick of her 'tall stories'. Even after attempting to kill herself six times, professionals still called me and moaned about her on the phone, claiming that she was a fantasist, a pathological liar, a drain on resources and that ritual abuse doesn't even exist. One social worker suggested it would be better for everyone if she did kill herself.

It wasn't until a few years later that I met a special ops detective team who confirmed to me that they had been investigating ritual and satanic abuse for years, and that this kind of abuse was more common than people liked to believe.

The research is sparse, but we do know that professionals working in mental health and psychiatry are one of the most likely groups to meet women who have been subjected to ritual and satanic abuse (Salter, 2012). Many academics, journalists and authorities have argued that ritual abuse does not exist and is instead the product of 'false memory syndrome', 'hysteria' and 'moral panic'.

However, there have been successful convictions of ritual abuse of children in the USA, UK, Europe, Australia and Africa. In studies between 1996 and 1999, mental health practitioners reported that they had each supported one to two clients who had disclosed ritual abuse during therapy (Salter, 2012).

Dr Michael Salter is a professor based in Australia. Refreshingly, he doesn't claim or assume that women who talk about being abused are mentally ill, delusional, attention seeking, suffering from 'false memories' or hysterical. Instead, he has interviewed many victims of ritual and satanic abuse, and encourages a trauma-informed approach to understanding their unique and distressing experiences.

Women as the crazy, obsessed ex

One of the most common stereotypes of a mentally ill woman is that of the crazy, obsessed ex-girlfriend (a story almost always told by men who claim to have done absolutely nothing wrong, but all of their exes are 'psycho').

As an aside, I believe it is generally a huge red flag when men work hard to convince you that all of their exes are 'psycho' and you should not listen to anything they say. This is a common tactic used against women and girls who have tried to report or disclose abuse or harm. Framing a woman like this makes her instantly unreliable and discredited, which is deliberate, because whatever she might have to say is probably of great importance.

In 2020, I had the privilege of meeting Maya. She contacted me for advice and support after her five-year-old daughter, Emilia, spontaneously disclosed that her dad, Martin, had been sexually abusing her and taking photos of her genitals on his 'special camera'. This would be a horrible, devastating shock to any mother, but it was made even more complicated and harrowing because several years earlier, Martin's ex-girlfriend, Debbie, had frantically tried to warn

Maya that he was a sex offender, and was abusing his then infant daughter.

Debbie had split from Martin and had tracked Maya down to tell her that he was a sex offender. Debbie was an experienced medical professional working in a hospital in the nearby city and had no reason to lie. However, Martin successfully convinced Maya that his ex was a 'psycho', a 'bunny boiler' and a 'crazy ex' who had remained obsessed with him since he broke it off with her. Debbie had a different story though, and tried to tell Maya that he was a violent and abusive man with a sexual interest in infant girls. She said she had tried to report him to the police but nothing had happened.

Maya was initially horrified and frightened, but Martin assured her that Debbie was delusional and obsessed.

> *Debbie didn't stop, though. She turned up at my workplace, and Emilia's school. She wrote letters and emails to me. Martin became more and more angry with her and encouraged me to report her to the police for harassment and stalking. After months of her not leaving me alone, she stopped and was warned by the police and given a restraining order.*

You can imagine Maya's devastation when her daughter disclosed a couple of years later the exact thing Debbie had tried to tell her. By this point, Debbie's testimony meant absolutely nothing – she was framed as a crazy, obsessed ex with a restraining order. Who was going to believe her? Maya couldn't use her in criminal or family court because she herself had sought to prosecute her for her behaviour years earlier.

Maya then found herself in the same shoes as Debbie, trying to report the abuse of her daughter whilst Martin left her for another woman and convinced her that Maya was his crazy, bitch, psycho ex who lied about him abusing his daughter for no reason. Suddenly, Maya was the crazy ex, and the new woman who quickly became pregnant with Martin's second daughter was so scared of Maya that she would never speak to her, open the door to her or go anywhere physically near her (because she was so utterly crazy, who knew what she would do to the new woman in Martin's life).

Keeping all of his exes apart by convincing them all that the others are crazy, obsessed psychos was a touch of genius – and worked wonders when the police came knocking. He easily turned the entire investigation on its head, to frame his exes as scheming, manipulative, calculated psychopaths who lie about him abusing his beloved daughter.

In this particular case, Maya was subjected to months of psychiatric and psychological assessments which he demanded – and naturally, she was 'found' to be mentally ill, emotionally unstable, delusional, dangerous to her daughter; and Emilia was sadly removed from her custody and given to Martin and his new partner days before Christmas Day 2020.

Diagnosis of women to prove and disprove crime

There is a strange dichotomy that arises when women or girls report a crime and do, or do not have, a psychiatric diagnosis. Firstly, there is the belief in many professional communities (police, social work, psychology, psychiatry and psychotherapy) that a psychiatric diagnosis will validate and prove the psychological harm that the criminal has caused to her. This is perceived to be a benefit, as the prosecution team can use medical records and mental health records to 'prove' that their client is so mentally disordered or disturbed from the rapes, abuse, trafficking or neglect that the crime must have happened, and the offender deserves to be found guilty.

I came across this fairly frequently when working in the criminal justice system, and again when managing rape centres, but never as frequently as I found it when working with teenage girls who had been sexually abused and exploited. In this group, there was a general belief by most professionals that referring the young girl to CAMHS to secure a psychiatric diagnosis would open the door for treatment, proof and official records of her mental distress.

On this basis, the process becomes political and strategic instead of choosing a referral in the best interests of the girl. In some areas of the UK, funding and resources are reserved only for those who have been diagnosed with specific mental health disorders, and so it is seen as beneficial to gain one of those psychiatric diagnoses in order to access therapy, funding and support.

During my interviews with adult women for this book, several of them told me that they completely trusted the systems they were accessing, and when they were told to go to psychiatrists and mental health teams, they thought that they were in capable, ethical and supportive hands. Both Naomi and Hannah told me in their interviews that they initially felt completely safe and supported by the mental health referral process and system, until they began to realise that they were being pathologised and medicated for being raped or abused – and their credibility was then being called into question.

Many times, I had conversations with professionals who did not believe the girl was mentally ill at all, but the police or social services had advised them to push for a psychiatric diagnosis so they could use it as evidence of harm.

In 2017, I spoke to several directors and managers of rape and domestic abuse centres who told me that they were often advised to refer girls and women for psychiatric and psychological assessment, and were assured that it would benefit the girls and women they worked with. However, they quickly realised that this often was not the case, and the psychiatric diagnoses were being used against the women and girls – to suggest that they were unreliable, psychotic, unstable, attention seeking or so distressed that their memory and recollection of events would be useless.

One of the rape and sexual violence service CEOs told me that girls and women with autism diagnoses were being discredited, ignored and failed frequently. In fact, she said that their local police force hadn't taken forward a case where the woman or girl was autistic in several years. In all cases, no matter how much she and her staff pushed and appealed, the argument was that victims of rape, sexual abuse and domestic abuse with autism were not credible witnesses and could not reliably take part in a trial.

There is absolutely no evidence for this assertion, and even if someone does have difficulties or a disability, there are still rights, protocols and guidance for how best to support them whilst giving evidence and reporting crime. Further, it would be pertinent to argue that the refusal to investigate a crime based on whether the woman or girl is autistic is discrimination.

Around the same time, I had interviewed a brilliantly intelligent woman named Sasha, who told me of her experience of being raped in front of witnesses, in broad daylight as she walked through a Midlands city on her way home from work. She was attacked by a stranger and immediately called the police. She told me that despite her reservations and concerns about the racism she might be subjected to as a Pakistani woman, she was absolutely certain that her case would be taken seriously because it hit all of the common stereotypes of the classic rape myth. It happened outdoors, she had witnesses, the rapist was a stranger, she had injuries and DNA evidence.

She was not prepared, however, for police to request her medical and mental health records, which showed that she had been sectioned twice, had sought crisis support several times and had reported being sexually abused in early childhood, too.

Sasha explained to me that as soon as her mental health was brought up, they started to question her version of events – despite all of the evidence. Eventually, they started to question her ability to give evidence and asked her why she had retracted her statements of child sexual abuse when she was much younger. They suggested that she had retracted them because she is delusional, and they decided to close the case against the man who raped her.

Cases like these are very common.

When I was working in the criminal justice system, I led two crown courts and five magistrates' courts, each one with multiple court-rooms within. This means that on any given weekday, I would be managing between eight and fifteen court trials of varying crimes from theft to homicide. The use of psychiatric diagnosis (both actual and implied) was commonplace. Where defence lawyers didn't have any 'proof' of psychiatric diagnosis, they simply made one up. Instead of relying on medical records, they would frequently suggest to the jury or magistrates that the woman or girl was delusional, depressed, unstable, deceptive, promiscuous, obsessive, crazy or out for revenge. It was frankly devastating to watch, and nothing could prepare the girls and women I supported for suddenly being confronted with a barrister accusing them of being mentally ill or malicious (or commonly, both). No matter what support work I had done before, and on the day of the trial, I witnessed girls and women break down in tears, become enraged or completely give up at the mere mention of their mental health.

It led me to think that women and girls know all too well what is coming next, when someone calls their mental health into question.

I decided to talk to a clinical psychologist about her experience of the pathologisation of women and girls subjected to male violence. Maryam* is an experienced psychologist working in residential care. She also leads a pathway in the NHS for 'personality disorder' and complex trauma. She began by telling me, much like Penny, that she hated the personality disorder diagnosis, and pushed for this to be dropped from all referral criteria into her pathway.

> *Not a surprise the main bulk of our referrals are females with a crazy label called EUPD attached to them. I've spent time across the trust telling people about how stupid PD and EUPD is – hence dropping PD from any of our referral criteria. I've just said, if its distress, that's good enough for me. I've dropped it from DBT service I manage as well, and informed people if you want to work on this pathway, then diagnosis and PD is banned. All the females have had experiences of abuse (sexual, emotional, neglect etc) hence being in services. So we work with the girls and women on what they are needing from services and work with them in the community. I also work privately in children's residential homes as an external consultant where the many females in care are there as a result of sexual abuse (by males).*

I was interested to learn that Maryam had chosen to make significant changes to the service she managed in the city, to try to stop the pathologisation of women and girls. She had noticed the same pattern as I had, that the women and girls were all victims of abuse, violence and neglect. She realised that personality disorder was a catch-all term that was being slapped on hundreds of traumatised women and girls, and so she used her power to create systemic change in the NHS.

We discussed misogyny and patriarchy in psychiatry, and the evidence of it in her own services. Maryam told me that mental health services are primarily governed by males in senior management. She said that the only way mental health services would challenge this patriarchal system of victim blaming and pathologisation would be to develop woman-only, women-led services.

Mental health services that are governed by males at senior management yes. In varying shapes and forms all services are. Blaming females that if they had dressed in a certain way they would not have got raped, or did it even happen as they didn't say anything at the time. All services have this unless we have dedicated services for women led and owned by women. In mental health services, medics are mainly male and they treat our girls and women like they are to blame for their problems. They get injected with medication and then are told they need therapy, and then questioned again to make sure the details match up. Heaven forbid a female get it wrong! I also feel services like mine where females get the diagnosis of 'PD', male and female staff blame the girls and women, and treat them like crap. They can't see beyond anything.

As my interviews with professionals and women continued, it became strikingly clear that women in mental health units were being dehumanised, and female professionals were bearing witness to this oppression and control. More and more women were waking up to the reality of psychiatry as a dangerous, risky place for women and girls to be – and were doing everything they could to subvert an established and powerful system of misogyny.

CHAPTER 6

Pathologising women and girls in the courtroom

The biggest let-down is that it doesn't matter if you are lying or telling the truth, you could have all the evidence in the world and they still won't believe you. They leave you to get abused and switch it all around, so you are the issue. My psychiatrist wrote on my records 'she is having issues with spouse' when I told him I was being beaten up, abused and raped. I did tell them but they didn't listen or ever record it.

For many women who are pathologised and diagnosed with psychiatric disorders, their worst nightmare is to end up in a courtroom. Whether they are going through a divorce, agreeing child contact or are a victim in a criminal trial – as I have touched on in the previous chapter, having a mental health disorder on file is usually a recipe for discrimination, gaslighting and injustice.

This chapter will examine the way psychiatric and psychological assessment and diagnosis are being used in courtrooms, often without any right to appeal or retract. In some cases, the mere suggestion of mental disorder is enough to frame a woman as totally incapable of telling the truth, and yet another misogynistic system finds a bedfellow with psychiatry.

Family court

In 2020, I had the privilege of interviewing Brianna about her experiences of being pathologised and mistreated in the courtroom. After being raped at university and suffering at the hands of a racist psychiatric system, Brianna was diagnosed with Emotionally Unstable Personality Disorder and depression. She was on several different medications including antidepressants and antipsychotic drugs which made her feel very ill.

'They made me feel numb. I couldn't feel anything. Like he could punch me in the face and I would feel absolutely nothing,' she told me as she reflected on the medication she was given.

In 2016, she met Matt. She described him as racist towards her, abusive and sexually violent. He would mock her and gaslight her for having a personality disorder diagnosis, and would frequently tell her that no one would believe anything she said, even if she did report him one day.

> *He was so sexually abusive to me, and racist. One day I just turned up at the A&E department and asked them to help me. I was desperate for help. I was pregnant with his child and I was so scared. I was shut in a triage room with a male nurse and he told me that they were going to section me. I was terrified. The next day they just released me and was like, 'There's nothing wrong with her, she's just got EUPD.' He kept asking me for sex in the car on the way home from the hospital and I kept saying no, like I didn't want sex. And he just kept on and on and on at me and then he raped me.*

Matt left her seven days later. Brianna was subjected to months of hell after she was raped by her partner, as he repeatedly reported her to social services and the police for being mentally unstable and claimed that he felt she was a risk to their baby. She was assessed several times and even sectioned once more, all whilst she told professionals that he was doing this on purpose to gain control over her and make her look like she was incapable of being a mother. When their baby was born, Matt immediately started action to get custody, and predictably, leaned on Brianna's mental health records to position her as dangerous and unstable.

He's done everything you can think of. He's turned up at my house wearing a GoPro strapped to his chest. He's reported me over and over for my mental health. He kept deliberately doing safe and well checks on me via the police; one time, they even sent an air ambulance and I was just there in my house. He stalks me on social media, creates fake profiles and sends messages to me. He infiltrated a domestic abuse Facebook support group I was in and pretended to be another victim. He even alleged that I stabbed him. At one point, when he was denying the rape and violence, he accused me of cheating on him and then submitted to the court a close-up picture of my vulva and vagina to 'prove' he hadn't raped me. He had that picture from my phone years earlier, and submitted it to the court. It was so embarrassing. Everyone saw my vagina. I just knew every lawyer and the judge in the case had seen me. No one stopped him or punished him – he shared nudes of me without consent to an entire legal team and I had no rights. He did it on purpose.

Luckily for Brianna, the judge in her case became suspicious of Matt's motivations when he changed his request and said he only wanted to see their baby once per week for six hours, but continued to position Brianna as profoundly mentally disordered. The judge ruled that their baby should stay with Brianna and the proceedings were closed.

However, even two years on, Brianna explained to me that she is still treated as a risk by social workers who frequently challenge her about her mental health, personality disorder and still write on her records that she stabbed Matt (despite there being no evidence, injuries or investigation).

I asked her what she felt the impact of being labelled with EUPD/BPD was, instead of her years of trauma from male violence being recognised and validated.

The biggest let-down is that it doesn't matter if you are lying or telling the truth, you could have all the evidence in the world and they still won't believe you. They leave you to get abused and switch it all around so you are the issue. My psychiatrist wrote on my records 'she is having issues with spouse' when I told him I was being beaten up, abused and raped. I did tell them but they didn't listen or ever record it. Everything I go to the GP for now is 'oh it's the BPD', BPD this, BPD that, 'you're over-emotional'. I don't go to the doctors anymore, what's the point?

What the BPD label has done is exclude me from services that are directed at DV and sexual violence, excluded me from obtaining jobs I applied for (police officer and fire brigade) and even excluded me from support to help with grief (miscarriage). I found out that MIND doesn't accept referrals of people with BPD as we are seen as too high risk, so I couldn't get therapy I needed. The BPD meant that they medicated my pregnancy (they gave me quetiapine for mood swings), they ignored all of my disclosures of sexual violence and forced me to take responsibility for abuse, they did not provide a way out of abusive relationships but forced me to stay in it and sort it out. The court told me that because of the BPD, I had to be seen to be working with Matt and giving him access to our child and being amicable otherwise they would start action against me. They all made me believe that abuse was my fault as I have a 'disordered personality'.

Brianna recently gained access to all of her mental health records and showed them to me. As I worked through them, I couldn't believe how absent her own experiences were: no mention of being raped or sexually assaulted at university, no mention of domestic violence or abuse, no mention of the constant harassment and stalking by her ex-partner. Just pages and pages of comments about her being 'unstable', 'emotional', 'tearful' and 'angry'. One entry, when Brianna was 38 weeks pregnant and having disclosed abuse several times even states, 'she is currently living separately from the father due to her mood swings'. No mention of abuse.

In reference to a time where he attacked her whilst pregnant, the psychiatrist wrote in her notes, 'following a verbal exchange between her and her partner, she rang the police and then she was taken to A&E'. That's the only reference to anything happening to Brianna in several pages of notes. The ignorance of the domestic and sexual violence that she had been subjected to was shocking, and it was appalling to see the language and tactics used within years of notes to reframe Brianna as the issue, without any relation to context or her own disclosures. It must be enraging for her to read back through the way she was described and treated for so long, knowing that she had repeatedly disclosed violence and abuse.

The question then, is why would so many professionals ignore a woman consistently telling the same stories of abuse and violence? Why would that detail become so irrelevant that it doesn't appear on any of her records? As Brianna quite rightly said to me, the whole reason she was seeking support was because of the male violence she was subjected to, and yet, it was never recorded. Instead, all there was were years of comments about her personality and emotions.

There are several possible answers to why this happened (and why this happens frequently to many women and girls who access mental health services).

The first is theoretical: the medical model of mental health is disinterested in social context, environments, abuse and oppression, and instead situates the issues within the person and specifically, within their brain. With all services that Brianna accessed subscribing to the medical model of mental health, their approach was rigidly focused on 'treating' her with increasing medications instead of exploring why she was so scared, low and suicidal.

The second is patriarchal: the BPD diagnosis is a misogynistic tool which is more likely to be given to women and girls, and has the toxic effect of positioning women as problematic, unstable and unreliable. This means that for a woman like Brianna, many of her disclosures could be dismissed as the complaining of an emotional woman, exaggerating or attention seeking. Male violence can continue, and women who disclose will be reported and assessed as mad – just as they always were.

The third is strategic: if professionals acknowledged that all of Brianna's 'symptoms' were caused by male violence, they would have to do something about it. Someone would have to step in, and protect her and her unborn baby. Practically, there is much more work to do, and organisations would have to take responsibility for the discovery of an adult or child in serious danger, abuse or oppression every day. They would have to work together to solve social issues and address years of misogynistic violence that has previously been swept under the rug.

The fourth, which is specific to Brianna and other Black women, is racism. For Brianna, there was years of racist comments about her attitude, her ethnicity, her afro and even how 'articulate' she was, which was often written as if it was a surprise. Women are up against an incredibly powerful system to begin with, but to be a Black woman in a mental health service is a very dangerous place to be.

Criminal court

Family court is not the only place where women have their mental health used against them. In 2020, I spoke with several women who had been pathologised and abused in criminal trials where they were supposed to be the victim. Instead, their mental health was used to position them as the problem, the cause of the crimes against them, or even as the perpetrator.

I was grateful to hear from twenty-two-year old Alice, who contacted me to talk about her experiences of being pathologised whilst she was a teenager. Between the ages of thirteen and fifteen years old, Alice was groomed by a group of men in her town, trafficked, sexually abused and raped. Her case become one of the biggest in the UK, and was reported widely in the media when the group of offenders were sentenced to multiple long sentences for their crimes against many young girls in the area. Her case was also subject to a serious case review due to the failings to protect her and the other girls.

What looked like a successful conviction to the general public was a life-changing and traumatic experience for Alice, who was diagnosed with borderline personality disorder and heavily medicated until she could no longer read, write, attend school or count coins to buy an item from a shop.

I was sexually abused and exploited from being thirteen years old. I had been put on fluoxetine, citalopram and sertraline. I was put in a secure unit between fourteen and fifteen years old and I was made to take 10mg of risperidone every single day. It made me sleep constantly. I would try to wake up for half an hour and the staff would make me go back to bed because of the side effects. The dizziness, and extreme disorientation. I was told that I needed the drug to keep me calm. I was missing out on my education, and after about six months I plucked up the courage to tell them that I couldn't keep taking it. After speaking to a psychiatrist many years later, I was informed that I should never have been given the risperidone and that I was on ten times more than fully grown men, who were typically given 1–2mg per day with extreme side effects, even for them.

Alice was given risperidone, a powerful atypical antipsychotic drug, used to medicate people with schizophrenia, bipolar disorder and autism. Current prescribing guidelines suggest that adolescents should not be given more than 2.5mg per day, and as she was correctly informed, most adults are given between 0.5mg and 3mg as an initial dose, increasing incrementally to a maximum adult dose of 6–8mg (The Maudsley, 2018).

The criminal trial took several years to begin, and Alice was seventeen years old when the CPS requested that she was given doses of diazepam to give evidence in court. Even with years of experience, I was shocked to hear this, as diazepam could easily be used by the defence barrister to argue that Alice was not fit to give evidence at all.

The CPS and police did in fact request that I was given diazepam. At that time, I was struggling to see any purpose in going to court and it was having such a detrimental impact on me that they suggested that I take it to be able to stand in court calmly. I refused this offer and this was something my mother spoke about in the serious case review as I was being asked to take

drugs to go through such a process after drugs were used by the
men that sexually abused and exploited me.

It is appalling that Alice had been pushed to take diazepam in order
to give evidence in court, especially as this triggered memories of the
sexual abuse and exploitation she had suffered. To her, it felt like a
strong contradiction – almost a continuation of her exploitation that
she was in court to give evidence about.

I asked how she felt about it all now, at twenty-two years old, and
whether she had anything she wanted to add to this book. Alice
thought about it for a while and then replied.

I one hundred per cent feel strongly about the book you're writ-
ing. I've suffered awful abuse from a very young age which has
made me respond in a lot of different ways through the years.
Not one psychiatrist, psychologist, police officer, or support
worker, or any professional has said to me, 'you endured awful
abuse which made you respond the way you did'. Instead I had
people telling me it was my fault. They said I shouldn't have put
myself in those situations, I should not have contacted those
men back, I shouldn't of gone certain places with certain people.
Every single comment made was what I could've done differ-
ently. As a victim of abuse this is already something you question
yourself about daily but when every professional is telling you,
you start to believe it. I was told several times through the court
process to 'think of all the other girls that could go through this',
yes, this is something I wanted to stop, but this was also about
me and the abuse I'd had to endure. This was something they
weren't bothered about though, they wanted their convictions,
and it was never about the victims. I've never had any psycho-
logical input and I've been told that I'm basically a lost cause
now and I will never get any better because of my experiences. I

never felt like a victim through the whole process. I felt like I was the perpetrator. I was being locked away and silenced because of my 'decisions'. Why weren't these men that were still allowed to continue to abuse young girls and women locked up?

This reply from Alice felt disturbingly similar to the many others I had heard over the years. Women and girls who had reported and disclosed abuse felt like they were mentally ill, and felt like criminals being locked up and silenced.

I also spoke to Hannah, who is a white forty-three-year-old Londoner. She described a life of pathologisation which ultimately resulted in the man who violently assaulted, raped and abused her and then sexually abused her daughter, being let off the hook without criminal charges. No charges were made for the rape of his wife, the rape of a child, or the attempted murder of his then-pregnant wife. Instead, he was charged and found guilty of GBH, he served 9 months in prison, was deported and fined £1,500 for the inconvenience.

Hannah was eighteen when she was first referred into mental health services. After several appointments with male doctors, she realised that she couldn't tell them what happened to her in childhood, and she was diagnosed with EUPD. Like so many other women, she was labelled psychotic and given medication. When she told them of flashbacks to her childhood abuse, they recorded them as hallucinations and increased her medication. Soon after, she was sectioned and placed on a ward where a doctor sat her down to warn her:

The doctor came to see me and said that I had to make sure my door was locked at all times because there were patients on the ward who would rape me. They said that there were a few very dangerous male patients. I tried to lock doors, but most of the locks were broken. My door was broken so I couldn't lock it. I

> *was given tranquillisers a lot whilst I was in hospital. I was sexually assaulted in my bed by a patient but because they had given me tranquillisers, I couldn't move or say anything. I thought hospital was going to be this magical place where they would cure me and I would be safe. My community nurse was so nice to me, so I expected everyone to be like that.*

Her experiences caused her significant trauma which was largely ignored, and put down to her personality disorder. Hannah was told that her case wasn't 'severe enough' for further support or therapy and that she would need to manage the personality disorder herself with medication, mindfulness and exercise. When she was married to her first husband, the doctors started regularly consulting him about her mental health, medication and treatment.

> *I felt like no one was taking me seriously so I cut all my hair off, almost like a symbol, like a cry for help – I did it on purpose. I wish I hadn't, cos that fucked me over for years. They treated me as even more unstable. The doctors started talking to my husband and telling him I needed more medication. They told him all my details and records. I told them I had little children and I didn't want medication to make me feel dopey – but they called me and said they had discussed with my husband and they all agreed that I should be taking more medication. Only a few years later, my kids were removed from me and placed with him.*

With a system that had positioned Hannah as mentally ill, she told me that she felt she had no choice but to try to move on – she knew she couldn't fight their decisions and portrayals of her. She met a new man who became extremely violent and abusive. He was charged with attempted murder, rape and assaults, but eventually, he was only convicted of GBH. Once he was in prison, Hannah's eldest daughter disclosed that he had sexually abused her.

What followed were years of Hannah attempting to fight for justice for her children, struggling with domestic violence, threats and abuse from her ex, increasing medication and psychiatric diagnoses – and ultimately, she was framed as a 'crazy ranting woman'.

> *I reported the abuse of my daughter, but no one believed me. They said 'Look at the medical records of the mum, look at her medication' and that was it, they just dropped the whole case against him for sexually abusing my daughter. He was in the country illegally though, so they deported him instead of giving her any justice. Now the professionals keep claiming that she isn't traumatised at all and she has anger issues. I have fought that with her, and they keep trying to put her on Ritalin. They've even suggested now that she's a risk to her younger siblings because she's refusing medication and diagnosis.*

There are countless stories of women who have been accused of lying about or 'believing' that they (or their children) have been abused or raped by men, but it never really happened. This is nothing new of course, women's stories have always been framed as just that, stories. Tall stories. Old wives' tales. Lies. Revenge. Delusions. Madness.

There are common ways that psychiatry and mental health language are implicated in this process, and in over a decade of experience, I have seen pretty much every tactic. I've seen serious head injuries to teen girls who have been raped by adult men being positioned as self-inflicted injuries that were deliberately falsely reported to police. I worked on a case in which a girl who was abducted, raped and imprisoned in an abandoned terrace house by a gang of men, set it on fire in order to escape. A young teenager, she had been stripped naked, chained to a bed and raped for days. Her sudden quick thinking meant that she lit some flammable liquid, set fire to the room and managed to escape. She ran through the street, completely naked, covered in injuries, and banged on the doors of anyone who might answer and help her.

She was later sectioned, arrested, charged, and then convicted of arson. She was fifteen years old.

The men were not charged.

Whilst these examples may sound far-fetched, professionals working on these cases will know how mental health is often used against girls and women to completely derail their experiences. Their disclosures will be ignored or written up as fantasy. Their injuries will be recorded as self-inflicted. Their fear will be diagnosed as anxiety disorder. Their sadness will be diagnosed as depressive disorders and mood disorders. Their trauma will be diagnosed as a disordered personality.

In the last few years, I have noticed a large increase in the occurrence of the 'delusion defence' in cases where women report men for sexual and domestic violence. This convenient accusation carries such weight, that perpetrators, professionals and authorities regularly wheel it out, even where there is no diagnosis or evidence of 'delusions'. Indeed, the weight of this accusation is particularly heavy, one sniff of the word and thorough assessments can be ordered.

I recall the case of an eighteen-year-old girl who was taken to hospital by police on the morning she was violently assaulted by her ex-boyfriend who was in his early twenties. She had injuries to the neck and shoulder, and whilst with police, disclosed for the first time that she had been subjected to extreme violence and rapes for several years by this man. In the police interviews, he simply suggested that she was delusional, had mental health issues and was addicted to drugs. Despite there being no evidence of any of these accusations, police referred her to social care and mental health teams for assessments. No charges were brought against the man, but the young woman was subjected to weeks of interviews and assessments which ultimately found nothing.

In 2020, I was contacted by a woman who had recently been accused of being delusional when her eight-year-old son disclosed to a teacher that his dad had raped him. In this case, the son never told his mother, but chose to tell his favourite teacher at school. The teacher sought advice and reported her concerns to social care and the police, and the police informed the woman of her son's disclosure. She instantly stopped her son (and her other children) from seeing their dad, and made him leave the family home, which was supported by police. Over a year later in court, she was accused of being delusional, paranoid and 'coaching' her son to deliberately disclose to a teacher about his dad, and the judge supported that assertion with no evidence.

In 2019, Marianne, a forty-five-year-old therapist who is a close friend of mine, was relentlessly stalked and harassed by her ex-husband. He hacked her social media accounts, her bank account, her Amazon account, her CCTV system and started to send parcels and items to her house. At the peak of his behaviour, he decided to call random local tradesmen from directories and leave voicemails to all of their wives telling them that Marianne had been sleeping with all of their husbands. He then left her full name, address and phone numbers. Marianne was inevitably bombarded with threatening, angry and upset phone calls and visits to her address by devastated wives and girlfriends who all believed their husbands had been cheating on them.

It took Marianne weeks to deal with each and every one of the women, and explain that the voicemails were malicious and she didn't know any of these men. Having worked for many years in domestic and sexual violence, and with good links to local police, she decided to report her ex-husband. However, she was quickly written off as delusional by officers who came to her house, and told that she should 'calm down' and 'have a cup of tea', whilst they tried to convince her that she was paranoid or delusional. No charges were ever brought against him, and his behaviour continued for months.

What is interesting about the quick and easy accusation of 'delusions', is how quick and easy it really is. Once said, it is for the woman to prove that she is not delusional.

How do you prove you are not delusional?

Another common term borrowed from mental health and psychology is projection. Projection was initially suggested and theorised by Sigmund Freud, who is often given the title the father of psychoanalysis. Projection is the act of putting your personal issues onto somebody else, and then accusing them of having that set of issues, instead of recognising it within yourself. Despite it being a highly contested and widely debated concept, it is used in abundance when women disclose sexual and domestic abuse – often by professionals who have no knowledge of what 'projection' is.

In 2020, I spoke at length with Maya about her experiences with her daughter Emilia, and heard how she was often accused of 'projecting her issues on to her daughter'.

I don't know why they keep saying it. It's written in the court reports about me, too. They keep saying I am projecting my issues around safety on to Emilia and then making her believe that her daddy has been abusing her. That's not what happened, I was shocked when Emilia told me he had been taking pictures of her vagina. I ran and got the iPad so I could try to record her saying it, I couldn't believe what I heard. I called my best friend after she went to sleep and I just cried and cried. I told the police and social services because I thought I was supposed to. Now, they say these are all my own mental issues and issues from my childhood being projected on to Emilia and that I'm a perpetrator of 'family violence' because I am 'projecting' on to her. They even said I abused Emilia by letting her be interviewed by police and by the social worker. But I had no choice – I had to let them interview her.

Damned if she did, damned if she didn't.

Maya, like many other women, found herself in the catch-22 where she would be pathologised and scrutinised if she didn't report the abuse of her child, but would also be pathologised and scrutinised if she did.

If she doesn't report, she's neglectful and dangerous. If she does report, she's delusional and malicious. If she continues to report, she's coaching her child. If she argues back, she's mentally ill.

Or there's the case of Natalie, who was told directly by the sheriff in her case that they didn't 'take kindly to women who bad mouth their kids' dads', which was said to her during a hearing about her ex-husband raping her daughter. The sheriff went on to warn Natalie that her disclosures were malicious and told her to drop her action against her ex-husband, and stated in court that, 'just because he has raped one of your children doesn't mean he will rape the others'.

The weight of madness cannot be underestimated for women who attempt to engage with criminal and family justice systems. It really is no wonder that perpetrators use this accusation as often as they do, especially when it is so successful in discrediting women and inverting the process. What begins as a report of violence against the woman or girl very often results in detailed scrutiny and assessment of the woman. In some cases, it is as simple as a man making an offhand comment about his ex-partner or victim being psychotic, obsessed, crazy, neurotic, depressed, anxious or disordered, and the entire process changes.

CHAPTER 7

Ignoring and minimising women's health issues

I couldn't believe it. I sat there and told the GP about all these symptoms since my little one was born last year. I'm just so unwell. There's something wrong. It's hormonal, I think. I'm tired, I'm lethargic, I don't sleep, my temperature changes – I've never been like this before. It all started after I had my fourth baby last year. I told her everything and she took one look at my medical records, and she must have skimmed down and seen that I've been in mental health wards before and that was it. She wouldn't refer me for any tests or anything like that, she just said I needed to go back to the psychiatric ward. And then I didn't know what to do. Do I refuse? Do I just do what she says? What happens if I refuse and they think I'm mad? Do I turn up to this referral and go back to psychiatry?

Zoe, thirty-two years old

A critical discussion of why so many women are labelled as mentally ill when they raise concerns about their physical health is vital.

In 2020, I created a TikTok video for a bit of fun, mocking the inevitable process that women go through when they report their health issues to a doctor. In the video, I pretended to be a GP who asked ridiculous questions about the woman's mental health, told her to lose weight and then told her to just go on the pill as a solution to her serious health concerns. The video was seen by millions of people and sparked tens of thousands of comments, messages and emails.

Women recognised this process in their millions, from all different countries.

But it isn't just anecdotes and memes on the internet, academic research has been reporting this phenomenon for several years. Women are routinely ignored, gaslit and diagnosed with psychiatric disorders instead of being sent for simple, cheap tests which could have explored their physical illnesses and injuries. Studies suggest that women and girls who go to their GP or to A&E departments are more likely to die or have life-threatening symptoms ignored due to pathologisation. A significant number of medical studies have shown that when women present with cancer, stroke and cardiac arrest symptoms, they are likely to be told they are due to mental health issues and be turned away without further tests (BBC, 2018; Chen et al, 2008). This chapter will also discuss hormonal treatments, the contraceptive pill, periods, postnatal period and menopause – and how women and girls are pathologised for cyclical periods.

Alongside dangerous and harmful psychiatric treatments and pathologisation during life-threatening violence and abuse, the dismissal of health concerns is yet another way that women's and girls' lives are put at risk by the belief that women are hysterical, emotional, exaggerators and attention seekers. When interviewing women for this book, every woman I spoke to had at least one story without even trying to dig deep and remember.

Viv had collapsed several times with dangerously low blood pressure which had been put down to mental illness. Megan had complained of serious stomach-ache, joint pains and migraines that were put down to depression and she was medicated. Megan's mum had been being sick for years, and sought help from her GP who accused her of having mental health issues, being bulimic and needing intervention and medication – she later saw another doctor who recognised that she had serious stomach ulcers caused by H. pylori which needed treatment. Brianna was getting more and more unwell due to dangerously low folate levels but they told her it was the borderline personality disorder and she was sent back to a mental health ward twice before someone would give her a basic blood test – which confirmed the folate levels were extremely low and treatment was started immediately.

Despite being a nurse, Natalie woke up in a high dependency unit because doctors would not believe she was in labour. After desperately trying to tell male doctors that she was in labour and needed to push, she was told to go home and stop overreacting and exaggerating. She haemorrhaged shortly afterwards and lost a life-threatening quantity of blood. At fourteen years old, Diana began with several health issues and bed wetting, and instead of any investigations into the onset of these symptoms, she was prescribed antidepressants and sleeping tablets. At seventeen years old, she began to develop digestive issues that made her stomach hurt when she ate, but she was diagnosed with an eating disorder and given Prozac.

Naomi had unsuccessful surgery on cysts as a teenager, but was ignored by doctors when she said it hadn't worked and she was still in agony. As the pain spread up her back, she was told that she 'needed to feel the pain to heal'. She argued back and became aggressive and was sectioned. In high school she was in a lot of pain, her IUD had slipped and she was bleeding heavily. The nurse told her that if it was so bad, she should just go and pull it out herself in the school bathroom. She did this, and then immediately haemorrhaged.

Jade spent seventeen years trying to get a diagnosis for her joint and bone pains and countless dislocations. No matter how much pain she was in, or how many times she had presented at A&E with a dislocated joint, she was accused of making it up or exaggerating the pain. She was thirty-five years old by the time she was correctly diagnosed with Ehlers Danlos Syndrome.

Despite her seeking help for her spinal pain and symptoms at fourteen years old, she told me of countless times where she was ignored, dismissed, belittled or abused by doctors. At fourteen years old, the doctor bent her over, punched her in the back where the pain was, and told her she would 'grow out of it'.

Much later on, she had approached doctors again for support with growing symptoms (including specific drug reactions, bone issues, dislocations and spinal pain). She had printed out thirteen pages of information about Ehlers Danlos Syndrome after reaching out to the medical society for support and advice.

A doctor asked her, 'So on a scale of one to ten, how would you rate the pain you are in?'

When Jade rated her pain as a nine out of ten, the doctor laughed at her and said, 'Oh, so your hand hurts more than childbirth, does it?'

Jade made an important point, in asking why male doctors and men in general always use childbirth as the benchmark for all pains – especially as she had had children, and argued that the pain she was in was much worse than the managed pain of childbirth.

The other issue is the curious process of asking women to rate their pain on a scale of one to ten. If women have always been positioned as emotional, exaggerating hysterics – what good would a numerical, metaphorical scale of subjective pain be? If a woman says that her pain is a ten, will she be believed? Or will she be accused of making it up? Will a doctor wearily shake their head at her, whilst they write down a four, or five?

Throughout my research for this book, the stories of women's illnesses, pain and health issues being pathologised and ignored only continued.

After years of being pathologised after sexual and domestic abuse, Zoe recently went to her doctor to raise concerns that her body and hormones seem to be seriously affected since having her youngest child one year ago. She complained of severe fatigue, weight gain, sudden body temperature changes and interrupted sleep and asked for a blood test. The doctor immediately referred her back to the psychiatric ward and refused to do any other tests.

There are two main patterns around women who seek help from medical services:

1. Their physical symptoms, illnesses and injuries are described as mental health issues, exaggeration or fabrication
2. Their trauma, fears, sadness or distress are passed off as physical, chemical or biological issues with the brain

What is most interesting about the two pathways to misdiagnosis is that they seem to be the opposite of whatever the woman is saying. When she says it's a physical issue, it's in her head. When she says she's being abused or harmed, it's also in her head – but with some biochemical cause. So, everything can be ignored and dismissed as if it is just a figment of the imagination, in the head of hysterical women.

Periods – madness. Pregnancy – madness. Menopause – madness. Endometriosis – madness.

Sexual trauma? Madness. Symptoms of cancer? Madness. Cardiac symptoms? Madness.

It's no wonder that so many women stop seeking help from medical services.

Menstruation as madness

Women's menstrual cycles have interested, baffled and disgusted men for centuries. Authors such as Schooler et al. (2005) write and speak frequently about 'menstrual shame' being central to men's control of women and their bodies. Throughout history, periods have been demonised and framed as evil and dirty. The church played a role in this (again) and taught Christians that men should never lie with women who were bleeding. Folklore and misogynistic jokes about women posit that 'you should never trust anything that can bleed for a week without dying'.

Consider for a moment the pathologising language surrounding periods and cycles:

The curse. The devil. Mother Nature. Code red. Bloody Mary.

A 2016 international study found over 5,000 euphemisms for women's menstruation in ten different languages, which included the Finnish phrase 'Hullum lechman tauti', which translates to 'Mad Cow's Disease'. Language has great power in constructing our understanding of experiences and the world around us, and so it is important to notice when language is consistently negative about something so natural and normal.

Women's reproductive organs, processes and cycles have been spoken about in such derogatory language for so long that it might be that we don't even notice it anymore. As poignantly written by Gottlieb (2020), 'words tell a story, and so do efforts to avoid words'. What she is saying here is important – society and the patriarchy have spent considerable effort creating euphemisms, explanations, mental illnesses and diagnoses which avoid ever talking about menstruation, bleeding or periods. She asks in her paper, why do factual words about female reproduction and menstruation – which impacts 51 per cent of the global population – hold so much symbolic power? Why do we go to such lengths to frame female reproduction and menstruation as pathology?

Whilst this originated from religious and cultural beliefs about women's evil, psychiatry quickly took up the baton when it came to their turn to utilise menstruation as a way to pathologise and medicate women and girls who didn't behave in desirable ways. Gottlieb cites writing by O'Grady (2003) who argued that biblical scholars and commentators often cite the Bible's third book, Leviticus, as the source of the euphemism 'the curse' for menstruation. In Leviticus, menstruation is described as the ultimate punishment for female sin and it then lists a series of prohibited activities for menstruating women and girls. Through the wicked actions and sins of Eve, she was punished with 'the curse' (which was originally described in Genesis to be pain during childbirth, but later changed to include menstrual pain in Leviticus). Therefore, menstruation became the 'divine curse' for women's evil and Eve's transgressions.

Whilst Pope Gregory and many Christian scholars across fifteen centuries used menstruation as a reason for why women could not hold high office in religious congregations, organisations and communities, the Qu'ran is often cited to prohibit menstruating women from taking part in events or activities. In modern Muslim communities, fasting during Ramadan, entering a mosque, praying, having sex and making the pilgrimage to Mecca are all forbidden for menstruating women (Ahmed, 2015). Gottlieb goes on to make an interesting point about the influence of Islam, Judaism and Christianity in the narratives of menstruation as 'the curse', which has meant that as their populations have grown to around 54 per cent of the global population (Pew Research Centre, 2015), virtually every community, country, language and culture has been influenced by this euphemism (even where the religious origin is unknown or rejected).

Beliefs around the world include those which state that menstruating women should be separated from everyone else until they stop bleeding, that they should avoid cooking for men, they should not be in contact with dead bodies and they should be kept away from natural vegetation and forests. In addition to these prohibitions, some cultures and communities believe that menstruating women should not enter sacred or religious places, or touch the belongings of men.

For centuries then, menstruation has been positioned as a wholly negative and dangerous event which positioned women and their bodies as the problem. This had an unquestionable impact on the development and conceptualisation of gynaecology as a discipline, which was founded in the early nineteenth century on the beliefs that women's reproduction and menstruation were a collection of illnesses and disabilities (Strange, 2000).

Old records from *The Lancet* show that physicians and researchers wrote about menstruation as a distasteful, unpleasant and unfortunate topic to have to discuss and explore, whilst describing the treatment of women as tedious and annoying (Strange, 2000). Menstruating women were described as physically weak, psychologically vulnerable – and given lists of activities that they should avoid whilst menstruating. This list of activities supported the pre-existing belief that a woman was not as capable as a man to live a full and useful life, as they were being told that they were suffering from an illness or 'curse' for one to two weeks per month for decades of their life. In many medical journals in the nineteenth and twentieth centuries, menstruation was framed as a 'failure' of a woman, as the shedding of uterine lining meant that she failed to become pregnant and fulfil her role as a mother.

Further than this, doctors such as Edward Clarke wrote in 1870 that women should avoid education as the brain would take up too much blood flow in thinking and learning, which should be being used in their menstruation (Strange, 2000). He did go on to argue that he didn't feel women should be entirely excluded from education for this reason, but they should have a special kind of education which was less mentally taxing, and would prioritise blood flow to the ovaries to ensure that education didn't cause them to become 'barren'.

This history is pertinent not only for its influence on medicine, but for its inevitable influence on male psychiatrists who were looking for explanations for hysterical, crazy women they were treating in asylums. Leading psychiatrist Henry Maudsley agreed with these views on women, education and their mental abilities and used them to argue that women who pursued education or independence were selfish and wicked, as they should focus their limited capabilities on reproduction.

Menstrual complaints such as irregular, heavy or absent periods were quickly entwined with diagnoses of hysteria, and psychiatrists in the late nineteenth and early twentieth centuries argued that women with 'repressed menstrual blood' were mentally ill and in need of marriage to a man. Medical and psychiatric texts about women linked menstruation to women's psychosis, violence, irrationality and superstitions, which inspired many famous books and stories about crazy women from the Victorian era (Lister, 2014).

From then on, psychiatry has always pathologised menstruating women in one way or another – either using menstruation as a sign or symptom of mental disorder, or creating mental disorders that corresponded with the menstrual cycle.

In 1993, the American Psychiatric Association released a statement in the *New Scientist* saying that they had decided to include premenstrual dysphoric disorder (PMDD) as psychiatric to, 'result in better care of women and reduce the suffering of women with this mental disorder'.

Leading critics included Dr Paula Caplan and Dr Jane Ussher who called the decision anti-feminist, anti-female and a move motivated by finance and misogyny which would ultimately lead to people saying 'it's your hormones, dear' when women were being harmed, abused or were distressed. Ussher added that women were being given drugs with serious side effects for a disorder that didn't exist.

Both women were absolutely right, and nearly thirty years later, that is exactly what has happened. Still to this day, when women are perceived to be acting out of character, becoming angry, upset, tearful, anxious, tired, irritable or annoyed, the question tends to be, 'Is she on her period?'

In summer 2021, Zoe noticed that she was developing symptoms around the time of her period that caused her concern. A professional woman with good understanding of her body, she noticed that her physical symptoms had started after the birth of her fourth baby in 2020. What may seem like a fairly simple trip to the doctor to discuss hormonal changes after pregnancy is made so much more difficult and risky when you have a long history with psychiatric services.

I had the privilege of speaking at length to thirty-two-year-old business owner Zoe, who was raped as a child and when she told someone, the perpetrator killed himself. Zoe has long felt that she was held responsible for the death of the man, and was blamed for much of her teenage years. Her mother, who was abused by Zoe's father, told her that 'sometimes, the mind plays tricks on us' and suggested that Zoe lied about being raped. At fourteen years old, Zoe was perceived by many as a 'naughty girl' who was always 'playing up', needed to 'grow up' and required medication to get control of her. She was prescribed the antidepressant citalopram and later diagnosed with bipolar disorder. She was prescribed lithium and a range of other antipsychotic medication which caused her many health issues. She now has an impressive knowledge of psychotropic drugs, having been on and off many of them for almost twenty years.

I couldn't believe it. I sat there and told the GP about all these symptoms since my little one was born last year. I'm just so unwell. There's something wrong. It's hormonal, I think. I'm tired, I'm lethargic, I don't sleep, my temperature changes – I've never been like this before. It all started after I had my fourth baby last year. I told her everything and she took one look at my medical records, and she must have skimmed down and seen that I've been in mental health wards before and that was it. She wouldn't refer me for any tests or anything like that, she just said I needed to go back to the psychiatric ward. And then I didn't know what to do. Do I refuse? Do I just do what she says? What happens if I refuse and they think I'm mad? Do I turn up to this referral and go back to psychiatry?

Her doctor suggested that she should take a strong antidepressant for two weeks of each month, which she instantly refused. In our conversation, we discussed why that would be offered as a treatment, considering the side effects of constantly stopping and starting a powerful medication. Zoe also spoke of her fear of refusing the referral, in case it triggered social care assessment or involvement. What she wanted, of course, was the relevant blood tests to explore whether she had a hormonal imbalance that was causing the symptoms – but instead, she was referred to a psychiatrist who would no doubt focus on her 'disorders'.

Despite studies from 2018 demonstrating that around 90 per cent of women experience differences in their moods, energy levels, weight, water retention and emotions around the time of menstruation, the DSM has always listed it as a mental disorder. As of 2021, the DSM-V lists 'premenstrual dysphoric disorder' as a mental disorder of women – which includes such a broad and comprehensive range of possible symptoms that almost every woman could be diagnosed with this psychiatric disorder.

Premenstrual dysphoric disorder (DSM-V)

Diagnostic criteria

1. In the majority of menstrual cycles, at least five symptoms must be present in the final week before the onset of menses (bleeding), start to improve within a few days after the onset of menses, and become minimal or absent in the week after
One (or more) of the following symptoms must be present:
   ◆ Marked affective lability (e.g. mood swings: feeling suddenly sad or tearful, or increased sensitivity to rejection)
   ◆ Marked irritability or anger or increased interpersonal conflict

◆ Marked depressed mood, feelings of hopelessness, or self-depreciating thoughts

◆ Marked anxiety, tension, and or feelings of being keyed up or on edge

2. One (or more) of the following symptoms must additionally be present to reach a total of five symptoms when combined with the symptoms from Criterion B

3. Decreased interest in usual activities (e.g. work, school, friends, hobbies)

4. Subjective difficulty in concentration

5. Lethargy, easy fatigability, or marked lack of energy

6. Marked change in appetite; overeating; or specific food cravings

7. Hypersomnia or insomnia

8. A sense of being overwhelmed or out of control

9. Physical symptoms such as breast tenderness or swelling, joint or muscle pain, a sensation of 'bloating' or weight gain

(NCBI, 2021)

Most women will read this list and undoubtedly think, 'Well, that's me. I hit enough criteria for this psychiatric diagnosis.' And they would be right; it's fair to say that most of us would. And so, the circular journey of medicine and psychiatry back towards framing menstruation as a mental illness is complete – with any and every woman being a potential patient, or customer, as it were.

This is something that did not escape the attention of pharmaceutical companies. Eli Lilly, the company that makes Prozac (a widely used antidepressant), repackaged their standard SSRI antidepressant drug Fluoxetine and sold it as 'SaraFem', with pretty pink and purple packaging adorned with a sunflower – aimed at 'alleviating' pre-menstrual dysphoric disorder. SaraFem now has FDA approval to treat depressive disorders, bulimia, obsessive compulsive disorder, panic disorder and premenstrual dysphoric disorder.

It is frankly amazing how many diverse issues one so-called anti-depressant pill can claim to treat. Especially considering it was also given to Brianna to 'manage her mood swings' whilst she was pregnant and being abused by her partner.

Pregnancy and birth have a worrying relationship with psychiatry and pathologisation, too. Pregnant women are often considered to be hormonal, crying, confused messes with a 'baby brain' and a short fuse. What is shocking to learn is how little is considered about the natural, social and cultural stressors of pregnancy and birth when women begin to struggle. Everything from worrying about when the baby last moved to whether the birth will hurt, to whether they will be a good mother to protecting themselves from abusive or absent fathers. Women and teenage girls experience (and are subjected to) many traumatic and frightening circumstances whilst pregnant and during birth, a detail which is again ignored by medical model explanations of mental illness during and after pregnancy.

In 2021, the MGH Centre for Women's Mental Health in collaboration with Harvard Medical School published a paper reporting that '1 in 5 women will suffer from a mood disorder or anxiety disorder whilst pregnant', and suggested that 71 per cent of women would 'experience at least one mood episode during pregnancy' and 85 per cent of women would 'experience at least one mood disturbance in the post-partum period'. In consistent medical language, the authors go on to report that women with bipolar and personality disorders have high rates of 'relapse' during pregnancy and should remain on psychotropic drugs throughout. This is despite their assertion that relatively little is known about whether the drugs are safe for pregnant women, which leads to many of them discontinuing their psychiatric medication when they find they are pregnant.

It is then of interest why studies do not consider the number of women who would be suffering from withdrawal effects throughout their pregnancy (something that is often brought up by critics of antidepressant studies in general). Many studies which claim to show patients 'relapsing' do not consider how many of them will be experiencing severe impacts from suddenly withdrawing from psychotropic medication that they may have been taking for many years. Rather than acknowledging the withdrawal, their symptoms are put down to a mental health 'relapse' and considered evidence that they need the drugs to remain stable and so they are swiftly put back on the drug, at which point all of their symptoms resolve, and the doctor and patient believe that this is proof that the drug solves the mental health relapse. In fact, all it has done is solve the drug withdrawal effects by restarting the drug.

Authors of the 2021 paper report that 'psychiatric illness and psychotic episodes can commonly begin in pregnancy' and they briefly mention that many pregnancies are unplanned – but then revert back to medical explanations of mental illness instead of considering the many different ways a pregnancy could occur that would cause significant trauma to a woman. The pregnancy could be unwanted, unplanned, or conceived in rape, sexual abuse, domestic abuse or incest. The pregnancy could be unwanted but the woman cannot or is not allowed to have a termination. The pregnancy could be in quick succession to a previous pregnancy and the woman is worrying how she will cope with two infants. The father might have left her, or could be completely useless and neglectful. She could be worried about her own body, her health and her life.

There is very little discussed about the impact of pregnancy on the woman in her own right. Just as it was in the nineteenth century, it is deemed socially unacceptable and selfish for a woman to be devastated that her independence, social life, career and life plans have been changed forever by pregnancy and childbirth.

Women are never allowed to publicly (or privately) discuss their regret at having children or becoming pregnant. They are supposed to accept every change to their body as a gift, whether it is damaged skin, damaged organs, damaged joints or damaged pelvic floors. The process of pregnancy and birth is one of the most dangerous and damaging a woman can go through, and yet, if she is anything but elated, she is likely to panic that there is something wrong with her.

The same can be said for those days and weeks after giving birth, which are socially portrayed as some sort of perfect paradise – but are often filled with sleep deprivation, anxiety, aches and pains, heavy postpartum bleeding, the healing of stitches and internal and external injuries, bruising from injections, catheters and IV lines.

Ultimately, women are expected to be completely selfless at the time of pregnancy and birth, they are not supposed to care what happens to their bodies and their lives, and only care for the baby they are carrying and giving birth to. No matter what goes wrong, or how many traumas the pregnancy or birth causes, they are supposed to feel that it was all worth it.

And what if it wasn't worth it? Would a woman dare even admit that?

Arguably, this creates an environment for pregnant women that is impossible to live up to. Women have many worries and concerns during pregnancy and childbirth, and yet, they are commonly diagnosed with mental disorders instead of professionals telling them that they are completely normal, and entitled to feel a range of emotions – from excitement to grief for their pre-motherhood lives.

In the majority of medical and psychiatric papers on 'maternal mental illness', there are long lists of the impacts on babies who are born to women with depression and anxiety. They include low birth weight, slow growth, learning difficulties and other illnesses after birth. Despite these risks, there seems to be no real effort to explore why the women are depressed or anxious, and instead, the advice seems to be that the women should be prescribed medication to manage their 'mood episodes', which, arguably, doesn't solve the alleged risks to the baby, unless the risks are caused by their mothers' moods, for which there is no evidence.

Despite this, MGH (2015) reports that women with bipolar disorder should remain on psychotropic medication even though there is evidence that several commonly used drugs will cause moderate to severe malformations of the heart and neural tube of the foetus. These findings are only for the small number of drugs that have been rigorously tested however, as the majority of drugs used for bipolar disorder in women have no studies or data to prove or disprove the risk to the baby.

Some SSRIs and anticonvulsants have been shown to significantly increase birth defects when they are started (or withdrawn) in the third trimester. This is in stark contrast to the advice and prescriptions given to several of the women I interviewed for this book, who were medicated in the third trimester, withdrew in the third trimester, or were told to take the drugs intermittently throughout the pregnancy. It is clear then, that information and advice is inconsistent and dangerous to women who are pregnant.

Many of the women I interviewed for this book had experiences of becoming pregnant, having miscarriages and giving birth. In at least half of the women I interviewed, their concerns or symptoms during or after pregnancy were ignored, put down to mental illness relapse or were medicated with more antidepressants. As discussed in other chapters, Natalie haemorrhaged and woke up in a high dependency unit because doctors ignored her, Brianna had dangerously low folate blood levels and was referred to a psychiatric ward twice, and Diana had a life-changing traumatic experience with her pregnancy and birth which was met with very little interest or empathy from doctors in 2017.

I was grateful for Diana's time in 2020, when we met virtually to discuss her experiences of being pathologised following her childhood abuse. Whilst I have written about Diana's experiences of being placed on a dangerous adult mixed-sex ward when she was just a child, here we hear from her again as she recounts her experiences of becoming pregnant.

My kids are three and seven now. As soon as I learned I was pregnant I knew the birth was going to be difficult, I just knew it. I told them all it was gonna be hard. I told the midwife and the doctors but no one supported me. I had to tell them I was sexually abused and that I couldn't cope with the pelvic exams but no one listened to me. It was sort of like, 'Well you got pregnant!' One doctor I spoke to about my fears of pelvic examination said that to me, like if you can have sex, you can deal with a pelvic exam, like they are the same. I begged them, desperately, for a C-section so I didn't have to go through a vaginal birth and they just said, 'We don't give C-sections to people like you.' I remember begging them and saying it would retraumatise me and they just said no, and ignored me. The birth was really really bad, I won't go into it. But they just said to me afterwards, 'You need counselling.'

Despite her experiences, when she became pregnant with her second baby, she was refused a C-section again, and was told to manage it herself. She told me of a brilliant trauma-informed community midwife she was lucky enough to meet – and she planned a home birth with everything she knew would make her feel in control. Unfortunately, when she went into labour, there were complications and an ambulance rushed her to hospital. She was given medication and procedures she didn't consent to, and she was resisting and arguing back.

Everyone was mad at me. They were all angry, but they didn't understand. All my plans had gone wrong, they were giving me medication I didn't want, doing stuff to me I didn't want and I just panicked. Then they told me that I had to breastfeed which is a huge trigger for me. You know, we don't talk enough about how breastfeeding can be hugely triggering for those of us who were sexually abused in childhood. As much as I wanted to breastfeed my children, as I am fully aware of the benefits, I was scared. I wanted to bond and be close to them, and give them all the other health benefits, but it was a huge challenge, and very lonely. My second child was very ill when she was only a few weeks old. I can still remember her coming out of intensive care and off the feeding tube and the consultant saying to me, with no notice or chat about it with me, 'Now we are going to put her to the breast.' As if I was a machine. My thoughts, feelings and emotions were not considered. There was a lot of pressure, as the breastmilk was seen as an important part of her recovery. I was also told that a formula-fed baby wouldn't have made it. I didn't feel able to not continue breastfeeding. Again, I felt my body existed to provide other people with things, and that my feelings didn't matter. I felt as if I had to do it at any cost to myself. I wanted to feed my children and I am proud that I did. But the impact on me of doing so has been huge. I would say I felt like a freak for finding it so challenging and difficult; the reality was not so much disgusting as scary, frightening and triggering. I always wanted to be a natural, earth mother type with dungarees and cloth nappies and breastfeeding. In reality, I felt like I was being expected to give my body to others, which meant I experienced trauma. It made me want to hide away. I persevered, and it wasn't always awful, but in honesty, at times it was. And I hate that it was.

I want to take a moment to thank Diana for her honesty and authenticity in this account of motherhood, breastfeeding and birth. It is vital that women are able to speak about the complexity of their experiences without being judged and punished. I know that many women will read this account and relate to her.

I must agree with Diana when she says that very little is spoken of the women who become triggered when attempting to breastfeed. With a culture which sexualises and objectifies breasts, and then the added trauma of whatever an abuser has done to her breasts and body, it is no wonder that so many women might struggle with their baby feeding from their breasts. The conversation I had with Diana was the first time either of us had had that conversation out loud with anyone, and we discussed how difficult it must be to find equilibrium between seeing your breasts as sexual objects for the abuser (or even for current partners) and also understanding them for their true purpose, which is to feed and nourish newborns.

Diana told me that the entire process of giving birth and all of the medical attention she received stuck with her to this day.

Still now, the memory of the medics inserting fingers up my vagina makes me feel physically sick and full of panic. It is as if I was abused all over again, given no choice but to allow it because of their need to check on my baby. When I am pretty sure this could all have been avoided if I had been heard and

believed and given a C-section. Over and over people would
enter or leave the room, the door was open, there was no privacy
and my body was on display for other people to inspect. The
number of ways this re-traumatised me, took me back to what
had happened before with the pain and terror and helplessness,
cannot be counted. And after it all, there was no privacy to cry
or curl up or talk it through, I was on a ward with many other
new mothers and their babies, all seemingly doing so well, and I
was lonely and hurting and struggling. When a nurse came to
check my stitches and I said I couldn't face it (I think we discussed
this before – it is a big deal to me), I was told off, I was told that
if I couldn't let them check then they couldn't help me – as if, if
anything went wrong because I couldn't let them do what they
wanted/needed/usually do, that it would be all my fault. At this
point it felt like they had had enough of me and given up on me.

The trauma surrounding pregnancy, birth and postpartum periods is
obscured by the flowery, cute, fluffy, excited narratives of becoming a
mother and 'having a baby'. The 'true calling' of women.

No matter what women have been put through, there seems to be no
consideration for how likely it is that they have been abused or traumatised – and how triggering all of these experiences can be. Even for
women without trauma histories, what Diana went through is a set of
traumas in itself.

The way this is all glossed over for pregnant women and girls sincerely
irritates me. They are only ever told that pregnancy and birth will be
an amazing, life-changing and beautiful experience in which all the
fear, injury and illness will be worth it. When women tell them the
horrors and experiences of birth and motherhood, they are scolded
for 'fearmongering'.

What is clear, however, is that many women will never want to experience pregnancy or motherhood at all, and many more experience this time as terrifying, traumatic and, unfortunately for some, as a period of their lives in which they find themselves medicated and pathologised for being scared, unhappy, anxious or irritated.

As if this wasn't enough, and at the risk of this chapter turning into its own book, women are also likely to be pathologised when they reach menopause, when they suffer from gynaecological complications, when they struggle with their sex lives, or when they try to report pretty much any other physical illness.

Especially, and this cannot be understated, if they had the audacity to Google it first.

Menopause as madness

The menopause has long been demonised, pathologised and linked to women's madness. In 1926, two professors wrote in *The Lancet* that menstruation and menopause were diseases or abnormalities of women. Professor Pinard wrote that normal women would never have periods or a menopause, because they would continually be either pregnant or lactating, whereas Professor Wallich argued that period pains could be completely alleviated if women were more positive, and periods and menopause were women being punished by nature for not conforming to their roles and environment properly (Strange, 2000).

Menopause has been considered and written about in negative and misogynistic terms for centuries. It is the time when a woman outlives her fertility, becomes older and therefore, in patriarchal terms, becomes completely useless to men. This was clearly demonstrated by many doctors and psychiatrists who diagnosed menopausal women with hysteria and other 'hystero-psychoses' but also wrote about the women as if they had passed their sell-by date.

Strange (2000) argued that the menopause was seen as opposite to puberty. Where puberty of females was seen as positive and desirable, the menopause was seen as the abnormal, undesirable, problematised decline of femininity and the breakdown of the female body. This should be considered within the patriarchal norms of sexualisation too, in which the female teenage body is objectified and idealised as the way all women should aim to look.

> *The negative ramifications of the menopause were further reinforced by medical descriptions of the process which used terms such as 'genital insufficiency', 'pathological consequence', 'crisis' and 'critical age'. In a culture which valued women primarily for the production of offspring, the medicalisation of the menopause abrogated any sense of celebration at liberation from this role. Rather, the 'change of life' was defined as the cessation of her social worth.*
>
> Strange (2000)

In 1855, Dr Edward Tilt, a pioneer in gynaecological medicine, went so far as to liken the menopausal woman to 'those animals who die when once they have transmitted life to others'. The menopause was defined exclusively in terms of loss; with the passing of fertility, women simultaneously sacrificed their social status as women with a purpose.

Into the twentieth century, doctors stated that a woman's mental illness was inseparable from her ovaries and uterus – and that gynaecological issues were always linked to psychiatric issues (and vice versa). Women who were unfortunate enough to be sent to asylums as they aged were routinely subjected to pelvic examinations and womb extractions right up until the 1950s. Treatments for menopausal mental illnesses included carbonated soda, plaster on the stomach and vaginal injections of lead. Yes, lead.

By the 1930s, menopause was being described as a deficiency disease of women, and they started to be prescribed synthetic oestrogen, which would later become one of the most common treatments in the western world.

To the present day, if you perform a simple Google search for menopausal symptoms or problems, you will be presented with thousands of articles about 'menopause madness' and 'menopause psychosis'. Blogs, videos, articles and self-help guides talk about women becoming crazy, forgetful, psychotic, insufferable and irrational older women filled with menopausal rage. It is of interest then, that society portrays older women as so problematic and in need of treatment – especially as the latest NHS data shows that women over sixty years old are the most common recipients of electroconvulsive therapy in the UK.

Centuries ago, witches were portrayed to be old, lonely women with no children, and they still are today in films and stories; in the thirteenth century it was believed that barren, ageing, evil women would snatch children and kill or eat them because they could not have their own. During the suffragette movement in the early twentieth century, when women fought for the right to vote, one of the most successful ways to campaign against them was to portray them as haggard, ageing, barren witches.

Posters, postcards and images in newspapers were spread across England to humiliate and terrorise the suffragettes, with cartoons of them looking like old, fat cartoon witches with sagging, damaged skin, missing teeth, wild expressions, unkempt grey hair and sagging breasts. Slogans from anti-suffragists included warnings to young women never to engage with the suffragettes as they were crazy, hysterical, evil and, most importantly, barren women. Anti-suffragists publicly described the suffragettes as women who were infertile and unmarried – as if political interest was a disease of the feeble female mind which caused them to become barren – and, essentially, of very little use to men.

When we really begin to consider how much women's fertility and women's menopause is wrapped up with portrayals of insane, uncontrollable and evil women, it is a shocking revelation. In addition to the psychiatric diagnosis and medicating of healthy women and girls going through natural cycles of hormones, doctors have been heavily prescribing contraceptive pills to women and girls as a cure-all for decades.

In fact, the pill has been positioned as the cause and solution to many women's emotional experiences. Many teenage girls are put on the contraceptive pill not to prevent pregnancy, but to control their moods and emotions. CDC (2020) show that around 53 per cent of US teenage girls are on the contraceptive pill, and a further 20 per cent of girls are fitted with an implant or given a LARC (long-acting reversible contraception) such as the contraceptive injection or IUD. In the UK, the statistics are lower with 43 per cent of women using the pill, injection or implant for contraception. Despite this, of all women who ask for contraception in the UK, 90% of them will be prescribed the pill (*Guardian*, 2019).

Ever since the contraceptive pill was introduced in 1961, researchers have been exploring what relationship and effect it has on women's moods and emotions. The pill (in all of its forms) has common and serious side effects including increased rates of breast cancer, blood clots, migraines, weight gain and skin problems. Despite this, it is heavily recommended to teenage girls in order to reduce teenage pregnancies (which at one point, was a major concern in the UK, with the highest rates of teenage pregnancy in Europe).

As a quick detour, even the issue of staggeringly high teenage pregnancy rates in the UK was dealt with by medicating and controlling teenage girls instead of looking at how and why so many teenage girls (often under the age of consent) were being made pregnant by men and boys (often illegally). Every teenage pregnancy under the age of sixteen is technically illegal, and yet, nothing was done to tackle the number of men and boys who were having sex with girls who couldn't consent. This is particularly poignant when we consider that there are around four to five times more teenage mums than teenage dads, which suggests that the majority of teenage girls becoming pregnant were being abused by adult men, who rarely appear in the narrative. Teen mums are often shamed, mocked and criticised for becoming pregnant as if it happened by magic, whilst the dads escape any comment at all.

In 2019, a study from the Netherlands published in a psychiatric journal found that sixteen-year-old girls taking the pill were significantly more likely to exhibit 'depressive symptoms' than girls who were not on the pill. The sixteen-year-old girls reported more crying, more problems with sleeping and more problems with eating (De Wit et al., 2019). Wildly, the authors concluded that they didn't know why this was, and suggested that it could be that girls with depressive disorders are more likely to take the pill – which was a shocking conclusion to arrive at.

So close, and yet, so far.

The female body appears to be something of a mystery to psychiatry and psychology researchers, who seem to regularly pathologise anything to do with hormones or female reproductive health issues. Alternatively, they ignore them all together, which was certainly the case for endometriosis. Gabrielle Jackson was the woman who started the global investigation by the *Guardian* into women's experiences of endometriosis in 2015. Despite one in ten women of reproductive age having endometriosis (176 million women worldwide), women are routinely told that their symptoms are psychological, that they are mentally ill or that they exaggerate their pain.

In her book, *Pain and Prejudice*, she writes about her findings of the pathologisation of women with endometriosis:

> *One gynaecologist wrote about how the disease can be cured by stress management because only women with certain personality type disorders get endo. Another gynaecologist wondered aloud to a researcher, 'Do mad people get endo, or does endo make you mad?' 'It's probably a bit of both', he concluded. An anaesthetist told a pain seminar that women with treatment-resistant endo have probably been sexually abused and need to see a psychiatrist ... sufferers from around the world face the same battles: long delays in diagnosis, having their pain doubted then normalised, having their mental health questioned and receiving bad medical advice.*

That quote is from 2015, and having read it you would be forgiven for believing that you had accidentally flicked back to the chapter on the history of the pathologisation of women; the reframing of women's reproductive issues as mental illnesses, the dangerous medical advice, the gaslighting of their pain complaints. Endometriosis is proof that we have barely progressed at all, and when women do raise concerns about their health, they are told they are mentally ill exaggerators.

I had a disturbing experience in 2020 when I was in A&E as a visitor, when a young woman was brought in by paramedics at 3 a.m. She was screaming in such pain, it made me feel sick. They were trying to ask her basic questions and she couldn't hear or respond to them in between the screams for her mum. The paramedics were weary of her already, and suggested to doctors that there was nothing wrong with her. She screamed relentlessly for hours, and they called for her mum. They grew impatient and started to shout at her, told her to calm down and that there was no need for such a racket. I am not a physician, but it was clear to me that this human being was in excruciating and uncontrollable pain. The doctors nipped around our curtain and apologised for her screaming – but all I could think about was how they were not doing any tests, no one had read her medical files, and no one was referring her anywhere.

I whispered to my wife, 'You would run emergency tests and a scan, wouldn't you?' and she nodded. We sat next to the young woman for hours whilst she cried and screamed. Eventually, her mother arrived and they started talking about police, and how much she had had to drink. They made some calls to custody to find out what they knew about her.

More than five hours later – with no tests, no scans and no empathy for her – the truth was revealed and she was given morphine to shut her up.

She was a young woman in her early twenties who had been out to Nando's for a meal with her best friends. A week prior, she had had surgery for endometriosis and polycystic ovaries. On her way home from the restaurant, she had suddenly become overwhelmed with abdominal pain and collapsed in the road. She had lain there for some time, screaming for help, whilst drivers and pedestrians had ignored her, until one person rang the police about the crazy woman, lying in the road screaming for her mum. The police had sent a patrol car out and arrested her for being drunk and for public disorder, and put her in a cell. The woman had not been drinking that evening, but she was held in a police cell for several hours where she screamed and writhed on the floor in pain.

Eventually, the custody officers rang an ambulance and told them that she was blind drunk and causing a fuss. Her mother had set the record straight with the A&E team, and told them that she required pain relief urgently.

I distinctly remember the moment that the morphine took effect, and for the first time, we heard the young woman's voice, finally able to speak. She thanked her mum, and told everyone what had happened to her. She cried and told the doctors that she thought something had ruptured from the surgery and that she needed to see a surgeon or consultant urgently. However, even with the full details, the weary doctors did not support the need for her to have any further investigations, and refused to refer her anywhere else. They told her that it was a weekend, and nothing could be done, and that she was 'fine', now she had been given a morphine IV.

Again, her mother argued for some time to try to convince them to admit her daughter to a ward where they could investigate what had happened, and feared that as soon as the morphine wore off, she would be back to excruciating pain. They were both ignored, and the young woman was discharged from the hospital. Her mother pushed her out of the A&E department, still in a wheelchair, looking visibly exhausted from her ordeal. They got in a taxi, and the doctors all breathed a sigh of relief that the woman who had been screaming for no good reason had been discharged.

This story will not come as a surprise to the many thousands of women who have had their bleeding, pain, swelling and any of the range of other endometriosis symptoms ignored or minimised for years. On average, women in the UK wait eight years for a correct diagnosis, with 95 per cent of them saying that their endometriosis had a significant negative impact on their well-being (All Party Parliamentary Group on Endometriosis, 2020). Of the thousands of women who took part in the APPG review, 58 per cent of them had been to their GP about their symptoms at least ten times, 53 per cent visited A&E with severe symptoms and 21 per cent saw doctors in hospital more than ten times before being diagnosed.

Women reported that they were consistently told that their physical symptoms were depression, anxiety, panic attacks – or simply, made up. The report found that many women were prescribed cognitive behavioural therapy (CBT) instead of being referred to gynaecologists or specialist endometriosis centres.

However, whilst some researchers were busy ignoring and minimising women, one group of researchers set about sexualising endometriosis in a peer-reviewed paper that I was certain was satire. In 2013, a now withdrawn study rated the attractiveness of women with rectovaginal endometriosis. The medical journal took eight years to remove the study, and the original researchers issued a half-apology saying that they felt their study findings had been misinterpreted and taken out of context (*Fertility and Sterility*, 2020).

In their original study, Vercellini et al. (2013) used two female and two male participants to rate the attractiveness of women with different forms of endometriosis, and then concluded that women with rectovaginal types were more attractive, had larger breasts, less body fat and first had sex earlier than women with other forms of endometriosis.

Additionally, researchers such as Hammerli et al. (2018) conducted in-depth qualitative research into the experiences of men who felt their sex lives were impacted by their female partner having endometriosis – and inevitably reported that the men felt they were not getting enough sex.

There is no way of reading research like that without laughing at the absurdity of it, and then raging at the sheer audacity. Whilst vital research into endometriosis receives little to no resource or funding, here were funded academics writing about how sexy women are with a painful disease, and whether men were getting enough sex from women who were struggling with chronic pain from endometriosis.

The mind boggles.

Everything else

It could be assumed that this dismissive and pathologising attitude towards women was confined to 'women's troubles', but research consistently shows that no matter what health issue women report to their doctor, they are still much more likely to be ignored, minimised or diagnosed with a mental health issue.

This experience is common to thousands of women, myself included. Like the women I interviewed for this book, I had been ignored for nine years whilst trying to find a cause for chronic chest pains that had ruled my life since I was eighteen years old. I had been to my doctor and to hospital countless times and told there was nothing wrong with me. I found that I was usually left for hours on my own with no information whilst in severe pain, until someone came along, did the bare minimum, and then told me that I wasn't having a heart attack. I used to say to them, 'I don't think I am having a heart attack, but there is clearly something wrong.' I never got anywhere.

I would be left alone on a hospital bed, not being able to take a full breath in due to the pain in my chest, whilst feeling completely invisible.

When I was twenty-three, I again went to the hospital when my chest pains caused me to lose sensation in my fingers and forearm. I was becoming increasingly worried about the pains, which would strike at random times and stop me in my tracks. I could be lecturing, driving, shopping, eating, running or resting and the pain would be so severe, it would stop me from taking full breaths.

One time, it happened whilst I was lecturing, and I collapsed from the pain. I woke up on the floor, surrounded by my delegates, and paramedics. I felt ridiculous, but scared that the issue that had been ignored for years was causing me to collapse and lose consciousness.

(If you are one of the thirty professionals who was in that room that day, I am so sorry!)

My first major breakthrough happened at twenty-five years old, when I learned to stop panicking when the pain struck. This did absolutely nothing for the pain, but keeping calm meant I didn't feel like I was wasting further time in a hospital or a clinic. I learned to cope, and learned to mask it. When it happened to me during lecturing or public speaking after that, I would regulate my shallow breathing and sip water – or I would give my students a break or an exercise to do.

Thousands of people who I have taught over the years have probably been taught by me whilst I was in agonising pain. It was once the reason I built interactive and interesting exercises into my lectures and training workshops, so I could rest.

My second, and final major breakthrough was meeting an incredible specialist physiotherapist who worked for major football and Olympic teams. Neil Sullivan lived locally, and at twenty-seven years old, I decided to buy myself a forty-minute appointment with him for my birthday (I know, I buy myself the best gifts). This gift, however, changed my life – and proved to me that when doctors and medical specialists listen to women and take their time, they can effectively diagnose and treat long-standing complaints.

He asked me questions about my life history, my medical history, my occupation, my lifestyle – and any injuries I had ever had or accidents I had ever been in. It was the first time anyone had ever asked me any of these things, and I did my best to answer. He then examined my neck, spine, shoulders and legs. He suddenly asked, 'Have you ever been in a car crash?'

I said that I had been in several car crashes as a child, but nothing recent. He pushed me a little further and asked again, 'Okay, so maybe not a car crash, but an injury or incident that injured your shoulder or neck?'

I thought about it, and then told him of the time I was beaten up at eighteen years old and taken to hospital with a dislocated shoulder. He asked me for details and then simply said that he knew what was wrong with me. I had sustained significant injuries which had never healed properly, and were causing spasms in my chest, back and shoulder. He prescribed manual physiotherapy for several weeks and told me he could address it and stop the pain. I walked out of that appointment and cried in my car. Seven weeks later, I was completely pain-free and have never had those pains again.

Neil was the first person to truly listen to me, and to ask the right questions.

Whether it is women reporting cancer symptoms or raising concerns about botched vaginal mesh surgery that has caused them serious health complications, research shows that they are still much more likely to be ignored, minimised or diagnosed with mental health issues.

Partially, this will be due to medicine and much of science being based on men and male bodies, with women and female bodies still being seen as too complicated and too much of a variable to be included in medical trials. The symptoms that medics are taught to look out for are all based on men's bodies, despite men and women responding differently to everything from heart attacks to water infections. Add that to the centuries of pathologising women and girls as mentally ill, and we have a perfect storm for women's illnesses and deaths being ignored and dismissed on a daily basis.

Misogyny still reigns supreme in medicine – and it is fatal to women.

When it comes to heart disease, the public are rarely informed that heart attack and heart disease symptoms present differently in men and women. Women are much more likely to be told that they have anxiety, and sent home from hospitals and A&E departments. In a study by Khan et al. (2018), women were found to be half as likely to be treated correctly for a heart attack, and were twice as likely to die within six months of being discharged from a hospital. Decades of studies have suggested that women have lower pain thresholds and increased reactions to pain, but they never look at whether women are simply ignored for longer, and left in more severe pain without treatment.

In a set of studies in the 1980s, researchers were interested in what became known as 'Yentl Syndrome', which was described as the notable finding that women with illnesses or pain would be treated less aggressively than men until they prove they are as sick as men. This resulted in several studies which noticed that women were often left much longer than men without treatment, were given inadequate pain relief for serious health issues and were usually referred to a specialist after many years of fighting for anyone to listen to them (Hoffmann & Tarzian, 2003).

In the early 1990s, a study of hundreds of men and women with AIDS found that the women in the cohort were prescribed much less pain relief than the men, and were left longer without treatment of their pain (Brietbart et al., 1996). This was echoed in a 1994 study of men and women with metastatic cancer, which found that women were prescribed five times less pain relief than men (Cleeland et al., 1994).

In 2014, Robertson found the exact same findings in a set of studies in Sweden, showing no change to the perception of women's pain – and in 2019, the *Independent* published an article which cited peer reviewed research gathered by Harriet Hall which found:

◆ Women are 30 per cent more likely to have a stroke misdiagnosed
◆ Women make up 75 per cent of all people with auto-immune conditions (a finding also discussed by Jackson, 2018)
◆ Women go longer with undiagnosed cancer than men
◆ 25 per cent of women with brain tumours present to their doctor for at least a year before diagnosis
◆ In hospital, women's pain is more likely to be seen as hypochondria

Despite research showing that autoimmune issues are more likely in women due to our immune systems being more flexible and more complicated than men's to enable us to carry and grow a foetus during pregnancy, half of women will receive a psychiatric diagnosis before being diagnosed correctly with an autoimmune condition (Jackson, 2018).

In 2020, a review into the vaginal mesh scandal in the UK found that thousands of women had been dismissed as having psychological and psychiatric issues when they raised concerns. Vaginal mesh is a piece of material that can be used in surgery to treat pelvic organ prolapse and bladder incontinence in women, usually after childbirth. However, when women started to complain that the mesh was causing them significant pain during sex and in their day-to-day lives, their concerns were met with the usual accusation: psychiatric issues. Many women were told that they were mentally ill hypochondriacs who were complaining about something small (*Guardian*, 2020).

It is clear that women are being failed – and ultimately, psychiatry has a lot to answer for. Women are routinely told that they are overreacting, exaggerating or lying about their pain or symptoms – and are often told that they have health anxiety. Despite doctors regularly ridiculing women for Googling symptoms and health advice, women are more and more likely to turn to internet forums, Facebook support groups and academic journals for their health advice. Sick of the process of being gaslit for ten minutes in a rushed GP appointment whilst a doctor tells them that it's all in their heads, women are now much less likely to seek help than they ever have been.

There is a powerful myth that women go to their GPs or hospitals much more quickly and with much more confidence than men, who are often reported to be too embarrassed to seek medical help. However, more recent research (and the interviews for this book) show that women are reluctant to talk to their doctors, or have stopped going to doctors and hospitals with their ailments, for fear of being told they are making it up, or worse, being diagnosed as mentally ill.

In 2019, I launched a study to explore the experiences of women who sought mental health support after rape or abuse. In total, 395 women took part, aged between eighteen and eighty-four years old.

The findings suggested that referral into health services was common: 74 per cent of women who had been raped or abused were referred to talk to their GP, and a further 7 per cent were referred to talk to their practice nurse.

Involvement with mental health services was highly likely, with 47 per cent being referred to a psychologist and 70 per cent being referred to a psychiatrist or psychiatric nurse within a mental health team. Of the 395 women, a third said that the professional they spoke to did not have a good understanding of sexual violence or abuse, and a further 53 per cent said that the professionals had a mixed understanding of abuse and violence – with some being good, and others being terrible.

Of the 395 women, 79 per cent of them had been diagnosed with a mental disorder after seeking support for their trauma from rape or abuse.

Key facts

◆ 63 per cent of women were diagnosed with depressive disorder
◆ 53 per cent of women were diagnosed with anxiety disorder
◆ 42 per cent of women were diagnosed with PTSD
◆ 27 per cent of women were diagnosed with a personality disorder (25 per cent of these were BPD and EUPD)
◆ 24 per cent of women had three or more diagnoses of different mental disorders

I wanted to understand what happened next, and so I asked the women what support they were offered when they were diagnosed: 67 per cent were given a prescription for medication, 42 per cent were referred for CBT and 8 per cent said they were never offered any support.

I was interested to hear from Carol*, an experienced and qualified doctor in the UK, who works in general practice several days a week, and in a busy inner city A&E department one day a week. She was also the gynaecology lead for her locality until recently. I took the opportunity to ask her what her views were of the medical misogyny so many women and girls were being subjected to. She told me that she knew there were excellent, caring and non-judgemental clinicians who treat women respectfully, but the system was misogynistic and sexist, including many more professionals.

I believe this is due to the persistent sexist and misogynistic clinicians who are still practising and still behave in a patronising and dismissive way. It's still depressingly unsurprising to hear women's experiences trivialised or dismissed – for example the 'crazy girlfriend' stereotype given to women with mental health and trauma-related problems. Only recently a new patient told me that her last GP had patted her on the head as he told her that her symptoms of body pain etc were 'all in her head'.

It is shocking to think that in 2021, doctors are patting women on the head and telling them that their pain is all psychological. Carol explained to me that the misogyny and sexism were embedded into the medical system at all levels, meaning that there are rapidly increasing numbers of female medical students, female doctors and female nurses – but their salaries are not the same as the males in the same posts. Somewhat ironically, she told me that female doctors like herself, working in general practice, were often discriminated against when they became sick, or pregnant.

Women are not supported once they qualify. For example, in general practice if you are employed in a practice by the partners, they are essentially a small business which means they do not have to abide by the NHS terms and conditions – they can refuse to provide maternity pay or sick pay for as long as they want! None of this was really explained to me when I chose to go into general practice, and it effectively discriminates and reduces the choices women have.

In August 2021, a report was released by the BMA stating that nine out of ten female doctors had been subjected to sexism in the workplace, and four out of ten felt that they could not report it. The report, entitled 'Sexism is Medicine', also found that women were subjected to sexual harassment, misogyny, unfair employment conditions, discrimination when they were pregnant, had children or were unwell – and were often ignored or dismissed in favour of male doctors' medical opinions. Over 70 per cent of the female doctors said that they felt their sex was a barrier to career progression, and 61 per cent said that they were discouraged from going to work in a chosen speciality because of their sex. Of those, 39 per cent were either prevented or did not go on to work in their chosen speciality because of the misogyny.

It is little wonder then, that women and girls are so commonly faced with medical misogyny. If thousands of doctors (both male and female) work in an industry with such a significant and obvious level of discrimination against women, then it would follow that women and girls as patients will be treated with similar contempt.

Carol told me that gynaecology referrals were 'ridiculously underfunded', leading to over a year waiting list to access a simple outpatient appointment for women and girls. She argued that there would be no way that men's health issues would be seen as so unimportant.

Cases of medical misogyny stayed with Carol, and she recalled the death of one of her female patients last year. We spoke about the way that women and girls who were subjected to male violence were pathologised and framed as the problem. Carol's patient was being subjected to domestic abuse, by her partner, who was a violent convicted criminal. Carol was shocked to see that her medical file had been flagged that she was 'dependent on alcohol', 'EUPD', and worse 'violent to her partner'. Carol explained that she had been labelled and treated as difficult, chaotic and disordered. She was found hanging at home in June 2020, during lockdown.

Whilst this may seem as though it could have been a one-off, Carol said this kind of pathologisation happened 'all the time, in different ways'.

I asked her if there were any specific diagnoses that were common in these cases of medical misogyny, especially where women or girls had disclosed abuse or harm. She told me that trauma was rarely ever acknowledged or addressed, and that women and girls were being incorrectly diagnosed with personality disorders and mental health issues, instead. She raised concerns that this further stigmatised them, and led to them being discriminated against.

My practice is based in the city centre where our population is largely twenty to forty years of age. I've found or noticed that typically women who have been abused as a child or teenager, will leave to go to uni, or get a job, and try and move forward. Unfortunately, their trauma response kicks in, and they often start drinking or using drugs and self-harm. They become labelled as 'difficult', 'manipulative' and eventually diagnosed with borderline personality disorder when really, they have complex PTSD (if a diagnosis is needed), and what they need is trauma-based therapy, but they never get it. We are so limited with what we can do to help and of course they are prescribed medication, but they need support, understanding and the right therapy. They are still afraid to disclose anything because of the fear of how they may be perceived. Furthermore, it's common to see chronic pelvic pain, non-epileptic seizure, or functional neurological disorders being pathologised as mental illnesses.

She went on to say that she felt strongly that all medical professionals should be trained in trauma, trauma-informed care and the impact trauma can have. Carol's experiences reminded me of the story of Lucy Dawson, a twenty-year-old woman studying criminology at the University of Leicester.

In 2016, having had no prior health issues, she developed a severe headache. For months, the real, life-threatening condition of auto-immune encephalitis was misdiagnosed as psychiatric illness, and instead of being investigated or treated, Lucy was locked in a psychiatric facility where she was given rounds of ECT, which ultimately left her disabled.

Her symptoms, and the onset, were sudden. It should have been obvious that such severe symptoms could be caused by some change in the brain. She had suddenly developed a severe headache that never went away, she would scream robotically, she would sometimes lose the ability to speak, her behaviour became unusual – so unusual in fact, that people around her thought she had been spiked with drugs.

Such a quick and severe change in behaviour and ability to speak, teamed with a headache, should have been a red flag to scan her brain immediately. Instead, she was sectioned and given antipsychotics, which, of course, did not make any difference other than to make her completely catatonic due to the sedative effects of the medication. For three months, she was medicated and treated as if she was having a 'mental breakdown'. When it became clear that the antipsychotics were not working, doctors told her parents that she needed ECT to 'shock her' into changing. They were told that she would die without treatment – Lucy now looks back, and amazingly, laughs at how illogical that argument is.

She was given ECT which triggered multiple seizures, and then left on a bed without rails, to come round from the treatment. Her mother and grandmother were there with her as she lay catatonic on the bed, and raised concerns to staff that when she did come round, she would likely fall off the bed. This was ignored, and shortly afterwards, Lucy came round from the ECT severely distressed, and fell on to an extremely hot radiator pipe. There she lay for some time, until an older lady in the ward noticed her and shouted for help.

Instead of getting her immediate medical attention, the staff of the psychiatric ward said that her screams of pain were a manifestation of her psychiatric illness, put an orthopaedic boot on her foot, and told her parents she had tripped. They left the large burn on her leg untreated, and when she was discharged a few weeks later, her mother discovered a 13cm, completely open wound, which was weeping and bleeding.

Another month later, Lucy had tests for acquired brain injury, and was then told that she had developed autoimmune encephalitis, which had slowly been causing more and more brain damage whilst she was medicated, subjected to ECT and left to scream in pain. She described her speech as 'ruinous' and said that sometimes, she couldn't form sentences, she would forget words and was really slow. Her leg became completely paralysed, and the neurologist blamed this on the encephalitis.

Lucy had never heard of encephalitis, and decided to contact the Encephalitis Society for more information. They were appalled by her story, and raised concerns that they didn't believe her leg paralysis was caused by encephalitis at all. They suggested that she seek a lawyer.

After several specialist appointments and meetings, she met a doctor who became curious about the link between the large burn scar on the top of her leg, near her bottom, and the paralysis. The doctor suggested that the burn injury from the hot radiator pipe was so deep and severe, that it had burned through her sciatic nerve.

Lucy recently talked to the British press about her experiences, and discussed what it was like to try to go back to university and everyday life. Not only had the brain injury changed the way she communicated and the way she understood the world, but the trauma of her experiences had changed the way she saw the world, saw frivolous gossip and celebrity culture.

She is now a successful model, influencer and ambassador for the Encephalitis Society.

Whilst I was learning about Lucy's story, and contacting her for permission to include her experiences in this book, I was interested to learn that *Guardian* journalist Simon Hattenstone, who had interviewed her about her life, had been subjected to the same misdiagnosis of his childhood encephalitis.

As Simon is a man, we could conclude that this is not a case of medical misogyny, and is more a case of the way psychiatry is used to pathologise medical issues. However, his own story is coloured by misogyny. Instead of being correctly diagnosed and treated for encephalitis, Simon was diagnosed with childhood psychiatric disorders; and his mother was diagnosed with Munchausen syndrome by proxy.

His mother had raised several times that she thought there was something wrong. The doctors had decided that Simon's mother had a psychiatric disorder herself, which caused her to fabricate his illness. Instead of support, Simon was put on antidepressants and his mother was diagnosed as chronically mentally ill. And so, misogyny did impact his diagnosis, too.

It should be becoming absolutely clear by this point that misogyny and pathologisation are putting millions of women and girls at risk. How can we possibly trust the medical profession, if we know that so many of their decisions and treatments are coloured by their beliefs that we are exaggerating, manipulative and emotional?

CHAPTER 8

Professionals who refuse to pathologise

Hello Jessica,

I am a consultant psychiatrist working in NHS. I've worked as a psychiatrist for around twenty-five years. The demand for diagnosis for female victims of abuse by males has increased dramatically over the last five years. Often they are not at all happy with me when I try to explain there is nothing wrong with them, and that their symptoms and behaviours are the completely natural result of the abuse they have experienced. I see very similar responses in the comments sections of your posts. I think it is lack of services for victims of abuse that drives them to want to see their problems in the light of an illness. Unfortunately, if they are labelled with a disorder the 'help' provided often only makes the situation worse. I really admire your work. It takes people like you with the fearless courage of their convictions to make change happen.

Regards,

Thalia

Whilst writing this book I posted several tweets, TikTok videos, Instagram and Facebook posts about the pathologisation of women and girls. They were shared across hundreds of thousands of people, and two GPs contacted me to discuss them. One was a woman and one was a man.

The woman contacted me to say that I was describing something that had been worrying her for a long time. She worked in a city where each year, thousands of young women came to university. She described it to me as the first time they had ever had freedom or independence. She suggested that sometimes, this is the first time young women are away from home, and able to process the abuse and trauma they have been subjected to. She said that it was common to come across young women in their first year at university who were struggling to cope, but that they were frequently being diagnosed with borderline personality disorder.

The second GP was a man who wrote to me to tell me that my posts had challenged him and made him feel uncomfortable about his own practice. He said that he had no previous knowledge of trauma-informed approaches, or the systematic referrals and diagnoses of women and girls subjected to abuse and violence. He wrote that he thinks he has been guilty of simply referring women and girls into psychiatric services which resulted in them being given personality disorder diagnoses. He wrote to say that he would be changing his practice immediately, and that he had developed links with local women's services so he had more information and better referral routes which avoided pathologisation. Change then, is possible.

Professionals working directly with abused and traumatised women and girls – whether they are police officers, social workers, lawyers, mental health nurses or support workers – tend to be exposed to, and susceptible to the same myths, stereotypes and misinformation as anyone else. There is an optimistic assumption that people who do these jobs are better informed or better equipped, well educated and well trained – that they would not hold harmful or biased views about rape, or abuse, or women, or marginalised groups.

But they do.

Studies have shown for decades that professionals hold harmful, stereotypical and oppressive views at the same rate as members of the general public – and education is often not the answer to the views they hold. Simply put, you can't train some of these views out of people. It's not as simple as teaching them about theories and practice, if they hold a deep-seated emotional belief about a group of people.

If they hold a deep misogynistic belief about women, a training course won't undo that. But large cultural, systemic change can tackle this issue. Just as psychiatry has been able to create powerful narratives and myths about mental health, it is possible that we could create equally powerful counter-narratives and spread them across the general population so that children and adults were more informed about theories and approaches to mental health.

After hearing from the two GPs, I decided to ask for the experiences of more professionals in a range of different settings. In early 2021, I put out a call for professionals who wanted to talk to me about their experiences of working with women and girls in psychology, psychiatry and mental health services around the world. I was inundated with emails and messages. Psychologists, doctors, psychiatrists, mental health nurses, prison officers, therapists, social workers and support workers wrote to me about their own concerns that women and girls were being pathologised, diagnosed, isolated, imprisoned and medicated. In this chapter, I want to explore the stories and concerns of a broad range of professionals from the UK, USA, Pakistan, Australia, Sri Lanka and New Zealand.

I asked four key questions of the professionals who wanted to contribute to this book:

1. Could you give some examples of pathologisation in your practice?

2. Could you give examples of good practice, and where pathologisation is being challenged?
3. What happens when you, as a professional, try to challenge the pathologisation of women?
4. What would you want to see change in your particular field, so we can end the pathologisation of women and girls?

In summer 2021, I caught up with an old friend who had worked primarily as a forensic psychologist in prisons for many years. She told me that she had been through a transformative process in her own practice, away from pathologisation and medicalisation, and towards trauma-informed, humanistic practice. She cringed as she remembered the way she was trained, and the emphasis that was placed on diagnosing young people with personality disorders. She told me that as she looked back on her practice from years ago, it made her want to cry.

Around the same time, I met a professional working in New Zealand who told me that she had recently worked in an organisation which had a system that would flag up women and girls with borderline personality disorder diagnosis. She told me that when she clicked on the file, a screen would pop up saying 'CAUTION: BORDERLINE PD'. We discussed this, both angry.

How could professionals and institutions claim that personality disorder diagnoses in women and girls were not pathologising them, when they had built systems that warned professionals before they could access their files?

Professionals I spoke to whilst writing this book had hundreds of examples of the pathologisation of women and girls, which often shocked, angered and exhausted them. I consider it vital to include their voices here, because there is a concerted effort from some professionals and institutions to position any dissenting voice as malicious or offensive towards psychiatry, psychology and mental health professionals.

Examples of the pathologisation of women

I was privileged to hear from so many professionals with experiences they wanted to share. Whilst reading their statements and responses, I felt reassured to know that they were in those roles, where they could protect women and girls from further pathologisation. Their understanding of what was happening was complex and insightful. They recognised that women and girls were being harmed, and they recognised that they themselves were being groomed not to connect with, or build relationships with the women they worked with, because they were so dangerous and manipulative.

> *My experience of services is that the overt focus is on women's risk behaviours, particularly self-harm and suicidal behaviours, and there is a lack of discussion about the woman's life experiences, trauma history, experience of distress, impact of residing within services, her strengths and resilience etc. Women's attempts to communicate their distress, or behaviours with other intentions and motivations (e.g. problem solving), are quickly labelled as 'manipulative' or 'splitting'. Staff are cautioned about 'getting too close' to women, because they will 'latch on' to you. I believe that medicating women in these services is often a form of chemical sedation, to alter her body chemistry so that she becomes lethargic and apparently compliant or concordant, with the primary (if not only) beneficiaries being the staff working with her.*

The quote above comes from Rose, a professional working within women's prisons and women's mental health services. Her experience is commonplace in these environments, especially when it comes to the reframing of women as manipulative, and the warning of staff members against getting too close or involved with the women they are supporting. Language like 'don't get too close or they will latch on to you' is something I have heard hundreds of times over the years.

It reminded me of a quote from 1885 in which physician Silas Weir Mitchell described women and girls with mental illness as 'vampires who suck the blood of healthy people around her'. How little had changed in over a century.

Professionals are often warned that women in their services are attention seekers, dangerous, chaotic, complex and devious – and so, whilst they should support them, they should also keep them at arm's length, never reveal any personal details about themselves, never spend too much time with them, and never 'collude' with their anxieties, paranoia, anger, distress, criticisms or questions.

Rose also raises her concerns about medicating women in prisons and mental health services, which she considers to be a form of chemical sedation – a way to keep them tired, confused, foggy and unable to remember or think clearly. Ironically, rather than making women become manipulative, this approach makes women and girls easier to manipulate, control and subdue. Further, it tends to make women question their version of events, their memories and whether they are indeed 'going crazy'.

Nora, a mental health social worker in the UK, had so many examples of pathologisation that her first words to me were, 'Where do I start with this?'

She spoke to me about a young girl who had been sexually abused, being pinned down by six members of staff and force-fed because she wouldn't eat. She told me how she felt like screaming when she found that doctors had decided to ignore the girl's trauma and disclosures and instead treat her as if she had a behavioural eating disorder.

She told me about the way she had challenged police and mental health professionals who had diagnosed a twenty-five-year-old woman with EUPD after she was raped, and then retrospectively claimed that her EUPD was the reason she was raped, and that she needed referring to Nora to 'reduce her chances of future sexual assaults'.

> *No other professional involved seemed able to make the connection between her being raped and her current distress. Rather they thought she was raped due to her EUPD. Which of course is the most bullshit diagnosis of all time. This woman's experience of rape was completely turned into mental illness.*

She went on to explain to me that in her many years of practice, she had noticed a pattern. Abused women and girls would be diagnosed with bipolar. 'Difficult' women and girls were diagnosed with EUPD. She went on to say that when women and girls with bipolar diagnoses became more challenging or critical of the services, or didn't want medication, or didn't seem to improve on medication, they were simply rediagnosed as EUPD and then refused therapy.

This point about personality disorder was echoed by almost every professional I interviewed, including Emily (a registered manager of mental health services), Rhonda (a teacher) and Sandra (an assistant psychologist). All three gave upsetting and detailed accounts of women and girls being pathologised and diagnosed with personality disorders before being reframed as problematic, delusional and paranoid. Sandra quite rightly pointed out that all NICE guidelines advise against diagnosing girls under eighteen years old with any personality disorders, which is being actively ignored all over the world.

Across the other side of the world, Selina, an experienced psychologist in Australia, shared similar stories and examples of pathologisation. She raised some important points that I had been thinking about for years. She was right, many autistic women and girls were being positioned as difficult and mentally ill, before being medicated for psychiatric diagnoses they never had.

> *Many of these women are autistic and share many horror stories of being misdiagnosed as Borderline PD, bipolar, etc. They have developed such a fear of professionals and a mistrust as their issues have been dismissed and denied as them being dramatic, over the top, avoidant and more. The increasingly apparent damage that therapies such as CBT can do to try to help people to 'think' their way out of problems. It's gross.*

Selina's point about cognitive behavioural therapy (CBT) is an important one, too. I often hear women and girls (and professionals) announce that 'CBT is shit' or 'CBT doesn't work'. When I was younger, I used to accept this uncritically, and thought that maybe it was just a terrible intervention. This was until I undertook an advanced training course in CBT myself in 2014, and realised that it was being completely misused – and thrown at everyone and anyone as if it was a miracle cure for everything.

The truth is, CBT has been, and still is, being used as a fix-all, six-week talking therapy intervention for everything from a fear of heights (which it would be great for) to years of complex trauma (which it isn't designed for).

Selina's appraisal is right too, that CBT is being used to encourage women and girls to 'think' differently about their abuse and oppression.

This is a conversation I had had with Dr Andrew Fox several years earlier, when he was supervising the write-up of my PhD. We were sat having lunch and talking about the outrageousness of victim blaming when I brought up CBT. As a practising clinical psychologist and academic, he had extensive experience of the use and theory of CBT, and we began a discussion which ended with us both agreeing that CBT was being used to victim blame and gaslight women and girls who had been raped.

Instead of validating their trauma as real, they were being prescribed six sessions of CBT to change the way they thought, felt and behaved in response to their trauma. We considered how that must feel, to attend a talking therapy session, thinking you could discuss what happened to you – only to be told that you were not there to discuss the trauma, but to change the way you keep behaving and thinking about it.

No wonder so many women and girls hated it.

The solution to this issue is simple, though – CBT was not designed or meant for processing complex trauma, so, it should never be used in that way.

However, even psychiatrists who pushed back against harmful and useless interventions were coming up against barriers within their own field. I spoke to several psychiatrists and mental health nurses who told me that they had recognised the pathologisation of women and girls, but were coerced, blackmailed or threatened into diagnosing, prescribing therapies, medicating and sectioning women who disclosed rape and abuse.

Thalia is an experienced consultant psychiatrist in the NHS, who gave me numerous examples of pathologisation, including one case where she was pressured to diagnose a woman in her fifties with a mental disorder so the police didn't have to arrest her elderly father who had been abusing her for decades.

> *A woman in her fifties was the victim of horrific physical, emotional, and sexual abuse, which started in childhood and was ongoing. She came to the attention of mental health services following an overdose, which he had encouraged her to take. While in hospital she disclosed the extent of the abuse. She was totally controlled by her father so wanted to return home to look after him, because he was elderly and physically frail. The police and social services response was to pressure me to diagnose her with a mental disorder and detain her rather than arrest and detain him. When I refused I was told it would be my responsibility if he killed her.*

I went on to ask professionals what they felt were the most common diagnoses in women and girls who disclose abuse and harm, and what their views were of this commonality. Every professional I spoke to answered in the same way: BPD and EUPD.

Rose told me that EUPD was used to diagnose women and girls when they had been repeatedly mistreated and abused – to pass them around like a 'hot potato' so no service has to help them.

> *So an abused woman turns into society's problem and because nobody is adequately trained in supporting these women, or willing to understand her distress, she is put into a box to give people the context that this woman can't 'appropriately' manage herself in the eyes of society, therefore for us to explain why she is like this, we will medicalise it. This makes it easier to then pass*

women on as a 'hot potato' from service to service, all the while she receives no help or support on a personal or systemic level.

I also had the privilege of talking to Dr Alexis Palfreyman. We discussed her work on self-directed violence in women and girls in Sri Lanka. Her work is one of a kind for a rather sobering reason: she is the first person to ask women how, why and with what consequences they choose to engage in self-harm and attempt suicide.

When she told me this, I was shocked. With so much research on self-harm and suicidality – how had there not been any work which simply asked women and girls about the thoughts which led up to their self-harm, or their decision to try to kill themselves?

Alexis told me that she had conducted the country's largest and most comprehensive research on mental health in perinatal women; and having spent a decade working on and researching the mental health of women and girls in Sri Lanka, she had some vital observations.

I have spent a significant amount of time over the years with frontline health and social care providers (from community through specialist tertiary care level), medico-legal actors, affected families and survivors of self-harm themselves, and in that time, I have observed a chronic over-pathologisation of women alongside an under-recognition and even active minimisation of the real drivers of their suffering and subsequent self-harm. The two commonest psychiatric pathologies we see routinely assigned to women and girls presenting with self-harm are Borderline Personality Disorder and Bipolar. But my observations are twofold: firstly, the proportion of women being assigned these diagnoses is considerable and well above what we see in other contexts, which begs the question what is going on? Are Sri Lankan women then somehow more biologically or socially programmed to have these disorders? The answer of course is that it is not rational nor defensible through the existing evidence on mental disorders to conclude Sri Lankan women who self-harm would be significantly more likely to have these psychiatric disorders than women who self-harm in other settings. The science just doesn't bear out. This takes me to my second observation, which is that alongside these diagnoses and in literally hundreds of interviews with girls and women, the key 'problem' identified is their 'irrational, disproportionate anger'. I can't tell you how many patients are told by medical staff, 'you have an "anger problem"'.

It seems that no matter where you are a woman in the world, you are never allowed to be an angry woman. Alexis agreed, and said that she felt that young women's anger was being used to medicate and diagnose them.

The medicating aspect is no joke – we know that because women have almost wholly been left out of clinical drug trials across the decades, essentially no psychiatric medication has been tested in trials on women's bodies and dosing is not titrated to their needs nor takes account of their metabolisms and hormones (this is really true for all meds by the way). The overwhelming majority of psychiatrists and certainly GPs have no education to understand they are over-medicating women to levels suited to male bodies and physiological systems. Essentially, we're still doping women in docility albeit in a different form to what Freud and co. advised for hysteria.

I was interested in this argument, especially as I always find it refreshing to hear academics and medics talk about the vital differences between male and female biology when it comes to medication (psychiatric or otherwise). There is not enough focus on this huge oversight – and how it continues to impact women and girls who are prescribed medications that have only ever been tested and measured on male bodies and brains.

Often when I talk publicly about the pathologisation and psychiatric labelling of women and girls, professionals who support medical model approaches to mental health will comment that I am stupid, unqualified, malicious or even lying about cases of women being medicated and sedated. I am certain that this will happen when this book is released. I imagine that these frequent social media pile-ons must look frightening for the professionals who agree with me, and also see this oppression of women and girls in their practice each day.

Why would they speak out, if they knew they would face the same ridicule and mass complaints that I do?

In my experience, this leads to professionals feeling alone – or feeling as though their views are not worthy of respect in an academic or professional environment. They are left questioning whether their trauma-informed approaches are quackery, or simply unscientific. When contrasting their own work against the giant of the medical model, it is easy to see why they become intimidated, not least because critical voices of medical models are very often publicly bullied and silenced.

Critical professionals such as Dr James Davies, Professor Richard Bentall, Dr John Read, Dr Lucy Johnstone, Professor Peter Kinderman, Dr Roger McFillin, Jo Watson, and Dr Jacqui Dillon are regularly trolled, harassed, stalked, threatened and abused online for their comments, approaches and arguments against pathologisation. Some of them have had to take extended breaks from social media and their academic work to cope with the abuse.

I spoke to many professionals, and most of them required full anonymity to keep themselves safe. This should give us pause for thought. Why do qualified psychologists, psychiatrists, psychotherapists, social workers and academics need anonymity in order to talk about the pathologisation of women and girls? What would happen to them, if they spoke out?

This was something I discussed with them at length.

Speaking out against pathologisation

When I discussed this with professionals, many of them told stories of being bullied, ridiculed, discriminated against, or even sacked for challenging the way women and girls were being treated. Some professionals told me that they were seen as a 'social pariah' since speaking out.

Several of the professionals spoke of a powerful group of male doctors who still had control over the narratives and treatments of women and girls, even when other professionals were trying to advocate against the medication and psychiatric diagnosis of women. Indeed, some professionals asked that I could ensure their identities were never revealed for this book, because they feared what the male doctors and management would do to them if they found that they had spoken to me about what was happening to women and girls in their services, clinics, wards and authorities.

Rose spoke to me about attempting to challenge the repeated use of ECT on a young woman. Despite her protests and arguments, she was ignored, and the treatment continued. As part of her role, she supported the young woman as she came round from the treatment – and this injustice stuck with her.

When I was a support worker in my early twenties, I voiced my disagreement and distress that a woman I was working with, slightly younger than I, was going for a course of ECT. This would be her second course of ECT. She presented with high levels of distress and frequently engaged in self-harm and suicidal behaviours. At the time, I didn't have the knowledge or understanding to articulate a reasoned argument, but I just believed it was wrong. Part of my dismay was that if she had had this 'treatment' before and it 'didn't work', why would we put her through this again?! I was told that this was the team's decision, and it would be going ahead. I had to escort her on leave to several of these appointments and will never forget holding her hand as she came round from the anaesthetic crying, every single time.

Many people who have never worked with women and girls subjected to ECT do not understand what it is, or how it works. Rose was faced with the reality that women and girls are being sedated with anaesthetic and then subjected to multiple electric shocks to the brain until they induce seizures. This is repeated a few times per week for a set of weeks, despite new research showing that much ECT treatment is conducted without the informed consent of the women. Rose is likely to have witnessed traumatic scenes of her client refusing the treatment – begging for the treatment not to go ahead, looking for someone to stop it from happening – and then have been forced to 'support' her to attend the appointments and undergo ECT repeatedly. It is notable then, that Rose remembers so clearly that her client would wake up from the anaesthetic crying 'every single time'.

I asked professionals about what happens when they try to challenge or change decisions about women and girls, and there was a clear pattern in their answers. If they spoke up, they would be told that they were not competent, qualified or educated enough. If they were women themselves, they would often earn themselves the label of 'aggressive' or 'difficult' to work with. They would be subjected to meetings and disciplinary hearings for refusing to support pathologisation – and in lots of cases, they resigned from their roles to seek more humanistic settings to work within.

Lauren, an experienced professional working with women in the UK, said that when she challenged the way that women were being treated, she was 'dismissed, my qualifications questioned, and I was told that I was not a therapist, not a doctor, and you can't have knowledge or opinions on this'.

I also heard from mental health social worker Nora, who told me that it was a 'mixed bag' – meaning that sometimes she had success in challenging pathologisation and sometimes she was positioned as problematic herself.

Sometimes especially when battling doctors I wonder about how I am being labelled. I like to think I am passionate and assertive though I know I have been called difficult, challenging, loud. I personally think it's worth it, as I have experienced a great deal of trauma within my own life and know of the power struggle when you are on the 'patient' side of things.

I noted that many professionals spoke about 'battling' or 'fighting' doctors, managers and systems that pathologised women. It certainly wasn't easy to get professionals to see women and girls as humans who had been harmed, traumatised and pathologised.

Shona is an experienced registered manager of residential care services, and spoke to me in 2021 about her challenges of working against a largely medical system. She noted that whilst her services focused on adult mental health, she often worked with women who had autism, but were being pathologised and medicated as having EUPD and BPD. That meant that rather than getting any support for autism as a neurodivergence, they were being told that they had personality disorders and required medication. When Shona and her staff challenged this, they came up against powerful established systems and narratives, which often meant that their concerns about misdiagnoses were ignored.

Psychiatric services are hierarchical and male-dominated, so very difficult to challenge. As someone who managed and delivered services, I'd feel coerced into agreeing with professionals when they pathologised women – but I would train, supervise and support my staff team using very different values!

The quote from Shona here also highlights the way that professionals are often working within dual narratives, in dilemmatic ways. She spoke about feeling coerced to agree with the psychiatric labelling of women and girls, but chose to train and supervise her own staff against this approach. This came up frequently.

In 2021, I met two professionals who worked within CAMHS in the UK, but disagreed with every theoretical and practical approach their own organisation took. They were constantly challenging the diagnoses and decisions of psychiatrists, which meant that they had earned a reputation for being difficult. They had noticed that the girls they were working with in their sexual violence support service were all being diagnosed with bipolar and personality disorders, and then medicated. They had also noticed that parents and carers were pushing for the diagnoses and medication as a 'quick fix'. This left them in a difficult position in which they would refuse to diagnose the girls, and would instead promote trauma-informed understanding and support for sexual trauma – but would then be expected to work within a medical model service which promoted the diagnoses and medications the parents and carers were asking for. Quickly, they were seen as the problem.

Dr Alexis Palfreyman was one of the only professionals I spoke to who did not want to remain anonymous. Her work is actively challenging the pathologisation of women who self-harm, attempt or succeed in killing themselves.

> *I personally continue to face a lot of pushback and disrespect from colleagues, other academics, and definitely service providers – perhaps unsurprisingly psychiatrists being the most disinterested or sceptical. Psychiatrists have had a monopoly on self-harm and suicide in many settings for a long time and I encounter a lot of territorialism over the issue. I also do think there is a very evident history of psychiatry taking a particularly dominating orientation to women and girls as compared to men and boys, so letting go of that hold to allow for non-clinical and more social explanatory models to complement or even replace their thinking where appropriate remains a challenge. My non-clinical status (I'm the 'wrong' kind of doctor), coupled with being a (relatively young) woman doesn't help.*

I reflected on this answer. This was my experience, too. Psychiatry often felt like the final frontier for feminism and women's rights. It was overtly patriarchal, and most of its victims were, and continue to be, women. Misogyny ran riot. Racism was unchecked in a historical white supremacist system that still had entire narratives and diagnoses borne out of hatred and oppression of Black communities. Homophobia had been supported for decades whilst lesbian women were treated as if they were mentally ill. Whenever this is brought up, professionals are labelled offensive, unprofessional and unworthy of attention.

Like Dr Palfreyman, I had experienced years of disrespect, accusations, and pushback for simply suggesting that women and girls are not mentally ill, but are traumatised by their experiences, abuse and oppression. It seems such an obvious thing to say, from one professional to another – 'maybe she isn't disordered, maybe she isn't ill at all' – maybe she's trying to cope with years of abuse and harm?

Maybe we had got it all wrong?

But far from acknowledging the issues, the layers of misogyny continue into the professional structure too, because not only are women and girls being pathologised and medicated – but female professionals seem to be dismissed and mocked when they argue back. Using traditional gender role stereotypes, the female professionals are described as 'soft touches', 'uneducated' or 'unqualified'. They are seen as weaker, unscientific, and too caring.

Selina is a clinical psychologist in Australia who uses trauma-informed approaches, and she spoke to me about the way she was disrespected and mocked for being too soft on the women she was working with, when other professionals deemed them to be mentally disordered and even manipulative.

> *In trying to advocate for the above client, I have been dismissed, eye rolled at and I think considered a 'soft touch' – fooled by the manipulation of that client, and others. That they believe they know better and with that narcissistic lens, anything I say or advocate for is considered as irrelevant and dismissed. I'm just a nice psychologist who the client has got wrapped around their fingers.*

This is a particularly interesting quote from Selina, as it raises the common issue of women with diagnoses of personality disorders and psychoses being positioned as evil, manipulative and conniving. I too, had noticed the way women and teenage girls were described as controlling, calculated and deviant. With this additional framing of them, professionals who speak against their pathologisation can be seen as naïve, or not being strict enough on their mentally disordered clients.

I was then particularly interested to hear from Thalia, an experienced consultant psychiatrist. She wrote to me whilst I was writing this book, as she had noticed I was writing about the overdiagnosis of borderline personality disorder in women and girls. Her email is included at the beginning of this chapter. It was vital to hear from psychiatrists themselves who were rejecting the medical diagnosis of women and girls. It struck me that Thalia had a clear understanding that whilst demand for personality disorder diagnoses was high, it was not in the best interests of the women or girls.

I wanted to ask her what it was like to be a psychiatrist who opposed medicalisation, and what happened when she spoke out against pathologisation in her own field of expertise. With twenty-five years working as a psychiatrist in the NHS, she was certainly well placed to deal with the accusations of not being qualified, medically trained or experienced enough to comment.

And yet, she spoke of similar responses. She was dismissed, ignored, criticised and even subjected to formal complaints.

'When I challenge things, the response is often a complaint. This is most often from the women themselves, who see me wanting a diagnosis, in the hope that it will explain their inability to accept and be cheerful about the abuse they have experienced or are continuing to experience. They want medication to make them feel okay with things as they are. I have a caseload of around 500 people so the expectation is that I will see them once, give a diagnosis and medication, and either discharge or a nurse will follow up. This makes it very difficult to do any

trauma-focused work. While I try to explain that there is noth-
ing wrong with them, it is a natural consequence of abuse, this is
often received as their problems being dismissed, which is
completely understandable as I have nothing else to offer them.
I think what needs to change is how the consequences of abuse
are viewed not only by psychiatry but more importantly by soci-
ety in general. There need to be resources available to offer
trauma-focused help. Most of the psychiatrists I know don't
want to be labelling victims of abuse as mentally disordered and
giving medication. They do so because they are expected to, and
because there is nothing else available for victims.

Thalia raised something important here: women and girls were
becoming angry and upset when they were not given a diagnosis
which would later harm them.

This is something that people ask me frequently – whether I support
the psychiatric diagnoses and medication of women and girls when
they ask for them directly.

Like Thalia, I do not. This may sound as though we are both putting
ideology or theory above the women we work with, but both of us,
like many of the professionals in this chapter, know the impact of
those diagnoses. Women and girls may well be convinced that they
have disorders and mental illnesses, and they may even think that the
diagnosis will help them to understand or 'recover' from them. They
may think that the diagnosis will lead to effective medical treatment,
and then they will be cured.

The reality is different, and as Thalia pointed out, the diagnoses and
medication for borderline personality disorders, psychoses and bipolar only lead to women being treated worse than before.

Many of us become aware as the years pass that supporting or passively accepting the psychiatric labelling of women and girls will harm them in the long run. They may feel better temporarily, whilst they feel in control, empowered and informed that they have been given a formal diagnosis and prescription which 'validates' their 'mental health', but what will really happen is that they will be pathologised, judged, stigmatised and treated as though they are going to be mentally ill for the rest of their lives.

It can be an unnerving experience to meet a psychologist like me, or a psychiatrist like Thalia, or an academic like Alexis – and realise that we will not support a diagnosis, and instead, we seek to explore the reasons, roots and meanings of the trauma responses and coping mechanisms that are troubling the person.

One of the most common complaints, as Thalia discusses, is the assumption that because we will not support diagnosis of a mental illness, we must not believe in human distress or trauma at all. Further, we can be accused of ignoring, dismissing or silencing women and girls who believe they are mentally ill. This must be one of the hardest criticisms to deal with, when we know that the future of that woman or girl will rest on whether they are diagnosed or not.

We are often acutely aware that the diagnosis will lead to doctors ignoring their health issues, universities rejecting their applications, schools isolating them or referring them to specialist provisions, employers sacking them or discriminating against them, police forces and ambulance services flagging them as dangerous, criminal justice systems positioning them as liars and non-credible witnesses, social services assessing their capability to be good parents and family court judges viewing them as a risk to their children, or lying about being abused.

When faced with these very real possibilities, many of us are reluctant to subject any of the women or girls we work with to psychiatric labelling and medication that they will potentially struggle with for decades of their lives. Unfortunately, women and girls are led to believe that diagnosis and medication are in their best interests, and that the organisations, charities and hospitals they are referred to will not harm them further.

There is comfort in believing that their feelings and experiences are a recognised medical (psychiatric) illness, rather than a result of years of stress, trauma, oppression, bullying, grief, poverty, abuse, inequality, injustice, discrimination and fear.

Thalia's responses reminded me of a professional I met in 2018, whose mother had died after years of psychiatric intervention, medication and inpatient treatment. I had given a seminar about the pathologisation of girls being sexually abused by men, and at the end of the session, an experienced social worker approached me to tell me that she completely disagreed with everything I had said. She told me that some people are simply mentally ill, and there is nothing anyone can do, and nothing that caused it.

She told me that her mother had always been mentally ill, and had been prescribed many different antipsychotics and antidepressants over the years. Despite this, none of them had worked and eventually, after refusing to take any more medication, and after many serious attempts, her mother had ended her own life by suicide. She told me that the psychiatrists had explained that sometimes the medication isn't strong enough, and it doesn't work anymore.

I asked her what her mother was like, and she told me that her mother was always tired, stressed, upset, chaotic and complained of physical health issues. She had been abused as a child by her dad, who had also abused her own mother in front of her. Her husband had left her, and she had spent years in and out of psychiatric hospitals.

When I asked whether she thought those experiences might have contributed to her mother's 'mental illness' and her suicide attempts, she became angry and told me that her experiences had nothing to do with it, and that her illness was due to brain chemistry imbalances that were too severe to treat. She said that her mother had a disease that couldn't be cured, and that it was no one else's fault. She said the doctors had done 'all they could for her', and there was no cure.

This narrative, of a woman being ill with some organic brain chemistry imbalance which was so difficult to treat that she killed herself, is arguably easier to accept than the reality, which was that her mother had been sexually abused for years by her dad, whilst watching her mother be beaten and abused, too. It is easier and simpler to blame an illness than her dad's actions. It is easier to believe that the doctors had exhausted all options, and had done everything they could possibly do to 'treat' her, than it is to understand that she was pathologised and sectioned over and over again, until she refused to take any more medication and killed herself.

Thalia refusing to pathologise the women and girls she works with is arguably an example of responsible, ethical and trauma-informed practice in psychiatry – despite it being perceived as problematic.

I wanted to learn more about good practice, and so I asked the groups of professionals for examples of practice where pathologisation was being challenged effectively.

Out of almost twenty professionals, sixteen of them told me that they had no good practice examples to talk about. Some of them said that they were surrounded by such poor practice that the only potential good practice they knew of was their own.

Nora told me about her team, and Alexis told me about her own work. Thalia told me about her own work, too.

Nora explained that since moving to a specialist social work team, she has been able to challenge doctors, medical models and pathologisation much more.

I work in a great team, we all regularly challenge discriminatory practice. For example, challenging the idea that anyone with a mental health diagnosis is unable to protect themselves from harm. We are social workers, we shouldn't be working to a medical model to start with. I used to work within an integrated community mental health team, and it was awful, the doctors have all the power. Now we are purely social workers in a specialist team, we are able to more effectively challenge the medical model and the continued pathologisation of women.

I am also part of the women's network within local government. We have organised a group event with the local police women's group to discuss women's safety with a focus on getting men to join the event as the change mainly needs to happen with them.

And Alexis discussed her own academic work as an example of good practice.

I'm tooting my own horn here, but my work is some of the only scholarship using living and deceased women's and girls' own explanations of their self-directed violence to challenge their pathologisation. I can think of only a few other researchers (all women) around the globe centring their experiences. Perhaps surprisingly, I have developed the world's first and only model explicating the process – the sequencing of factors – experienced by women and girls as they move towards and, importantly, through a self-harming event. This model is currently termed The Pain Pathway and I'm in the process of making a short animated trilingual film about the model in the Sri Lankan context; a website is being developed to accompany it and I hope it becomes a place where people can find early resources and take the model to explore how useful and suitable it might be in many other settings. The fundamental takeaway for the Pathway is that self-directed violence is chiefly a consequence of the accumulation of oppression(s), mistreatment and actual violence levied upon girls and women across their life course. In sum, self-directed violence is really a response to interpersonal gendered violence. It is not about psychiatric diagnoses.

As a psychologist who has worked with women and girls throughout my career, I was interested to learn that Alexis had found that there was very little academic research which asked women and girls what their own understandings and experiences were of self-directed violence and harm. When I reflected however, it seemed all too familiar.

In my own field of expertise, women and girls had not been given voices about their experiences of being blamed and blaming themselves for sexual violence, as the field had over-relied on quantitative studies and decades-old theories which positioned women and girls as passive sponges that would absorb any belief that anyone gave them. This resulted in oversimplified, misogynistic and unhelpful approaches to victim blaming and self-blame of women and girls.

In her field, Alexis had found virtually the same thing: that women and girls had never been asked what led to their self-harm, why they did it and what it meant to them. There were a lot of theories, risk checklists and assumptions, but very little lived experience.

It seems so obvious – to learn about the mental health and trauma experiences of women and girls, we need to ask them and then centre their voices. And yet, so much of our practice and research is based on theories, observations, stereotypes, assumptions and cultural norms.

How could we end the pathologisation of women?

The professionals I interviewed for this book had hundreds of years of experience between them. They were exhausted, disillusioned and ready for meaningful change. They were challenging their workplaces, their managers, their registration bodies and their colleagues. I wanted to finish my interviews with them by asking how we could end this global effort to pathologise and medicate millions of women and girls – and in general, they all had the same answer for me.

Trauma-informed practice and theory is at the top of the priority list for professionals who are looking for alternatives to psychiatry and medical model thinking. They have had enough of traditional mental health, and are ready to break down imposing power and control dynamics. Many of the professionals regarded pathologisation as a form of victim blaming, and wanted to challenge the insidious nature of woman blaming in mental health, which is a view I share with them.

Rose explained that we need radical change in the way we perceive and treat women and girls. In her view, the broader issue which underpins psychiatry is misogyny and the oppression of marginalised people.

I would like professionals to have meaningful and genuine conversations with the women we work with about their experiences, what their needs are, what support they want to receive from services, and genuine co-production of trauma-informed/ responsive services. I would like to see the seed of trauma-informed work grow exponentially across all health, social care and criminal justice services. I would like to see alternatives to the medical model be seriously invested in and nurtured within these settings and a massive culture shift in the language, narratives and practices within services.

It is hard to believe that it is so controversial for professionals to be calling for 'meaningful and genuine' conversations with the women they work with. However, it appears that we are here, at this place in our history and our practice which requires us to acknowledge that our systems and policies are not in the best interests of women and girls we work with. The conversations we have with women and girls are somewhere between misinformation, professional grooming and emotional blackmail.

Women and girls are regularly given misinformation about having brain chemistry imbalances and incurable personality disorders. They are also frequently – and professionally – groomed and blackmailed into complying and submitting to doctors, nurses, psychologists, therapists, police and social services.

I started teaching about professional grooming in 2018, to the utter horror of hundreds of professionals. When we talk about grooming, people tend to think of sex offenders, paedophiles and child abusers. They think of weird old men grooming kids in chat rooms, or getting them to meet them at a park.

In my view, this is not a useful conceptualisation of grooming behaviour or tactics. Instead, I teach professionals that grooming takes place in every arena of our lives, from the moment we are born. I have written about this at length in my article 'Why grooming is so hard to spot: The truth' which has been read over 26,000 times at the time of writing this book.

Psychiatry and psychology are not exceptions to this.

Grooming is a process which combines multiple tactics and approaches to force a person to do something you want them to do. Therefore, grooming could be used to convince someone to quit smoking, move to another country, convert to an extremist ideology, perform sexual acts they don't want to do, start a weight-loss programme or run drugs for a dealer. Grooming can manipulate anyone into anything, if it is done successfully.

Grooming can include complimenting, protecting, persuading, selling, gaslighting, harassing, threatening, manipulating, deceiving, insulting, intoxicating, injuring or even showering someone with gifts. It can include making someone feel a sense of belonging or safety. It could be threatening them that something will happen to someone they love if they don't do something. It could be emotional blackmail.

You can be groomed into thinking you are mentally ill. You can be groomed into taking medication that is making you feel worse. You can be groomed into believing that without the medication, you will die. You can be groomed into doubting your own instincts and decision making. You can be groomed into believing that your personality is disordered, and your fears are a mental illness.

You can be groomed into thinking that everything you have been through is irrelevant, that the medication will make you feel better, and if it makes you feel worse, it's because you need more medication, and if a higher dosage doesn't work, you need another kind of medication, and if that doesn't work, it's because you have an untreatable, 'treatment-resistant' form of the disorder.

And eventually, you will begin to think that the problem sits with you. In your body. In your brain. Not only are you then groomed to accept that new narrative, but you are encouraged to see yourself as part of a 'community', or to 'identify' with the disorder. When you think about it like this, it is an incredibly powerful form of grooming.

Going back to the point Rose made then, how many conversations with women and girls in mental health services are, in fact, grooming and manipulation? How many are meaningful and genuine, as Rose wants?

Couldn't it be a form of grooming to tell a young woman that if she doesn't take the medication, she won't be referred for therapy?

Couldn't it be a form of grooming to threaten to remove the children of a woman subjected to domestic abuse, unless she stops reporting and complaining that she is being abused?

Couldn't it be a form of grooming to lock women and girls in wards, convince them that they are mentally disordered, prescribe them strong medications, sedate them when they don't comply, and then suggest that their experiences of rape and abuse are all in their heads?

It's no wonder that women and girls report feeling controlled, groomed and punished when they are in mental health services. Especially, when they quickly learn that their mental health can and will be used against them whenever necessary.

This is something that Selina feels strongly about. Her work in clinical psychology in Australia has led her to believe that the control and grooming of women and girls is central to psychiatry.

Psychiatry just appears to be so damaging. Since learning about ritual abuse, I have this big theory that psychiatry is all about controlling women and girls, deliberately undermining them and their agency, making society believe they are weak and crazy and hysterical so that psychiatry can continue to abuse their power and privilege and build their power and networks. I know there are some great ones out there – and those are the ones who subscribe to relational-based therapies who believe trauma is something that happens to someone, not inherently that there is something bad about a person's personality.

Nora felt that the pathologisation of women and girls was a form of victim blaming that needed to be eradicated in psychiatry and mental health. I agree with Nora. After all, this is the exact reason why I ended up writing *Why Women are Blamed for Everything*, and what inspired this book. Pathologisation is blatant victim blaming. When I asked Nora what she thought needed to change, she replied in all capital letters, 'NO MORE VICTIM BLAMING'.

She argued that women were being held responsible for male violence, and she had reached the end of her tolerance with this heavily embedded and widely accepted approach.

Women are not responsible for being victims of sexual assault, rape or domestic violence. They do not need to learn how to not date shit men. Men need to not be shit. MARAC meetings need to focus on more perpetrator-led interventions for domestic abuse. Rather than ways we can make women leave men, because if you don't improve the man he will just continue to abuse women. A woman who has experienced or is currently experiencing abuse does not have 'depression, anxiety or EUPD', they are experiencing trauma and trying their best to survive. The police need to take more action against perpetrators instead of no further action and referring the woman to statutory services.

Shona also focused on EUPD and BPD. She wanted to see the end of it – so no more women and girls could be diagnosed with a personality disorder. However, she also raised an important point that I agree with: that male perpetrators are also being diagnosed with personality disorders to explain or excuse their offending.

This is of interest to me, as a trauma-informed psychologist. I agree with Shona, and with other professionals who argue that male perpetrators are not mentally ill or psychopathic. I don't believe that sex offenders, child abusers, paedophiles, domestic abuse perpetrators or traffickers have personality disorders or mental health issues. Decades of research suggests otherwise: perpetrators commit these crimes because they want to, and because they are motivated to do so. Further, they live in a society that normalises, minimises or glorifies their crimes. It would make sense then, that they went ahead and did what they wanted to do, safe in the knowledge that there would be no real prospect of conviction or consequence.

I would like to see the eradication of personality disorder as a 'diagnosis'. I have worked with (typically) male perpetrators who have 'psychopathic PD' or 'antisocial PD' diagnoses and these labels are as unhelpful to them as the emotionally unstable or borderline ones are to (typically) women. A trauma-based approach is essential. A values-based approach should be encouraged within professional teams – unconditional positive regard and understanding that a person's response is usually proportional to their experience – so when that response seems unusual to us, perhaps we should consider how they are experiencing the world and see things from their perspective rather than our own. Community Mental Health Teams tend to have big caseloads, they are medical model based, and they need to see as many people as possible in as short a time frame as possible. Medication is given for reasons unrelated to illness – this doesn't work, or causes further problems that may be labelled as non-compliance or treatment-resistant. The system creates situations where personality disorders become an inevitability – like a self-fulfilling prophecy, in my personal opinion.

Personality disorders seem to be the sticking point for many professionals who are tired of seeing virtually anything being reframed as a personality disorder diagnosis. Often, the criteria for diagnosis are so broad and loose that anyone could be diagnosed with one. Because there are no tests or scans, or objective measures of personality, there is no real way of ever proving that anyone has a disorder of personality.

I often wonder why no one else is noticing the strong relationship between gender role stereotyping and personality disorders. The men get the 'psychopathic' and 'antisocial' personality disorder diagnoses, and the women get the 'emotionally unstable', 'histrionic' and 'borderline' personality disorders. Doesn't that just scream stereotyping?

No matter whether people are offenders or victims, male or female, it's hard to agree that there are people in the world with disorders of personality which they will have for the rest of their lives. And that's without dipping into the controversial discussion of what a personality even is, and how it's defined and constructed with different psychological theories.

We have long been taught that key concepts of mental health, personality, attachment and psychology are 'proven', as if they are closed for discussion. Having spoken to others who took an undergraduate degree in psychology, it alarms me how many of us are taught popular theories and repetitive modules as if they are facts. At undergraduate study level, there is often not much room for critical thinking or appraisal outside of course materials – which leads to thousands of students being taught the same old, contested (sometimes debunked) theories and studies as everyone else.

Dr Alexis Palfreyman wants to change that, and I think she's right.

> *I have openly declared that it will be the hill I die on to get history of medicine to become core curriculum for medical and nursing programmes, with intensive focus on its propagation of misogyny, racism and other forms of discrimination and maltreatment which have been baked into the past and present. It's a critical way to ensure there is a clear and standardised expectation for all future clinicians of every level and specialty that we will no longer accept healthcare that harms instead of heals on the basis of someone's identity.*

We need to educate professionals urgently; and we need to redesign the curriculum for many disciplines around the world. As new students come through to begin their journey as a nurse, doctor, police officer, therapist, psychologist, psychiatrist, teacher, social worker or researcher – they need to know that the medical model of mental health is harming millions of people, and that it is founded and built upon dangerous and oppressive beliefs about marginalised groups.

Additionally, Alexis wants to see misogyny attitudinal assessments – which is something I enthusiastically agreed with her on. As a psychologist and psychometrician who is trained to construct and validate these attitudinal measures, I have been working with police forces and schools on creating them in the last twelve months or so. They are tricky to get right and require years of careful reliability and construct testing, validation and exploration before use – but if we can create a way of screening applications and professionals for misogyny, it could protect millions of women and girls.

Perhaps controversial, but I also believe that attitudinal assessments for signs of serious misogyny in applicants to clinical programmes – as with things like the police – could be hugely beneficial for reducing maltreatment and misdiagnosis of women and girls later on under those graduated clinicians' care. That's not to say we reject people who show any signs of internalised misogyny – I think we'd struggle to take anyone if that were the case – and we know we can improve people's attitudes through education. But it is possible to identify people with truly concerning views and we have to be brave enough to say that it's too risky to take a chance of those people hoping their attitudes may change. We know, for example, that domestic violence is much more common among police officers than the general population; we also know sexual violence is the second commonest offence by police officers in the US and UK while performing their roles – these offenders remain in post to harm for years and yet those signs and histories of misogyny and even violence were likely there before applying to the academy. We could reduce so much professionally sanctioned harm against women and girls in mental health and beyond, if we were better at asking key questions for high-risk, high-consequence jobs before permitting people into them.

Alexis is right to point out the prevalence of abuse and violence amongst professionals, including police officers themselves. I do wonder what we could achieve by screening these worrying attitudes before professionals were given access to women and girls at some of the most vulnerable and scary times of their lives. However, plenty of psychological research in psychometrics and attitude measurement shows that people will engage in socially desirable responding, meaning that they may deliberately answer the way they know they should answer, rather than how they actually feel about the issue.

This is likely to be the case with misogyny, as many of the measures used to screen these attitudes are outdated, too obvious or too specific. It's one of the many reasons I love creating and testing psychometrics myself, as it's such a challenge to get them right.

Alexis finished by saying that there is a growing collective of professionals out there who are ready to challenge the medical model of mental health, in order to protect as many women and girls as we can.

> There are others out there working on various issues within global mental health who are keen to shake up who is in the space and how we work together and to move away from pathologising anyone when it's inappropriate. That's the thing to focus on – and that small but growing tribe includes a hugely diverse pool of clinical and non-clinical experts including some fabulously inspiring psychiatrists, psychologists, social scientists, social workers, journalists and more. Those of us really making noise about this gender-ignorant orientation to mental health, I hope will grow too. It must – it's costing women and girls their health, and sometimes their lives.

CHAPTER 9

Sexualising 'crazy' women and sectioning sexually non-conformist women

Grab a cop gun kinda crazy / she's poison but tasty /
Yeah, people say, 'Run, don't walk away!' /
Cos she's sweet but a psycho / A little bit psycho
At night she's screaming / I'm out of my mind
   Sweet but Psycho – Ava Max (2018)

In the last few years, I have noticed an exponential increase in the sexualisation of psychiatric disorders and diagnosis, and it is this that inspired this book (and its title and covers). If psychiatrists are right, and their diagnoses constitute serious mental disorders which affect the daily lives of their sufferers, why is it deemed so sexy by men – and by society at large?

What's so sexy about being psychotic?

This chapter will explore the public positioning of women and girls with psychiatric disorders as sexy, desirable and edgy. On the reverse, this chapter will also explore how women's non-conformity to sexualisation, sexuality or sexual activity has often resulted in them being diagnosed with psychiatric disorders, which, weirdly, are not sexualised.

Could it be that so-called mental illness is wrapped up in heteronormative portrayals of sexy, helpless, vulnerable, damaged women that men want to take advantage of?

Back to the beginning (again)

As discussed in earlier chapters, women's sexuality has always been of interest to patriarchal psychiatric and religious systems. If 'of interest' means 'control at all costs', that is. Since the church began to frame women's sexuality as evil, sinful and dangerous to men, all women and girls across the world have been duped, manipulated and deliberately held back from understanding their own bodies, pleasure and sexuality. Sex has always been for men. Pleasure has always been for men. Reproduction has always been for men. Women's bodies have always been for men.

It is evidenced from thousands of years of these tactics that men have sought to control what they do not have and cannot understand. They desire women, but they hate them (the core tenet of misogyny). They recognise that women hold the power to reproduction, and therefore, the continuation of the human race. They are capable of creating life, growing life and then giving birth. They can withhold reproduction and sex, or allow that to happen on their own terms. This is an incredible amount of power, should women ever get it in its true form.

Men do not seek to oppress women because they are inferior, mentally unstable, unreliable, childish and stupid – they seek to oppress women because they recognise our power. No, men have systematically and strategically spent time and money in *saying* that women are inferior, mentally unstable, unreliable, childish and stupid – so that they can oppress us. In order to control women, they needed to convince billions of people that we were in need of control. Millennia of smear campaigns against women which have successfully positioned them as 'less than', were only required because women are not less than at all.

It is astounding to step back and consider how much collective effort goes into daily global misogyny, and how much of that is about controlling women's sex lives. The church played a central role in warning the public that female sexuality, female sexual pleasure, female reproduction and female masturbation were all the work of the devil, and/or witchcraft. The impact on both men and women was immeasurable, and still reverberates around the world to this day.

However, whilst these harmful views impacted both men and women, they only oppressed one half of the population, whilst the other were free to enjoy, exploit and control sex however they wished. Men were given free rein on their use of sex, rape, abuse, masturbation and pleasure, whilst women were entering the twenty-first century not knowing what an orgasm was, not being taught about their own clitoris, being shamed for masturbating, being called 'promiscuous' if they had casual sex and 'frigid' if they didn't have enough sex, being sexually abused as children, being persecuted if they were not sexually attracted to men at all, and having their genitals mutilated, cut off and sewn up to control their sexual pleasure.

After the church had played its role, authorities and physicians stepped up to take the baton and push the narratives of evil, sex-crazed (or evil, sexless) women who needed to be controlled, locked up, punished or medicated. The crux of this is, what was once myth and legend about the devil possessing women to make them desire sexual pleasure became enshrined in medicine and psychiatry as mental illnesses in need of treatment and medication. Psychiatry legitimised the pathologisation of women's sexuality and sexual desires.

By the nineteenth century, women were diagnosed and treated for psychiatric disorders if they were not having enough sex with their husbands, if they were deemed to be sexually frustrated, if they were lesbian, if they were bisexual, if they didn't want sex at all, if they were traumatised by rape and sexual abuse, if they wanted too much sex and if they masturbated. There was very little left that a woman could do freely with her body, for her own sexuality, that didn't result in a diagnosis of delusions, hysteria, homosexuality or psychosis.

Lesbian, bisexual, asexual, celibate, traumatised, non-consenting, too sexually active = mentally ill.

Having sex when you are told, with your husband, as an act of obedience, to pleasure your husband, to make a baby, without ever reaching orgasm = not mentally ill.

How did 'psycho' become 'sexy'?

To understand this phenomenon, and the journey towards women and teen girls being perceived as hot but crazy, sexy but psycho, beautiful but manipulative – we have to understand the way men objectify and sexualise women and girls.

Objectification is defined as using people like tools or toys, as if they had no feelings, opinions or rights of their own. According to Fredrickson and Roberts, sexual objectification is described as the valuing of a woman exclusively on the basis of her body and on her sexual parts, rather than on her full identity. When a woman is sexually objectified, her body becomes a mere instrument for satisfying sexual male desires. Sexualisation is the act of sexualising someone or something, seeing someone or something in sexual terms. Long (2012), argues that media representations of women and girls reduce women to an object for sex, holes to be filled or a body to be used. This has direct links to the victim blaming of women and girls who have been subjected to rape or sexual assault because it reinforces the notion that they are insatiable sex objects for men and boys to conquer and use. This systemic representation of the sexual purpose of women means that rape is often seen as an act of sex, not as an act of violence.

Attractive female characters were found to be more likely to be victims of sexual crimes in television shows than male characters (Cope-Farrar and Kunkel, 2011), and Loughnan et al. (2013), found that participants presented with a case study of an objectified, sexualised woman who had been raped were less likely to feel moral concern for her. She was more likely to be held responsible than women who were not objectified or sexualised. Not only this, but the hyper-sexualisation of groups of women can be absorbed and accepted by the women themselves (Loughnan et al., 2013), meaning that they can buy into the popular misrepresentation of their own gender roles and self-worth; thereby increasing self-blame when they are raped and abused by men (Taylor, 2020).

Sexualised and objectified women and girls are dehumanised, dementalised and therefore perceived as less worthy of moral concern. Consequently, when women and girls are sexualised and objectified either directly or indirectly, they are more likely to be blamed for rape and sexual assault and less likely to be perceived as suffering from the experience of being subjected to sexual violence (Loughnan et al., 2013). This process of dehumanisation and dementalisation is important when considering the way that women and girls who have diagnoses of psychiatric disorders are sexualised for two reasons.

Firstly, if women and girls are diagnosed and stigmatised, it furthers the aim of sexualisation and objectification. Women and girls with psychiatric disorders are ultimate sex objects: they are female, they are vulnerable, they are perceived as damaged, no one will believe them, they might be on drugs which sedate or disinhibit them and they might be perceived by men to have no boundaries, no limits and no morals. This is all meticulously and successfully wrapped up with moralistic views of female sex and pleasure. Mentally sound women will have rules, boundaries – and can therefore be perceived as stable, but boring. Mentally ill women might have no rules, no boundaries, and might be 'psycho' enough to do whatever a man wants them to do.

Maybe, she's so disordered that he can fuck her however he likes, abuse her, discard her, harm her, ignore her, exploit her and then dismiss her as his crazy, psycho, bunny boiler ex?

Secondly, women and girls can be duped into believing this narrative of crazy, sexy, psycho women. They can be groomed and taught that their value lies in presenting as disordered, damaged, and sexually available to abusive men.

Arguably, one of the most devastating effects of buying into the representation by the mass media of women as crazy sexual objects is that women can learn that their self-worth lies within sex and remaining constantly sexually available to men and boys (Garcia, 1999; APA, 2007b). This can lead to women and girls judging and blaming themselves using common rape myths for why they were raped – or not even realise that their sexual encounter was non-consensual, forced or exploitative (Ullman, 2010; Eaton, 2019). Indeed, Fairchild and Rudman (2008) have shown that young women who were subjected to sexual harassment and objectification in the street by unknown men had a variety of coping mechanisms – but those young women who responded to sexual harassment passively or by blaming themselves were much more likely to self-objectify.

The hot-crazy matrix

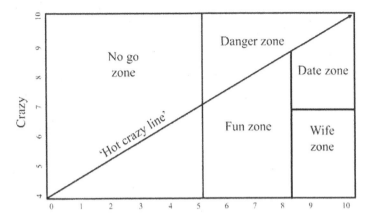

Before I begin to discuss this utter atrocity of men's objectification of women, and science attempting to support it – I must start by saying that the hot-crazy matrix is/was supposed to be a misogynistic joke dreamt up by men on the internet who argued that women were a mixture of hot and crazy.

The original YouTube video (now at over four million views) began by stating that all women were naturally crazy and psycho, and the real challenge for men is in finding a woman who is hot enough to fuck without being so crazy that 'you end up in prison'. There's a specific nod to killing or harming her, because she's so insufferable.

The basic theory is that men want a woman who is hot (and naturally crazy), but not so disordered that you can't date or marry her. As you can see in the diagram, millions of people who have viewed this are led to believe that the majority of women are so mentally unstable that they are confined to the 'no go zone'. These women are psychotic, but not hot enough to justify having sex with. Basically, if she is crazy but hot, this is okay, but if she is crazy and unattractive, she holds no value to men. She's a psycho.

Another sizeable chunk of women are confined to the 'fun zone'. This is described as the zone in which the man gets great, crazy sex from the woman, but she is so unhinged that he cannot possibly date or marry her. She is for casual sex and nothing more. She's a psycho, too.

The third largest proportion of women form the 'danger zone'. These women are considered extremely crazy and very hot. In many articles on the internet, these women are described as the type who would give men limitless, crazy sex, however and whenever they wanted it, but were so disordered that they would ruin a man's life. Think psycho, stalker, bunny boiler ex stereotype, slashing his car tyres, cutting his brake lines and burning his clothes (which I would like to add, is such an inverted stereotype considering that 97 per cent of all violence is committed by men, and 99 per cent of all violence towards women is committed by men – and yet, they have no psycho stereotype or matrix).

Finally, we have the date zone and the marry zone. Of course, men only date or marry women who are over 8.5 on the hot score, but they must be between a 4 and a 7 on the crazy score to marry.

This might be the first time you have noticed, but the y-axis of the scale which measures 'crazy' begins at a 4, whereas the x-axis which measures 'hot' begins at a zero. This is commonly explained to mean that there is no such thing as a sane woman, and that all women are at least a 4/10 insane.

You might be reading this section thinking, why on earth is she giving so much space to such misogynistic claptrap?

Well, my committed reader, you made it to chapter eight to discover that academics chose to research this hot-crazy matrix using public funding to 'prove' that it exists, and to argue that men tend to be more attracted to women and girls with borderline personality disorder and psychopathy.

In 2018, this study, by Blanchard et al., featured in top academic journal, *Personality and Individual Differences*. The paper features the diagram above, which is presented by the authors without any clarification that it comes from a YouTube video. It also uses women with borderline personality disorder as the category for exploration as 'crazy', which, in itself, should tell us what academics and researchers really think about this psychiatric diagnosis. At no point during ethical approval, study, write-up, submission to publication, peer review and then publication did anyone challenge the authors conceptualisation of women with diagnoses of borderline personality disorder as hot but psycho. Not once.

Blanchard et al. conflated women's personality disorder diagnoses with stereotypes found on a YouTube video and a set of internet memes and then wrote a serious scientific paper about it – to further the myth that men will be 'willing to date women with BPD as long as they are physically appealing' and that 'women with dark triad personality traits and psychopathy offer thrilling short-term relationships'.

Excellent use of money and time by the departments of psychology at Bishops Gate and Nottingham Trent University. What a profound and ethical addition to the literature on women's mental health.

Sexy but psycho – on a T-shirt?

The concept of women being sexy but psycho has spread across the world in recent years, with millions of search results including song lyrics, T-shirts, memes, articles, accessories, posters, celebrity endorsements and sitcom references.

There are currently 320 sellers on Etsy making women's clothing, key rings, earrings, phone covers, socks, mugs, and posters which have the slogans 'cute but psycho', 'sexy but psycho', 'hot but psycho', 'don't let this cute face fool you, I'm a total psycho', 'psycho is an understatement', 'psycho as fuck', '1% sweet, 99% psycho'. There are a further 850 sellers making similar items which say 'borderline personality disorder' on them. Items for women and girls also include slogans such as 'I am chemically imbalanced'. All adorned with sexualised images of women and girls, lips, lipstick, cherries, peaches, hearts, flowers, unicorns and all manner of hyperfeminised decorations. And these items are not confined to internet sellers. T-shirts with these slogans have been found in mainstream and designer brands across the world including Boohoo, ASOS and MissGuided.

Men's T-shirts contain slogans about their girlfriends being 'hot but psycho' and simple statements such as 'my girlfriend is psychotic'. More wordy T-shirts for men include those on Amazon, Instagram and Facebook which state, 'I'm married to a freaking awesome wife who is crazy and scares me sometimes, but I am the lucky one because I get to be her husband and she bought me this tee shirt.'

In the music and film industry, the portrayal of sexy but psycho women has been ramping up for nearly two decades. Films now frequently portray sexualised, psychotic, delusional ex-girlfriends and wives stalking men whilst men stalking women is portrayed as 'true love' and 'persistence pays off'. In 2006, *My Super Ex-Girlfriend* grossed $61 million at the box office as a film about a man whose psychotic, bunny boiler ex-girlfriend was a superhero who ruined his life.

In the DC universe in 2016, Harley Quinn is portrayed as an unhinged, psychotic, violent and hypersexualised woman who becomes part of the *Suicide Squad* in a globally successful film grossing over $133 million in the opening weekend. Harley Quinn (a named which plays on 'harlequin girl', meaning a fool or clown who gives men what they want), is the 'love interest' of famous antihero The Joker. Her backstory is horrific, as she was groomed, abused, beaten and controlled by The Joker, who was one of her patients when she was a psychiatrist intern in the Arkham Asylum. She is also depicted as having come from a broken home with an abusive family. The Joker gaslights and grooms her until he has control of her mind and body. Later on, her skin became bleached when her boyfriend, The Joker, kicked her into a vat of boiling acid. She is consistently depicted as wearing high heels, fishnet stockings, short skirts, ripped clothing and the classic hairstyle – infantile bunches.

This depiction of Harley Quinn became an instant hit, and women and girls bought merchandise, Halloween costumes and adult lingerie to liken themselves to a woman who was sexualised for ultimately being an extremely traumatised, sexualised, controlled victim of torture and abuse.

As the years progressed, the phrase and concept of 'sexy but psycho' became more and more accepted into popular culture with song lyrics of highly grossing songs encouraging and sexualising 'psycho women'. The lyrics at the beginning of this chapter are from smash hit 'Sweet but Psycho' which talks of warning men about women and girls who are hot, but psychotic. Famous artists who glorify and sexualise mental disorders of women who are depicted as sexy but psycho in their songs also include Bon Jovi, Charlie Puth, The Kinks, Iggy Azealia, Taylor Swift, Kardinal Offishal, James Blunt, Michael Jackson, Christina Aguilera, Ashnikko, Nelly Furtado, Bruno Mars, Rihanna, Lady Gaga, Kasabian and Beyoncé.

What this comes down to is that women and girls are experiencing a slow, steady and successful normalisation and sexualisation of their traumas. Psychiatric diagnosis, trauma from abuse, becoming a 'crazy ex' and being non-conforming is quickly becoming a trend, a goal, a way to be sexually objectified by men.

There is absolutely no benefit to women and girls in being typecast as psychotic, unhinged, mentally ill sex objects with no rules, no bound-aries and no stability; and yet, it is a sexualised stereotype which is taking the world by storm. Men can now comfortably talk about women as psychopathic and women will giggle and wear their cute T-shirt which advertises their borderline personality disorder. Men can make YouTube videos telling men to only fuck hot-crazy women, and psychology academics sanction it as the truth about borderline, psychopathic sexy women.

No, rather than being of benefit, this incredible sleight of hand supports the mass psychiatric diagnosis of women and teenage girls as being cool, sexy and edgy. What may seem like a joke about hysterical, emotional, unstable women is actually founded on centu-ries of psychiatric propaganda, torture and the deaths of real women and girls – and the mass medication of millions of women and girls globally. But women don't know this. The public don't know the history of the diagnoses and the lack of science for all of them.

It's starting to look eerily like marketing. And it's working.

I have learned recently that when I speak about the deliberate pathologisation of women and girls, I am frequently met with accu-sations of 'pill shaming' and 'denying' women and girls their psychi-atric diagnosis which 'validates' and 'supports' them to understand themselves. I initially found this distressing – I didn't want women and girls to think I was shaming or invalidating their diagnoses, after all, they tell me that being called mentally disordered is empowering, right?

However, as I have thought about this more and more, I have decided that invalidating the misogynistic psychiatric diagnoses is exactly what I am trying to do.

I am definitely 'denying' their diagnosis, and the centuries of pseudoscience, racism, misogyny and homophobia which underpins it. I am not shaming individual women who have been prescribed medication, but I am shaming and exposing the thousands of professionals who have routinely done this to women and girls around the world who are distressed, traumatised and in need of human compassion.

Many of the women I interviewed for this book were not sexualised at all as part of their psychiatric diagnoses, instead the opposite was true; they were diagnosed with mental disorders because they did not want sex, or were scared to have sex. If that is not proof of how much control psychiatry aims to have over women and girls, I do not know what is.

In 2021, I discussed this at length with Diana who told me that being sexually abused had left her traumatised by sex and intimacy. She didn't desire sex, she didn't enjoy sex and she was pushed to access psychiatric support.

The psychiatrist referred me for 'psychosexual problems'. I was terrified of sex and I was married at the time. Sometimes I did want sex but my body wouldn't cooperate. I had flashbacks, panic attacks, and vaginal spasms which really hurt. The psychiatrist said to me, 'how hard are you prepared to try for your husband?'

and I thought . . . this is not for my husband. I am not a vessel for his sex life. I stopped going to the sessions and didn't get any more help. The psychiatrist said to me that I probably enjoyed the sexual abuse and I should be grateful for it. I made a formal complaint to the NHS trust. The NHS trust said that he is a senior doctor and no other complaints have been made like this. He denied it and said it never happened. I was treated like a silly little girl who needed to grow up and stop wasting everyone's time.

Diana told me that she always wanted to be intimate with her other half, but her body wouldn't cooperate. Her vaginal spasms (which are common after trauma and distress) caused her terrible pain and meant that nothing could go inside her vagina, even if she wanted it to. She explained to me that she couldn't use tampons, have a speculum for a smear test or have sex.

Interestingly, me wanting to have a healthy sex life was never seen as a good enough reason to access 'support'. This was seen as a luxury, not a medical issue. But me not being able to have a medical procedure like a smear test (what the doctors wanted to do) or my husband not being able to have penetrative sex with me, those were seen as justifiable reasons. My vagina in those terms, in that discourse, seemed to exist so others could put things in it, for their needs and expectations to be met, and if they couldn't, I was defined and seen as broken. It still upsets me, this conversation. I was trying hard. So hard. That was why I was there asking for help, as humiliating and traumatic as that conversation could have been, even with a compassionate and supportive member of staff. And I just got told I wasn't trying hard enough, that sex was for the benefit of men, and that the abuse that had terrorised a large part of my childhood as a daily threat/reality, and every day since with its echoes, was some-how, unbelievably, enjoyable. I am livid that anyone could think, let alone say that. It is so far from the truth. I barely survived alive.

I also spoke to Anushka about the way her traumatic birth stopped her from having sex for several years, only to be diagnosed with depression and personality disorder. She was twenty-three when she suffered complications during the birth of her second son. She was seriously injured and had to have surgery to repair the damage from a neglectful forceps intervention which she shouted several times that she didn't consent to.

I just never wanted sex. I just never wanted it ever again. Me and my husband just stopped sleeping together. I hated sex and I felt nothing. It just felt like nothing. I stopped masturbating as well because it made me feel disgusting. I knew it was all about the birth and what happened. I sought help and I cried to the doctor that I was so upset about not being able to have sex anymore. And they diagnosed me with depression, and then later, personality disorder. I was told that I had to take the pills every day because I had a chemical imbalance in my brain. I was told that the pills would make everything easier. But I still never wanted sex again. It's really impacted my marriage but I can't imagine having sex with anyone else either.

What is clear, is that when women don't want to, or can't have sex, even where there is clear evidenced links to significant trauma, they are still deemed to be dysfunctional and disordered. They are still referred into psychiatric services and they are still likely to receive a diagnosis and medication which ignores the reason they sought help. No woman accesses services about needing help with her sex life and sexual pleasure in order to be told that she has a chemical imbalance in her brain and a personality disorder.

This is blatant misogyny. Psychotic women are sexy. Non-sexual women are psychotic. As a woman, you cannot escape the inevitable psychiatric diagnosis which will come as soon as you disclose abuse and trauma.

The sexualisation and pathologisation of Britney Spears

The world has watched whilst Britney Spears rose to fame dressed in 'sexy schoolgirl' uniform dancing in a school gym, singing 'hit me baby, one more time'. They watched as she become a global phenomenon and sex symbol. They laughed as she was chased endlessly by the press. As she struggled to cope. As she shaved her head. As she struggled to keep custody of her children. As she was sectioned and medicated. As she was forced to perform in Las Vegas whilst being regularly medicated to control and subdue her. As she was locked into a conservatorship for thirteen years by her abusive father.

Prior to her solo artist career, she had been a famous child star of Disney's *The Mickey Mouse Club* along with Ryan Gosling, Justin Timberlake and Christina Aguilera. She regularly performed songs and dance routines and acted. At fifteen years old, she signed a record deal.

I was eight years old when 'Hit me baby, one more time' came out. I watched it on the TV and didn't know she was just a child until much later, when I was an adult working in child sexual exploitation services. I looked back on the video and wondered how old she was when they sexualised her and sold her to the world. I did a quick Google search.

Sixteen.

I thought about her song titles and music videos. 'I'm a Slave 4 U' was curiously released on the same album as 'Not a Girl, Not Yet a Woman' when she was eighteen years old. Interestingly, both produced by Pharrell Williams, the producer of 'Blurred Lines' with Robin Thicke – widely considered to be a misogynistic, pro-rape song about objectifying women.

In 'I'm a Slave 4 U' and 'Boys' (again on the same album), she is positioned as a sex-crazed woman who will do anything for men. Yet 'Not a Girl, Not Yet a Woman' positions her as a child, coming of age, and being stuck in between childhood and adulthood.

I'm not a girl (Not a girl, not yet a woman)
Not yet a woman
(I'm just trying to find the woman in me)
All I need is time, a moment that is mine
While I'm in between

Between 1998 and 2001, her management released an incredible number of songs and music videos that clearly portrayed her as sexy, sultry and out of reach. Sometimes, I wonder how much of that was deliberately paedophilic and illegal. The 'jailbait' trope. That men knew she was a child, but she was being positioned as a sexual adult.

This included being interviewed several times about whether she was a virgin, when she lost her virginity, and whether she had a boyfriend yet.

My next strongest memory of Britney was in 2003, when she released 'Everytime'. The video was harrowing. I was thirteen years old, and even I noticed that something was very wrong. She was singing about pain and trauma. The music video featured her dying of an overdose in the bath and drowning. I watched it with horror. She wanted to die. Her portrayal of suicide was calm, peaceful and final. She is shown as having an out-of-body experience in which she sees herself being pulled out of the bath by a man and rushed to hospital, whilst paparazzi scramble to take pictures of her body.

This video still haunts me; in fact, it hurts more to watch now than it did then.

Here was a very young woman, shot into global stardom, sexualised and sold as a teenage sex object, struggling to cope with the pressure, and now depicting her own death. In 2008, her mother Lynne told the press that her daughter had 'lost her virginity' to an eighteen-year-old man when she was just fourteen years old, and way below the age of consent. She had started drinking at thirteen years old whilst working on *The Mickey Mouse Club*, and had started taking drugs at fifteen years old. In her memoir, Lynne recalls finding cocaine and weed in her daughter's bag as she was boarding a private jet around the time 'Baby One More Time' was released.

For some, this might just look like a teenager experimenting, having fun, and pushing boundaries – but to me, it looked like a teenager who was struggling to cope with something; a theme that would continue for another couple of decades.

In her book, Lynne looks back on the way she was told by managers and music producers that the only way sixteen-year-old Britney would be able to compete with stars like Mariah Carey would be to sexualise her, and frame her as a 'Lolita'. She writes that she was told that they wanted to deliberately manage Britney as a teenage sex object, and that Lynne regrets giving up control of her daughter's career.

Less than a year after Lynne gave this interview, in 2007 Britney was filmed having a 'public breakdown' and shaving her hair off. A month later, after being hounded by tipped-off paparazzi, she hit a car with an umbrella. This led to global media outlets framing her as violent, psychotic, insane and a bad mother to her children. Despite everything she was going through, and previously being regarded as a national treasure, she was framed as dangerous and disordered. She was then reportedly in and out of 'rehab' for years, sectioned several times and placed on psychiatric medication.

At the end of 2007, her father, Jamie, placed Britney under a 'temporary conservatorship' which lasted over thirteen years.

During this time, concerns slowly mounted amongst her loyal fanbase, who believed for years that she was being exploited and controlled. They argued that she was in danger, and being treated like a prisoner. They pointed to evidence on her social media which suggested that she was trying to carefully get messages to her fanbase that she was in danger. In 2009, they created a FreeBritney website, and demanded that her conservatorship was ended.

In November 2021, Britney filmed and posted a video to her fan base, and specifically thanked the FreeBritney movement for 'saving her life', and 'noticing that something was wrong'.

I started to become interested in Britney's journey around four years ago, when I noticed that she always looked disconnected in her social media videos and photographs. Her communication seemed odd. Her eye contact and body language weren't right, and I had commented that she was extremely traumatised, but likely to be taking medication of some sort. I wondered whether she, like many of the women and girls I was working with, was being subjected to the same process of pathologisation and control.

In 2019, one of the attorneys in the conservatorship case claimed that Britney was so mentally ill that she was like 'a comatose patient' and that she couldn't make any decisions or sign any statements because she was the equivalent of an unconscious person.

I started to feel that my worries were being confirmed. How could she simultaneously be so lacking in capacity that she was the equivalent of a person in a coma, and also be performing at a residency in Las Vegas every single night?

How could people around her be claiming that she was so mentally ill that she needed round-the-clock supervision and medication, but she was still well enough to perform for hours?

Something wasn't right.

Whilst many laughed off the idea that she was trying to send out messages that she was being abused and controlled as a conspiracy theory, I looked through her social media for hours and found that I agreed with her fanbase. There was something about her social media. The captions seemed strange, but purposeful. Were they being written deliberately by her social media managers to make her look insane? Were they being written by a woman who had been forced to take high dosages of medication? Were they coded messages to her fans, to keep campaigning for her to be released from her conservatorship?

Maybe one day we will know the truth, but in 2020, I wrote on my own social media that I was very worried about where her life was headed, and what the conservatorship was doing to her. I looked back over the life of a girl I had grown up at the same time as, and saw nothing but trauma, fear, confusion, pressure, harassment, abuse and pathologisation. It made sense to me that she struggled so much, but like so many others, she was diagnosed as mentally ill, lost custody of her children and was positioned as disordered and psychotic.

The 2021 documentary, *Framing Britney Spears*, was the first time I had seen an angle taken by mass media outlets (*New York Times*) which clearly demonstrated that Britney was being abused and exploited. I watched it with my wife and we both cried as we watched the journey of a young girl being controlled and abused, financially exploited and framed to the media as a danger to herself and her children.

At the time of writing this book, her father has recently announced that he will eventually step down from the conservatorship which controls her entire life, and she has recently been allowed to drive again after over fourteen years of not being allowed to drive her own car.

I sincerely hope that the world supports her no matter whether she decides to tell what really happened, or whether she quietly disappears from public life forever.

Her life story and case should serve as one of the most public examples of sexualisation, exploitation and pathologisation of women that has ever occurred.

Sexy but psycho – the Disney legacy

In 2014, I came across a video on YouTube which seemed to suggest that there was a link between the Disney franchise and the sexualisation and then subsequent 'breakdown' of female child stars. It wasn't much, but it was implied. I have been interested in this process ever since.

Britney was part of that cohort, but there have been many more girls since her era. As the years have passed, I've watched as rising child stars such as Miley Cyrus, Selena Gomez, Ariana Grande, Demi Lovato and Lindsay Lohan were taken down similar pathways of hypersexualisation and then pathologisation that were publicly discussed, but for some reason, not publicly scrutinised.

Well, the girls were scrutinised, of course. Not so much scrutiny was afforded to the managers and corporations who had clearly developed a blueprint for transforming their cute child stars into pornified sex objects overnight. Sometimes it felt like they had deliberately removed their successful female child stars from the limelight for short periods of time and then relaunched them as sex siren pop stars – when they were barely seventeen years old.

Miley Cyrus became famous for her starring role in *Hannah Montana*, in which she played a young famous popstar who has to disguise herself to enable her to live a normal life. However, by the age of fifteen, she was relaunched from actor to solo artist. Her songs were carefully constructed to be sexy, but almost acceptable – a teenager singing about her relationships or her crushes.

In 2010, at seventeen years old, her management released 'Can't Be Tamed', a song which describes her as crazy, sexy, wild, damaged, jagged and uncontrollable. In the video, she is dressed as a wild, exotic, sexy animal in a large cage, that rich people have paid to see. She becomes uncontrollable and difficult to tame, the rich people become frightened of her, and so the video is designed to position her as sexy, but out of control. Her clothing is ripped and shredded. Her makeup is dark. Her hair is wild.

It is vital to remember that she is not only a child at this point, but is still starring in a Disney children's programme with a viewership of millions of small children. It is therefore interesting that some critics have speculated that this could be a deliberate process that Disney use to move their young audience towards their pop stars as they age with them. This journey towards sexy, but ultimately, mentally ill, continues for years in her career.

By 2013, her music videos regularly showed her almost naked, taking drugs, and being encouraged to be as sexualised as possible. Huge smash hits such as 'We Can't Stop' and 'Wrecking Ball' deliberately portrayed her as sexy, but disordered. Naked, but crying into the camera. Beautiful, but aggressive. Laughing but angry. Intoxicated. Exhausted. Messy. Wild. Uncontrollable. Sexy.

I also have to wonder what the significance is of Miley crying into the camera with a shaved head in 'Wrecking Ball'.

Why, and how, was she positioned as sexy but psycho?

In 2019, tabloids reported that Miley's family were considering having her sectioned, in order to save her marriage to Liam Hemsworth. A source told the *NW* that 'it was clear she was back in a dark place, and her family are telling her to face up to her demons and seek psychiatric treatment before it's too late. If it saves her marriage, it will be a small price to pay.'

This is particularly distressing to read, considering that around that time she had come out as bisexual, and less than a year later, she came out as lesbian, and was in a relationship with a woman.

The tabloids and celebrity gossip blogs continued to position her as acting out, crazy, wild, promiscuous and problematic for years. It was reported by *Star* that she was 'acting out' to 'get attention' from her on-off partner, Liam. *Heat* magazine reported that her relationship with Kaitlynn Carter was a 'fling' to 'get attention' and that she needed to be sectioned or sent to rehab for 'social media addiction'. In 2020,

NW published a criticism of Miley, claiming that she had a 'mental breakdown' due to jealousy about her ex moving on, and that her current partner Cody Simpson was going to have her sectioned or sent to a mental health facility.

This targeting of a young woman is not unique, in fact it is a pattern which many young women have been subjected to.

Selena Gomez recently announced that she had been diagnosed with bipolar disorder, anxiety and depression having been put through the same process of sexualisation and framing as sexy, but psycho. Again, after being sent to a psychiatric hospital, she was told she was mentally ill.

In 2011, after yet another career which took her from Disney child star to sex object popstar in a matter of months, an eighteen-year-old Demi Lovato was 'sent to rehab' and diagnosed with bipolar disorder. She quickly became the poster child for many mental health organisations looking to 'raise awareness' of bipolar disorder. In 2018, she took a near-fatal overdose. However, she gave an interesting interview in 2020, in which she stated that she had been misdiagnosed with bipolar disorder, and that it seemed easier for doctors to slap a label on her anger and behaviour and tell her it was bipolar disorder. In her own words, 'bipolar was used as a convenient excuse' for what was really happening.

Similarly to Miley Cyrus, Demi gave an interview in 2021 in which she said 'I hooked up with a girl and was like, "I like this a lot more." It felt right.' She went on to say, 'I know who I am and what I am, but I'm just waiting until a specific time to come out.'

Demi said that she would feel a 'visceral reaction to being intimate with men', and 'blamed herself for ignoring red flags that she was not heterosexual'. This strikes me as important, that young girls and women who might not even be heterosexual were having their young female bodies exploited, sexualised and moulded for the male gaze by multimillion-dollar corporations – causing serious psychological trauma that would later be diagnosed in terms of psychiatric disorders.

Ariana Grande was quickly sexualised as a young teenage girl, and then put through the exact same process as the others. She has spoken publicly about her depression and anxiety, and says that since the terrorist bombing of her Manchester concert in 2017, she hates performing. What is interesting about Ariana's experiences is that rather than being labelled as bipolar or psychotic like the others, the public sympathised with her trauma from the terrorist attack, and see that as a real, tangible trauma. Instead, then, she was diagnosed with PTSD and her loyal fanbase promised to support her, even if she cancelled her tour dates.

Lindsay Lohan, on the other hand, was bullied for years for her public 'breakdown' and drug dependency, despite disclosing domestic abuse and other traumas related to child stardom, sexualisation and pathologisation. Lindsay was diagnosed with ADHD after 'erratic behaviour', which UCLA have argued is a misdiagnosis, leading her to be treated with Adderall. This drug is known to have similar effects to cocaine and amphetamines. However, she was also diagnosed with bipolar and alcohol dependency, which led to her living for several years on a cocktail of Dilaudid, Ambien, Adderall, Zoloft, Trazadone and Nexium. When she was twenty-four, doctors who felt she had been misdiagnosed helped to wean her off these drugs using careful tapering methods until she was completely medication-free.

Her story – of yet more abuse, trauma and pathologisation – is a sobering read. A young child star who was struggling was diagnosed with several psychiatric disorders she never had, medicated for years and then publicly mocked and criticised as crazy and promiscuous: a hot mess.

Throughout her childhood, Lindsay was subjected to various traumas. Despite having a complex relationship with her mum, which the tabloids have mocked for over a decade, in 2013 her mother stated to the *New York Daily News* that her trauma was all connected to things she witnessed and experienced in childhood.

This important detail seems to have slipped past the general public, who focus on her wild nights out, legal troubles, financial issues and addiction. Despite there being a possible root of her trauma, it has been ignored for decades. Even after all of the years have passed, she has stated several times in interviews that she has been harassed and lied about.

In an interview with the *Daily Mail* in 2016, Lindsay stated that her her mobile phone number had been shared on the internet, and several news outlets had been told that she was pregnant.

But it wasn't just the constant reports in the media.

In 2016, footage surfaced which appeared to show Lindsay being assaulted on a public beach in Greece. In the video which was widely circulated, she ran from the attack to be followed, grabbed, exposed and forced away.

It should be becoming painfully clear by now that what we are witnessing is a pattern of rising fame, sexualisation and then pathologisation of women and girls who are in fact being subjected to abuse, trauma and stress, and struggling to find how to cope, and who they really are in an industry which expects them to be happy, sexy, heterosexual objects of desire for men.

Speaking of sexuality, Lindsay is yet another woman subjected to years of pathologisation who has had long relationships with men and women. Her relationship with DJ Samantha Ronson between 2008 and 2010 was met with scepticism, jokes and even outrage in the press. It is little wonder that she denied it and refuses to confirm whether she is bisexual or not. Sadly, I have come across several LGBT outlets who published articles and blogs blasting her for 'bi-erasure', 'harming bisexual people' and 'denying being queer' which seem to have very little insight into how traumatic and frightening it might be for her to talk openly about her sexuality after years of press harassment, ridicule and male violence.

Whilst I have focused on Disney stars here, it would be wholly inaccurate to state that this journey is limited to their franchise. The 'Sexy but Psycho' blueprint has led to the abuse, harm and death of many women including Amy Winehouse, Whitney Houston, Kate Spade, Carrie Fisher, Anna Nicole Smith, Peaches Geldof, Bobbi Kristina Brown and Tina Turner.

I know how that list might look to some, but maybe it is time we take a step back and reanalyse the lives and deaths of these women?

All of them struggled with their traumas, stress, abuse or pressure of some kind. All of them were, at some point, positioned as wild, out of control, mentally ill, problematic or attention seeking. Instead of a humanistic response to what had been done to them, the public were encouraged to laugh along, gossip, harass them and speculate about their 'breakdowns'.

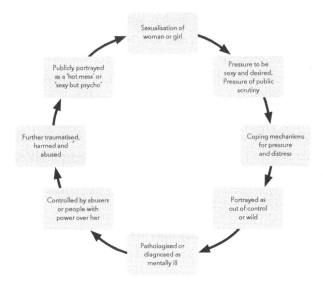

A cycle of sexualisation and pathologisation of women and girls

Sexualisation of woman or girl

Pressure to be sexy and desired. Pressure of public scrutiny

Coping mechanisms for pressure and distress

Portrayed as out of control or wild

Pathologised or diagnosed as mentally ill

Controlled by abusers or people with power over her

Further traumatised, harmed and abused

Publicly portrayed as a 'hot mess' or 'sexy but psycho'

The more I think about this cyclical, repetitive pattern of sexualisation, social pressure, pathologisation, traumatisation and then further sexualisation, the more it becomes clear to me that this is a deliberate, tried and tested process.

In many cases of pathologised and exploited women in the public eye, they have been abused or exploited for years. Their lives have become 24/7 reality TV shows they can never leave. They live in a real-world version of *The Truman Show*. Their trauma and distress are ignored, and we often see comments from people saying that if they want to live in the public eye, they should accept that they are public property, and will always be hounded.

When they speak out about not coping, being distressed, exhausted, or traumatised by the industry or by other factors in their lives, there is very little sympathy for what people perceive them to be: hot messes, devoid of emotion, attention-seeking whores, sex objects who have lost their prowess or angry women with a drink or drug problem.

For some of these women, decades of abuse and trauma have been ignored or turned into entertainment. They become caricatures of the sexy but insane woman stumbling out of a taxi whilst the paparazzi try to get an up-skirt shot. And for the average woman, who is not living in the public eye, who does not have a hoard of photographers following her to the supermarket – her lifelong story of sexualisation and pathologisation is alarmingly similar to Britney, Lindsay, Selena, Demi and Ariana.

The pathologisation of women seems to transcend many different categories and life experiences.

And in this ultimately harrowing realisation, women from all different walks of life are united in their oppression via psychiatry.

CHAPTER 10

Lifelong trauma reframed as incurable madness

There have been some positive things as I've got older, all of my experiences got better and worse at the same time. I got out from under erroneous diagnosis and medication. I was able to figure out the abuse and my marriage and the divorce. I think so much more clearly and I'm a lot more unapologetic now. But things have got worse, like my health plummeting. I've lost forever the chance to share in the magic years of my son's and daughter's childhoods on my own terms, without our interactions – even our happy ones – being diminished and laced with an invisible layer of anguish and fear. All I ever wanted in my heart of hearts, was to be a mum. I wanted to be a loving mother, do volunteer work, create a nice home – but I couldn't. I have to process the finality and the ending. I'll never get to do that and I grieve for my living child and have done for decades and my trauma is not even recognised.

Instead of pathologising trauma as a set of mental disorders and illnesses which, once diagnosed, only ever move from 'remission' to 'relapse' and then back to 'remission' with no cure, I prefer to teach people that processing, understanding and learning to work with your trauma and distress is a lifelong process.

Women's memories and feelings of trauma are naturally triggered and reprocessed at different stages of life (pregnancy, marriage, relationship breakdown, death of parents, death of abusers, illness, successes, relocation, child rearing, older age, etc.) but this is often taken as evidence that psychiatric diagnoses are incurable, lifelong issues.

I will never forget the phone call I took on a rape helpline back in 2013, when an eighty-six-year-old woman rang us after watching a rape of a young woman in a soap opera. She had been raped when she was fifteen years old, and never told anyone. The impact of the rape, and the fact that she could never talk about it, had meant that she had spent her entire life on antidepressants and antipsychotics – but had never had therapy.

She told me that the scenes from the soap opera had made her wonder whether it was the trauma from the rape that had made her so anxious and upset, which seemed to have impacted her periodically throughout her life. I spoke to her about trauma being something that stays with us and changes us, often for the rest of our lives. She pondered whether she ever really needed all those years of medication.

She spoke of how she felt when she got into her first sexual relationship after the rape, and how it impacted her. And then how it impacted her when she became pregnant and gave birth. And the way it made her feel when she saw the perpetrator occasionally. And then how it felt when he was diagnosed with cancer and the whole family rallied around him. And finally, how it felt when he died and her mother told her what a wonderful man he was.

Trauma isn't a one-off event, and so, processing the trauma is not a one-off event either. These are not medical 'relapses' of a mental disorder which require an increased dosage of psychotropic drugs to manage, they are just natural responses to environmental and psychological triggers. However, this deliberate and enduring use of medical descriptors such as 'diagnosis', 'symptoms', 'disorder', 'treatment', 'relapse' and 'remission' is enough to convince women (and the wider public) that their mental health diagnoses are lifelong diseases.

The assumption about trauma is that if it is long lasting, or keeps being retriggered, then there must be an underlying psychiatric cause. However, it is in fact common and purposeful to process and reprocess trauma memories and feelings. It is not a failure, and it is not akin to 'going backwards'.

Many of the women I interviewed had long and complex relationships with trauma, pathologisation, trauma processing and reprocessing. Contrary to what might be said, it is less about resilience and more about endurance.

I once sat in a small restaurant in China Town with a young woman who had been sexually abused, trafficked, addicted to drugs by the perpetrators, and had been in and out of care for years. She was sat in front of me in a different stage of her life. Safe, recovering from the addictions, processing her traumas and studying for her degree. She was incredibly intelligent. We talked about the sensationalisation of the concept of 'resilience'. The fact that the longer you stay in abuse, the 'stronger' you must be. The way professionals tell women and girls that they need to 'build their resilience' when they are being abused by men. The 'resilience' workshops and worksheets. We both hated the misuse of the word 'resilience'.

She looked up at me, over the food, and said, 'You know what, Jess, there is no such thing as resilience, only endurance. There is nothing resilient about a human who is abused and harmed for years, they are just forced to endure more and more harm.'

She changed the way I looked at resilience and endurance in trauma forever.

Some women I interviewed had battled with pathologisation for decades, and were frankly amazing to talk to. I want to use this space to tell you their stories and examine the levels and layers of gaslighting, dismissal, misogyny and pathologisation each woman was subjected to, and what they had to say to professionals.

Naomi's story

In the first week of January 2021, I was grateful to spend a significant amount of time talking to Naomi about her life story and her experiences of pathologisation. Naomi is a fifty-eight-year-old woman who currently resides in Israel and has American dual nationality. She began the interview by saying that she had half a century of these experiences of being pathologised. Her dad was a psychiatrist who worked for the authorities in America. Despite him being a respected mental health professional and lecturer, he abused his wife and his children, including Naomi. By eighteen years old (in 1981) Naomi had been admitted to a long-term locked ward in an asylum where she would remain for eighteen months. When she was in there, she realised that others in the asylum were also sons and daughters of psychiatrists.

Although technically Naomi was a voluntary admission, her admitting doctor told her that if she did not sign the papers, he would have her committed. Despite signing them, Naomi would discover that her legal 'voluntary status' meant nothing. Any time Naomi requested submitting her three-day notice to leave the hospital, which was her legal right, she would be told that if she submitted it, she would also be committed. During her stay, Naomi observed that there were a significant number of other patients who were also the children of psychiatrists. Naomi felt strongly that this was no coincidence. When they shared their experiences, it became clear that they all had fathers who extended their best selves to their patients, then abused and neglected their own children.

> *When I was much younger, I had a sexual relationship that was initiated by my high school history teacher. The abuse started in tenth grade and continued until I graduated. Just a few years ago, around forty years later, my former high school reached out to us all, inviting any former students who were sexually abused by their teacher to come forward and share their experiences. When I discussed this with my psychiatrist who was also my therapist here in Jerusalem, he said to me, 'I wonder what it was about you, that the teacher knew he could play with you?'*

The invitation to alumni to come forward and talk about abuse by faculty members came in response to a recent disclosure by another student. Naomi gave her story to an investigative team. Not only did she report the teacher, but she called out the response of the administration when they protected, supported and defended the teacher, even when he admitted his abuse. They placed the blame on Naomi, and she felt overwhelming guilt and responsibility for what had happened. These feelings continued long after her graduation and were a dominant factor in her cutting herself repeatedly over a number of years.

She continued self-harming. Although the asylum had a reputation for having a psychoanalytic and therapeutic approach, Naomi felt this was far from the truth. They focused more on behaviour modification approaches and other therapies which were 'nothing short of a farce'.

Patients were given more power over other patients than the doctors themselves. When patients wanted to sign out, the other patients would vote as to whether they could leave. Only once all other patients agreed this could a doctor agree the sign out.

They relied on psychiatric diagnoses, lithium and other heavy medications, locked-door seclusion, and wet sheet packing. Naomi was prescribed many drugs before she left, including 1400mg of Thorazine, and a strict seclusion programme which lasted for six months.

Initially I completely trusted psychiatrists and I felt like the hospital was the safest place I could possibly be. And I kept thinking I was safe because I was surrounded by doctors. But then I realised that the doctors barely spoke with me, and they just loaded me up with drugs. I had so many bad reactions to the drugs. Those doctors would have let me rot in seclusion. Even the head nurse found my treatment exceptional and disturbing. When the doctor finally admitted that locked-door seclusion was not working, they released me but put me on six-month mandatory staff escort. Other professionals questioned this. The same doctor told me that I looked like a prostitute when I was stood waiting for my therapy session. Despite both me and the doctor being Jewish, the doctor asked me during therapy who I thought the best Nazi in the room was. This was during a discussion about my self-harming behaviour. I did wonder why they were so invested in putting me down.

Prior to being admitted long term to the asylum, Naomi spent four months on another psychiatric ward. When on the ward, she developed cysts on the bottom of her spine which caused her serious pain. A surgeon came to her, lanced the cysts without any pain relief, and Naomi screamed in pain. She recalled apologising to the doctor for screaming. The next day, the pain returned, and Naomi asked to see a doctor, or to see the surgeon again in case there were other cysts. The ward staff refused and instead told her that she needed to feel the pain.

Naomi became angry and threw a chair, so she was put in seclusion. She was in too much pain to lie on the bare concrete floor and so she stood up the entire time she was in seclusion. When she came out, she called her mother in tears and asked for the surgeon to return to check the site of the cysts. The surgeon did eventually return and confirmed there was another cyst. The second time, the doctor took her to the operating theatre and she was put under anaesthetic correctly. However, she was forced to wait over a year for that surgery, by which point she was already living in the asylum.

> When I was in high school I had an IUD fitted. But it slipped and I kept bleeding very heavily. The nurse in the emergency department was a pro-lifer and was very angry that I had an IUD. She told me to go in the bathroom and pull it out myself. I tried, but I realised I was at risk of seriously damaging myself. So, I went back and told the nurse that I really needed a doctor to do it. Three male doctors came into my room, never uttered a word to me. One doctor removed the IUD whilst the other two stood and watched, and then they all left.

Naomi was subjected to many abusive, oppressive and harmful medical procedures both in the US and in Israel. It was interesting to hear how much she trusted doctors and medical systems until she had been harmed over and over again. Her dad, whilst being abusive and controlling, was a highly respected psychiatrist who practised psycho-analysis. She described him as being a much-loved, ethical and humanistic analyst and teacher in academia, but an abusive man behind closed doors. She was brought up to have trust and respect for medical professionals and systems, and so it was devastating and confusing to be pathologised and harmed by them.

Before his death, her father told her that he would not become a psychiatrist if he was picking a profession today. He said that psychiatry was fraudulent, and psychiatrists were no longer doctors, but only prescribers. Naomi remembers him coming home from a psychiatric conference, extremely angry at the content. He often refuted the biochemical theory of mental illness and lectured on the importance of the therapeutic relationship. Despite this, he never took Naomi to a non-medicating psychiatrist and even used her psychiatric medication induced weight gain to publicly humiliate her. In reality, where her father's abusive behaviour was more obvious, she was sandwiched between two abusive parents and an abusive husband.

Her ex-husband was college educated, but Naomi told me that his childhood had been one of abuse, abandonment, neglect and trauma. By age eight, he had been placed in foster care. Despite this, he became well connected and learned to use the psychiatric systems against his ex-wife and both of his children. Despite having joint custody he often pushed for complete control over the children, and would stop her from seeing them. Naomi was frequently framed as the perpetrator, or told that she should be on psychiatric medications for diagnoses she didn't even know she had. He would often claim that she needed to be on medication in order for her to 'get better', otherwise he would take the children away from her for good.

Eventually, he succeeded in removing both children from Naomi, although their joint custody was never officially revoked.

> *My ex-husband was extremely abusive after the divorce. When my daughter was six, there was an incident where my ex-husband wouldn't give my daughter back to me, although it was my weekend to have her. My lawyer said to me that I needed to set boundaries and go to the police. She said that she wouldn't ordinarily recommend calling the police, but in this case, she felt it necessary to send my ex a strong message that his behaviour could not continue. The police spoke to my ex-husband – I was present too – and they told him that he had to give my daughter over. As soon as we left, my ex drove downtown and obtained an emergency*

order that the police should take my daughter away, and have her taken to an inner city locked-door psychiatric ward for an emergency assessment. He had claimed that my six-year-old daughter was suicidal and was going to kill herself. We hadn't even been home for more than an hour. My daughter was quietly playing, and I was fixing her a meal in the kitchen, when suddenly there was banging on the door. Police were yelling, 'Open up!'

I took my daughter with the police, and when we got there, she was taken to be evaluated. In the ward my ex and his wife turned up with Chinese food and presents for my six-year-old daughter, to demonstrate to the staff what caring and doting parents they were. When my daughter emerged from the doctor's office, my ex asked her what the doctor had said to her. She looked up and said, 'He says I can go home with Mum'. My ex glared at her, and said to her, 'I'm so disappointed in you.'

This response by her ex-husband confirmed for Naomi that this whole stunt was premeditated, using the connections he had with the judge. She was horrified to realise that her ex was willing to have their six-year-old committed to a psychiatric ward, just to get back at Naomi.

Across the years, Naomi tried to protect her children from abuse (and from psychiatric systems), but ultimately, her ex-husband had more power and authority than she did. He finally succeeded in removing the children after years of threatening that if she didn't take psychiatric medication, he would permanently remove her access to her children. She was told by her Rabbi and her psychiatrists that she needed to continue taking the medication in order to parent her children, even though it was making her cry from exhaustion, making her very unwell and causing massive weight gain. She didn't feel safe enough to drive a car under such heavy sedatives and anti-psychotics, but this was ignored. When she raised that she wanted to get divorced, her Rabbi would not support her.

Both her Rabbi and psychiatrist discouraged Naomi from getting divorced although she had disclosed incidents, to both, of abuse to the children by her husband that she had witnessed.

When Naomi expressed her reluctance to go on medication which required her to abruptly stop nursing her infant daughter, both her doctor and Rabbi told her she had her priorities wrong.

All fingers were pointed at Naomi with no questions asked, or discussion of her husband's behaviour.

The day her husband brought her home from a short-term hospitalisation he threatened her and said, 'Look at you, you aren't getting any better. I'm going to take the children away from you for good!' Naomi felt like he was holding a gun to her head.

Finally, once she was extremely ill with a pulmonary embolism and had a 50 per cent chance of surviving, she realised that she must seek a divorce no matter what – otherwise her children would have no mother at all.

As an Orthodox Jew, she spoke to me about the way God would become entwined with psychiatry and medicine, which often resulted in her being given incorrect medical advice, or being given no advice or tests at all.

There was a lot of bad advice from doctors. The doctors often told me to just go back on the meds and stay on the antidepressants. When I told my psychiatrists about the bad treatment I was receiving from the medical doctors, because I was so physically ill, he said to me, 'You must be bringing negative energy to your interactions with the doctors'. They told me no matter what the doctor says to you, you should always remain obedient and

do what they say, even if the recommendations seemed danger-
ous. When I thought I had Crohn's disease the doctor said to me,
'You don't want a diagnosis in physical illness, because once the
doctor makes that diagnosis, God has to work within the diag-
nosis, and you're going to make it really hard for God to heal the
patient.' When I heard this, I was speechless, with my eyes as big
as saucers. I remember thinking I had just entered the five-year-
old mind of my doctor. Despite him being an Orthodox Jew, I
realised we obviously did not pray to the same God. I had a hard
time imagining that the God who created the world and split the
sea, would find it hard to heal a human being no matter what
diagnosis they received. I came to the conclusion that the mental
health and medical practitioners were merely mental and physi-
cal illness manufacturers and managers. How could they claim
being health practitioners when they didn't believe that help was
ever obtainable for their patients? As far as the religious ones
were concerned, if they didn't believe in the ability to heal, and
made statements like that, how could they claim to believe that
God is the ultimate healer?

Naomi explained to me how much she had struggled when her children started to show signs of trauma from the years of abuse, control
and psychiatric referrals. Both children's behaviour became extremely
difficult to deal with. She devoted herself to fighting for education and
resources for her son, while her psychiatrist, on hearing that she had
won funding for her son, asked, 'How did you manage to win? I have
professional colleagues who didn't succeed in getting that funding for
their own children!'

Her husband was abusing her and the children, whilst convincing
professionals and the public otherwise. Tragically, her son was misdiagnosed as having Tourette's, ADHD and paranoid schizophrenia
instead of a response to the trauma from the abuse. One medication

followed another as misdiagnoses continued. When Naomi questioned the diagnoses and the safety of the medication, her concerns were dismissed and it was suggested that she could be accused of negligence if she did not administer the medication. Her ex continued to control and abuse the children into adulthood.

Naomi spoke to me about her memory of deciding to leave America, hoping her teenagers would follow her to Israel.

Saying goodbye to my children and stepping on to the plane alone was one of the most excruciating days of my life. Eventually, my kids did come over to live with me in Israel, but so did my ex and his wife. Despite having gotten total control of the children, and a new wife, he has never stopped trying to punish and destroy my life because I divorced him. When my grown son became a client of a psycho-social programme in Israel, my ex-husband and his new wife went to tell the professionals that I was violent and abusive. The director barred me from having any contact with my son for eight years. The failure of the psychiatrists to help me understand the abuse of my parents and the failure of the psychiatrists, Rabbi and community to protect me and my children from classic instances of post-divorce abuse and domestic violence by proxy that continue till today, not only robbed me of years of my own life, but damaged and continue to damage my children's lives.

Reflecting on her life and spiritual journey, which culminated in becoming an active member of the Orthodox Jewish community for thirty years, Naomi said:

Prior to becoming an Orthodox Jew, I studied Catholicism very deeply as a theology major. I never formally converted to Christianity, but I instead became an Orthodox Jew. It wasn't until I got to Israel, that I realised I had to walk away from Orthodoxy too. I deeply identify as being Jewish, but I don't support anything organised anymore. I strongly believe in God and The Torah, but I am no longer part of a Jewish community. I realised that I really don't fit anywhere. I am neither secular nor religious. I have no longer any faith in psychiatry, doctors, the medical system. I don't partake in anything organised anymore. I cannot stomach the hypocrisy, the misogyny and the patriarchy in it all. I do believe in God, but my trust in God was truly shaken last year when my beloved dog died on Yom Kippur, after a cruel vet had tricked me and lied to me. I couldn't understand why my sweet, innocent and loving dog had to suffer in the last moments of her life, and why I had been sentenced to an existence filled with unresolvable grief, guilt and agony.

After decades of being pathologised, medicated and harmed, we had a discussion about where she finds herself now at fifty-eight years old. It is clear that so many years of trauma and distress have taken their toll on her health and emotional well-being. However, she told me about finding a trauma-informed therapist recently and how much progress she has made in such a relatively short period of time.

I was just an American-Jewish girl, the daughter of a doctor. At age eighteen, I walked into a psych hospital and I thought I would find people who would see me and understand me. I desperately wanted to get well and step into adulthood. I wanted to fulfil my dreams and contribute to repairing. Not only did I lose years of my own life, but the failure on the part of the psychiatrists and hospitals to help me heal from the abuse of my parents, not only robbed me of years of my own life, but damaged my children's lives. It is devastating to realise that my children and I were harmed most by our own people, who harmed my children in their desire to harm me. It would be easier to accept this tragedy if the perpetrators were an external enemy. It is heart-breaking and horrifying that this was not the case.

Helen's story

In summer 2021, Helen* wrote to me from Australia to say that she wanted someone to read her story. The subject of her email was 'My horror story in the mental health system'. I clicked on her email, sort of knowing what was coming. Thousands of women write to me, and when they describe their experiences as 'horror stories', they are not exaggerating. They are often trapped in systems that abuse them, gaslight them, control them and forcibly medicate them.

Helen was no exception, and after years of being subjected to domestic abuse, she had incredible insights into her experiences of the psychiatric services she was in and out of for decades. She told me that she had been told that she had been diagnosed with bipolar disorder as a 'result of domestic violence'.

She described how she was 'incarcerated against my will' in a hospital in Sydney, and her language intrigued me. Throughout her emails to me, she talked about being a prisoner, a criminal, being punished and imprisoned. These are all words that are usually associated with the prosecution and sentencing of serious criminals serving time in a jail – but her experience wasn't dissimilar. She described being put in 'a mental prison for thirteen years – not for any crime I had committed, but for crimes that my former partner and his colleagues committed.'

Her reports of his abuse were dismissed, minimised and ignored – and the hospital often liaised with her abuser, meaning that many of her medical records are based on his opinions and the hearsay of others.

She told me how it had all started, and how she had met her partner in her workplace. They were together for twenty-four years (working together for eleven of those), but he was already much older than her. He seemed the perfect partner at first, but quickly showed his true colours.

It began the way many such relationships do: I met my ex-partner in the workplace, where we developed what seemed to be a solid professional and personal relationship that turned to romance. Initially very heady and romantic, the relationship moved very quickly, with promises of marriage and children all within the space of a few months! He was quite a deal older than myself, was far more educated and astute, and very wealthy. He was also incredibly charming, witty, and had a great intellect. It seemed like he ticked every box for a wonderful partner and future husband. I felt that I had literally met my lifetime soul-mate. And he frequently referred to me as his. However, within about six months, he started to become increasingly more controlling and abusive, both psychologically and physically.

They started living together and got engaged. But despite the way the relationship appeared positive, his abuse was escalating and Helen learned the truth about his abuse of women.

During this time, he abused me on all levels: psychologically, physically, financially, and sexually (via exploitation and servitude). I also came to learn that he had a history of violence against women, porn addiction, and sex offending. Why did I stay with him? I was 'trauma bonded'. Trauma bonding, as I learned too late, is when the intense cycle of abuse and reconciliation makes the victim feel increasingly dependent and connected to the victimiser. During this time I sought counselling with a forensic psychiatrist. He told me he thought I had 'Battered

Woman Syndrome', which means I believed I deserved my
mistreatment and felt hopeless to escape. He also diagnosed me
with Stockholm Syndrome.

It is important to note here that Helen was subjected to the same
pathologising process that many women are: professionals told her
that she stayed because of so-called 'trauma bonding', 'battered
woman syndrome' and 'Stockholm syndrome'.

It may be a shock to some readers to discover that all three of these
diagnoses are based in misogyny and victim blaming – and that I
don't support the existence of any of them. Battered woman syndrome
is a concept developed in the 1970s by Lenore Walker. It became the
go-to diagnosis in the 1980s and 1990s alongside Seligman's concept
of 'learned helplessness', which is still being taught to social work
students in the UK.

What most people do not know, is the origin of 'learned helplessness'.
I myself was staggered and sickened when I found out.

Learned helplessness was theorised in 1967, after American psychologist Martin Seligman administered random electric shocks to dogs
who were strapped into harnesses. I would prefer not to go into
detail of the harm done to the dogs in this book, as it serves no
purpose other than to further traumatise readers; but his conclusion
was that when the dogs were harmed repeatedly, some would
develop a 'maladaptive passivity' to the pain, and eventually give up
trying to escape.

These frankly appalling studies lay the foundation for many other theories and studies which suggest that women and girls who are abused by
men don't escape the abuse because of 'learned helplessness'.

Even to this day, sources such as HealthLine and the International Classification of Diseases (ICD) list it as a 'serious mental health condition'. This is one of the most blatant examples of pathologising the response to being beaten and abused by men.

It's amazing to think that there is no such thing as 'men who batter women syndrome' but there is 'battered woman syndrome'.

If that wasn't problematic enough, Stockholm syndrome is another diagnosis that is widely accepted as real, despite being based on misinformation. People tend to know that the term 'Stockholm syndrome' was coined by psychiatrist Nils Bejerot, and was spread by the media in 1973 after four hostages were taken during a bank robbery in Stockholm, Sweden. The story, as it is told, is that a woman who was taken hostage by one of the bank robbers formed a positive relationship with the perpetrator, and a psychiatrist 'diagnosed' her with a syndrome which meant that she developed feelings for her captor.

It has been referenced and romanticised in music and films for decades since, including Bond film *The World is Not Enough*, in which a woman who is kidnapped falls in love with the perpetrator. *Beauty and the Beast* is said to be an example of 'Stockholm syndrome' too.

What is often ignored, however, is that Nils Bejerot never spoke to the woman, and when she publicly criticised him for his distance diagnosis of her – he told the press that this was part of her syndrome. Her criticism of him, making up a psychiatric syndrome, was part of the psychiatric syndrome. Now, where have we heard that before?

Trauma bonding on the other hand, is a more modern and common term, but one which unfortunately has similar connotations. As with Stockholm syndrome, this term suggests that victims of trauma and abuse bond with their abusers or oppressors, and become emotionally attached to them. What all of these syndromes seem to ignore is that women who are being controlled and abused by men have very little choice but to stay and form some sort of attachment – if it wasn't there already, caused by the deliberate grooming process of the man abusing them.

The description of a woman who is too scared to try to escape a violent and dangerous abuser as having a 'syndrome' is the epitome of victim blaming.

Despite these labels, Helen, like many other women I interviewed for this book, had total faith in the mental health system, and felt that it would be the safest place she could be. Instead, she spoke of arriving in what felt like a prison, where her belongings were confiscated and she had no way to contact friends and family.

When I was first admitted to my local public hospital, I breathed a sigh of relief, believing in all the hype you hear in the media of mentally unwell and traumatised patients receiving the 'help' they sorely need. However, this could not be further from the truth. What I encountered instead was a mental health system that treats patients like they are criminals. In place of a quiet, peaceful, therapeutic place of healing, I encountered something more akin to prison, and the hospital staff more like prison screws [guards]. I quickly learned the routine. The moment you arrive, all of your bags are searched, including your personal handbag. Your mobile phone and purse are immediately confiscated and not returned to you for your entire stay in hospital, nor are you allowed access to social media. You can request your purse later – that's if you don't mind lining up in a queue and waiting for up to four hours for your purse to be released from the hospital's safe. In the end, you just stop asking for it.

Helen went on to discuss an intriguing experience which I have found to be common: the illusion of 'voluntary admission' to psychiatric services. Many of the women I interviewed were not directly sectioned, but were told that they were in the mental health unit 'voluntarily'. Despite this, none of them were actually able to leave the hospital, and all were threatened with formal sectioning under the Mental Health Act if they did try to leave. That has never sounded very 'voluntary' to me.

> *If you admit yourself to hospital as a 'voluntary patient', presumably you are free to go anytime you wish, and to refuse psychiatric medication and other treatment, so long as you inform the staff of your refusal and that you plan to leave the hospital. As a voluntary patient, you supposedly have the right to change your mind. However, if you try to assert that right, the hospital just 'schedules' (sections) you under the Mental Health Act. In my case, the doctors kept harassing me about accepting the high dosages of medications they wanted to force on me. Otherwise, I was told, I would be scheduled. In other words, accept excessive treatment you do not want, and remain incarcerated against your will, but do it as a 'voluntary patient' under duress. Or as one doctor put it, 'We can play this game all day if you like, but the result will be the same.'*

The phrase 'playing a game' is appalling to hear from a doctor – almost like they knew they were in total power, and women trying to assert their freedom and rights were just part of a silly power dynamic game that women played, but would never win. The doctor in Helen's case knew that no matter what she tried, or what she said, she would be sectioned and medicated anyway, so she had no real power.

Helen explained that when she tried to report or talk about being a victim of domestic and sexual abuse, it was cast aside as another delusion of a crazy woman, and that she was often told by doctors and medical staff that she was making it all up for attention.

> *Nothing can sway them, not even physical evidence of abuse. At one point, I turned up to the emergency department visibly distressed, with medical evidence of a serious sexual assault by my former partner that even required surgery to stem the bleeding. But it made no impact. They treated my sexual assault in a rather cavalier manner, and then later reverted back to referring to my domestic violence as a 'fixed delusion', labelling me with a 'persecution complex'. The assault was bad enough, but their disbelief and attitude re-traumatised me.*

Helen spoke of something that was, again, common to so many women – the experience of being called delusional, or told you have some form of victim complex. In Helen's case, her obvious injuries were ignored and then her disclosures were reframed as delusions, and she was described as having an irrational and obsessive belief that she was subjected to hostility and abuse by others.

> *For example, at one point, a doctor writing a medical report on me described my domestic violence experience as a 'persecution hallucination'. Other doctors referred to it as 'having some adjustment issues with her boyfriend'. Yeah, I was having trouble adjusting to my partner's horrific abuse. If it weren't so serious, it would be funny.*

I agreed with Helen. This level of outright denial of her abuse by professionals, to the point where they invented syndromes, complexes and delusions – repeatedly – is ridiculous. Would it really have been so hard to simply listen to her, and believe her?

What she described next truly chilled me; however, it was not uncommon. Helen was advised by mental health nurses that she was irritating doctors by talking about being abused, and if she wanted to be released, she would need to stop talking about her abuse, and her desire to report her partner to the police.

Here's the thing: Helen's desire to report her abusive and violent partner to the police was being used as evidence that she was delusional and manic – so her choice was made for her. She either had to shut up about being abused, or remain in the psychiatric ward indefinitely.

I was told by nursing staff that when I kept talking about my domestic violence to my doctors, this 'irritates them', and if I wanted to be released, I had to 'learn to play the game'. If hearing about unpleasant things is irritating, maybe psychiatry isn't the job for you. I also found that even when you try to cooperate, you can't win. During one hospital admission, I made the mistake of telling one of the male doctors 'caring for' me that I was feeling better and ready to go home and that I planned to report the abuses to police. For this confession, I was met with a disapproving glare and hauled before a medical tribunal on the pretext that I was 'manic'. The male magistrate at the tribunal upheld the doctor's decision to section me for a further three to six weeks, or at the doctor's discretion. Since they didn't take my reports of abuse seriously in the first place, articulating that I was going to report my abuser was further evidence of derangement in their eyes.

After weeks more of forced medication and imprisonment simply for stating that she wanted to report her partner to the police, the staff started talking to her partner and his professional colleagues – and took their word above Helen's.

As much as this may come across as repetitive by this point, this is also not uncommon. During the research for this book, I interviewed several women who were sectioned and medicated because doctors and nurses kept calling or meeting their abusive partners who, of course, agreed that their victim was totally crazy, and lying about being abused.

Then, after the hospital staff had numerous chats with my abusers, they started siding with them, after which they started systematically brainwashing me into believing that the abuses 'aren't real' and that they're all due to a manifestation of 'a chemical imbalance in your brain'. Which ultimately lets your abuser off the hook. To use a spurious, unproven 'chemical imbalance theory', which this hospital heavily promotes, to discredit a person's experience of domestic violence is another vile injustice. Year after year, the hospital continued to communicate and collaborate with my ex, to zombify me with drugs – even after Victims of Crime (a government tribunal to whom I reported my abuse) had concluded that my account was truthful and compensated me for personal injury due to my rape.

Despite a review which investigated her case as a victim of crime, and after Helen was financially compensated for years of abuse and torture at the hands of her ex-partner and his colleagues, she was still treated as though she was a delusional, attention-seeking mental illness patient who was regularly forcibly injected with antipsychotics and sedatives.

If you remember, the subject of Helen's email was 'My horror story in the mental health system'. She repeatedly described her experiences as being akin to being imprisoned and punished for serious crime, and in some ways her email returned full circle when she finished by writing about a quote from the influential Thomas Szasz.

Social critic and psychiatrist Dr Thomas Szasz once said: 'Mental hospitals are the POW camps of our unarticulated wars.' What I and other female victims of domestic violence I met endured at the hands of the patriarchal psychiatrists at this major hospital were nothing short of human rights abuses.

Having reflected on the life stories provided by Helen and Naomi, I felt exhausted and angry for both of them. Such articulate, dedicated, intelligent women had been consistently medicated, diagnosed and gaslit for so many years, it was hard to understand how either of them coped for so long. Their strength amazed and confused me. They were both up against so much, with abusers that used psychiatric systems to control and harm them by proxy.

Both women had been subjected to so many life-changing traumas, and yet they were ignored. They were told that they were mentally disordered, and given medication which harmed their bodies for years. Both women were threatened and coerced into taking medications which caused serious side effects, often by using their children against them. Both Helen and Naomi had reached older age without having their original traumas of sexual abuse validated or addressed. They never received justice or support, and instead spent decades being told that their issues were chemical imbalances in their brains, delusions or mental disorders. Both women had abusive partners and families who learned to use their mental health records against them.

It is nothing short of a miracle that they are still here today – and a testament to how much they, and women like them, are able to push through against all odds. Throughout the interviews, the women I spoke to had many similar experiences, and messages for readers of this book. They want an end to pathologisation, and for their traumas to be recognised and responded to with dignity and empathy. It seems such a small ask, but it certainly isn't being achieved by any of our systems at present.

Some women, however, are not still with us. Many die by suicide or accidental overdose. Some die from the side effects of dangerous medication. Some are killed by abusive partners.

Euthanasia as a 'cure' of women's madness

One other way that women who are diagnosed with mental disorders die, is by the relatively new practice of 'psychiatric euthanasia'. At present, this practice (of giving people permission to die by lethal drugs) is only legal in the Netherlands and Belgium. The laws surrounding this form of euthanasia state that the person must be in unbearable mental pain, in which three psychiatrists agree that there is no reasonable prospect of improvement, and there is no reasonable alternative than dying.

So far, all of the young women who have died by euthanasia and had their cases reported in the media have been subjected to sexual abuse and significant trauma. These cases are devastating, not least because they represent the worst possible outcome for women who are pathologised by a system which convinces women and girls that they have incurable mental illnesses that will affect them for the rest of their lives.

Had anyone considered that this narrative, based on centuries of misogyny, dodgy science and myths about the brain would lead to young women seeking euthanasia to kill themselves with the approval of three doctors who agreed that there was nothing more anyone could do for their psychiatric illness?

This is a vital question for everyone. It is especially pertinent to those who believe that women and girls have mental disorders, brain chemical imbalances and genetic predispositions. Do you really believe in the medical model of mental health to such an extent, that you would treat trauma as a terminal illness from which the only escape is death?

In the Netherlands in January 2018, twenty-nine-year-old Aurelia Brouwers drank the lethal mixture of poisons which would voluntarily euthanise her. She said in a statement, *'I'm twenty-nine years old and I've chosen to be voluntarily euthanised. I've chosen this because I have a lot of mental health issues. I suffer unbearably and hopelessly. Every breath I take is torture. When I was twelve, I suffered from depression. And when I was first diagnosed, they told me I had Borderline Personality Disorder. Other diagnoses followed – attachment disorder, chronic depression, I'm chronically suicidal, I have anxiety, psychoses, and I hear voices.'*

There are several key arguments for why I believe this should never have been allowed to happen. The first is that the diagnoses themselves are highly contested, biased, misogynistic and are utilised when women and girls are subjected to significant trauma and abuse. If the diagnoses are so contested, and have such a controversial evidence base in the scientific literature, how can they be used with such lethal certainty to argue that there was no hope of improvement for Aurelia?

Secondly, it is absolutely normal for women and girls subjected to significant trauma to frequently consider suicide and death. This is a normal trauma response, and arises for many different reasons including helplessness, hopelessness, powerlessness, exhaustion, oppression and closure. This is not a psychiatric illness, or mental disorder, it is a common and explainable reaction to extreme harm. It is clear from Aurelia's many media appearances, and the blogs and articles that she wrote in the lead-up to her death, that the psychiatric diagnoses, medication and sectioning were all contributing to her distress and trauma. She wrote that her diagnoses got more and more complicated, until she was told that there was no realistic hope of improvement for her, and so, she decided that she didn't want to live a life like that.

And that would make sense, if psychiatry and the medical model of mental health were not but mere theories. However, they are just theories, and there are competing theories of mental health and mental illness.

Many doctors would never sign off the death of a person and legally agree that they had no prospect of improvement from trauma and mental distress. In fact, Aurelia's own doctor refused to support her application for voluntary euthanasia. I believe it is impossible to prove that her experiences would never get better, and that she would be better off dead.

Therefore, this is not the same as someone being told that they have a terminal, late-stage disease that is causing them severe pain and suffering, by which they would surely die within weeks or months. And herein then, lies the truth: mental illness is not the same as physical illness. Mental health is not the same as physical health. It is not the same as a broken leg or a headache which we take painkillers for. No matter how much money, celebrity and palatable language has been pumped into public campaigns to assimilate mental health with physical health, this is factually incorrect.

Thirdly, this worrying approach sets a precedent which has already seen more and more young women come forward to end their lives by voluntary euthanasia on the grounds of psychiatric illness with no prospect of improvement. Why would any professional want to see an approach to women's trauma which encourages or supports voluntary euthanasia as a legitimate option for 'treatment'?

Noa Pothoven was seventeen years old when she starved herself to death in 2019, after she was subjected to sexual violence. She had talked about wanting voluntary euthanasia, but had not been granted the licence to die. Instead, she made the decision to stop eating and drinking until she died, and announced this on her social media accounts. Rather than attempting to protect and save her, it was agreed by doctors that there was no realistic prospect of improvement, and they withdrew her feeding tubes and granted her wish to die.

Another unnamed Dutch woman in her early twenties died by voluntary euthanasia after she disclosed that she was sexually abused between the ages of five and fifteen years old, had been diagnosed with multiple psychiatric disorders and was deemed to be so mentally ill that she too had no reasonable prospect of improvement (*Independent*, 2016). She was told she had 'incurable PTSD and chronic depression'. This decision was made despite her records showing that intensive trauma therapy before her death had 'significantly improved' her mental health. Doctors stated that she had multiple psychiatric conditions that could not be cured, and therefore agreed to the euthanasia.

As hard as it is to believe, this particular case was released by the Dutch government as a best-practice example to showcase the high levels of care and the stringent decision-making process for euthanasia.

How stringent can the process be, when it doesn't even take into account how problematic the evidence base is for so called psychiatric conditions being incurable? And what about the evidence base which suggests that women and girls are significantly more likely to be diagnosed and medicated with these disorders, instead of having their traumas and experiences validated?

Are we really witnessing the beginning of psychiatry using death as a treatment for women's trauma?

It appears that we already did.

CHAPTER 11

Curing a sick system

We now have a new lens with which to view women's distress and coping strategies – as perfectly normal responses to trauma. There is nothing 'mad' or 'bad' about the women, their responses make complete sense and are logical given what they have been subjected to. That's not to say that we minimise their struggles or diminish the distress they may be experiencing; we acknowledge that they may be finding it hard to cope, they may be feeling scared, angry, and sad and the feelings may be overwhelming. But by moving away from pathologisation, we are able to position these 'symptoms' outside of the woman, and send the message to her that there is nothing 'wrong' with her.

Kellie-Anne, CEO of Kairos WWT

Women and girls are being pathologised, discredited, mocked, humiliated, gaslit and then diagnosed as mentally ill. Women are being told that their psychiatric disorders are so incurable that they would be better off euthanised. All the while, the 'end mental health stigma' brigade fail to understand the history and context of psychiatry, or the systems of oppression they are supporting. In addition, women and girls are now having psychiatric diagnosis sold back to them as validating, edgy and sexy.

We are looking at the most insidious and intelligent rebranding of oppression and sedation of women that we have ever seen. It's oppression, but make it sexy.

How do we tackle the enormity of the issues I have raised in this book?

First, I will discuss why professionals support this practice – and how this became so acceptable. Second, I will discuss my own ideas and theories of how to create lasting and meaningful alternatives and changes to this archaic and dangerous discipline. Third, I will argue that feminism must divorce itself from psychiatry, pathologisation and the mental health movement. Fourth, I will suggest an independent system that could protect everyone from this practice in the future.

Why do professionals support this practice?

With such alarming examples, it would be understandable to question if, and why, professionals support the pathologisation of women and girls at all. Do professionals really support the medicalisation and psychiatric diagnosis of so many women and girls, and if they do support it, why do they support it?

In my experience, the vast majority of professionals working with women and girls do not set out to pathologise or harm them. They don't even consciously subscribe to the medical model of mental health; in fact, most of them don't know what the medical model of mental health is. In years of teaching and training professionals, I have only come across a handful of them who know there are any theories of mental health at all.

The sad reality is that rather than there being a vast, deliberately abusive workforce hellbent on sectioning and medicating women and girls, there is instead a massive gap in knowledge and skill. A gap better described as a canyon. Or The Grand Canyon.

For decades, professionals have been trained in the dominant model of mental health – the medical model. Even those who don't fully agree with it find themselves lacking in alternatives. They pathologise women and girls without knowing what pathologisation is. They push for 'support with their mental health' without knowing that it will lead to the psychiatric diagnosis of their client, which will have lifelong consequences for her. They think that they are doing their best by 'validating' the mental health experiences of a woman or girl and 'empowering' her to seek medical help. They seldom understand the system they are referring her into, or what 'mental health' is a misnomer for.

When retraining professionals, I like to use a description of a woman who was abused in childhood. It is written as they would commonly see it in day-to-day practice.

> *Mandeep was abused and exploited through childhood and into early adulthood. She has been diagnosed with attachment disorder, borderline personality disorder and agoraphobia. She is difficult to engage, refuses to talk to staff, denies any abusive experiences and has some problematic behaviours.*

This type of referral is common, and is based on medical model language. I show this to professionals and ask them how this referral makes them feel.

In every session, thousands of professionals tell me that it makes them feel powerless, overwhelmed, inadequate, out of their depth and stressed. They tell me that they feel they could not work with Mandeep and she would need referring back to the mental health team. They say she is too complex, too problematic. They fear that her mental health issues would make her too unstable to make any real progress with her.

Then I show them the second version of the referral, written from a trauma-informed perspective, and ask them the same set of questions.

> *Mandeep was abused and exploited through childhood and into early adulthood. She is frequently scared, she struggles with trauma responses and she feels overwhelmed by our services. She is very scared of small spaces and rooms. She does not want to talk about the abuse, and is not ready to talk yet. She does not trust professionals and often backs away when people probe too deeply or make her feel unsafe.*

Interestingly, the same professionals who moments earlier were feeling that Mandeep was beyond help are suddenly feeling much more empathy and understanding towards her. Professionals often tell me that the second description is more human, more useful and more respectful. They tell me that they feel they can help her, and that her responses to the abuse are totally understandable. They don't feel a referral to mental health teams is necessary anymore.

And herein lies the issue: professionals hold views about mental health diagnoses and psychiatric disorders which stigmatise and stereotype women and girls as difficult, problematic and stressful – so they pass them to someone else. But when we remove the stigmatising labels and the diagnosis from the descriptions of the very same women, they relate to them and want to help them.

For many professionals, this exercise is the lightbulb moment in our module, where they realise that they work in a system which has always pathologised women.

But what about the abusive, power-hungry professionals that women and other professionals have talked about in this book? Do they exist in our services?

The answer is, of course, yes. Yes, we have abusive professionals in our services. We have racists in our services. We have misogynists in our services. We have dangerous people in our services.

The problem is, if the entire model is based on control, power, misogyny, racism, homophobia, grooming and gaslighting towards the clients, how on earth could you pick out a bad apple?

Or maybe, as American psychologist Philip Zimbardo often argued, the issue isn't one of a 'few bad apples', but of a bad barrel. If the system exists to stigmatise, pathologise and control non-conforming and traumatised people, then how could we even argue that those people are bad apples at all? Aren't they just behaving in the way the model has always taught them to?

Don't these professionals see themselves as superior and more worthy of human rights because that's exactly what psychiatry has been suggesting for over a century? How could we ever claim to be able to rid mental health of these dangerous and abusive people, if the entire framework supports them?

Whilst I was writing this book, I was working with an organisation who contacted me and asked me to support them with their practice, policies and approaches to working with women in prostitution to be non-pathologising and trauma-informed.

Kairos WWT, based in Coventry, had already been working in a woman-centred way for many years, but they wanted to challenge themselves to reject pathologisation, and encourage their partner agencies to follow their example.

When I first started working with them, their staff members discussed many case studies and examples of the pathologisation of the women they worked with. Emma Mitchell runs the 'A Home of Her Own' project, which supports women in prostitution with their accommodation and safe housing. She told me the story of Kayla, who had a diagnosis of bipolar disorder. She was released from prison without her medication. The supported accommodation knew that she did not have her medication; therefore, any time she was distressed it was blamed on her bipolar and the fact that she was not taking her medication.

However, her distress was valid. Kayla was in female-only accommodation, but her room could be accessed at any time by both male and female staff as part of the licence agreement. The staff would enter if they wanted to carry out a safe and well check, or to do a room inspection. Kayla had been subjected to domestic and sexual violence, including being held hostage and forced to do sex work.

The staff made this worse when she set up a camera to prove that, in her words, 'she was not going mad'. For months, the staff had argued that Kayla was paranoid and no one was coming into her room. The staff were seen on her camera entering the room and waving at the camera whilst laughing. This caused her extreme distress, not only because they were laughing into her camera, but because this proved that she was never 'suffering from paranoia'.

The final incident at the accommodation was when she had been drinking. She had barricaded herself into a room as she felt unsafe, the police were called and demanded she open the door. When she did, the male police officer shouted at her and said, 'Look at the fucking state of you, you need to get your shit together!' She was then taken to a new accommodation by a police car.

I asked CEO Kellie-Anne about the pathologisation of the women they work with, and why she chose to lead the organisation towards systemic change.

At Kairos Women Working Together we support women who have been subjected to or are at risk of sexual exploitation. Many are involved in street-based prostitution. As an organisation our values centre on meeting women where they are at, passing no judgement, respecting women's choice and providing services and support that the women themselves identify as what they need. Almost all of the women disclose to us that they've been subjected to historical or current sexual and/or domestic violence and abuse, and other traumatic experiences. We see that so many of them are labelled as 'chaotic' and 'complex', 'addicts', 'engaged is risky behaviour' and are so often diagnosed with or presumed to have various mental health disorders ranging from anxiety and depression through to bipolar disorder and personality disorders.

I worked with Kellie-Anne and her team of staff and volunteers to reach their goal of challenging the victim blaming and pathologisation of the women they worked with, which involved weeks of interactive education and training sessions. This work is not easy to do. Change is not easy to accomplish. Even in this relatively small team of women, many of them had been subjected to years of male violence and had themselves been pathologised. This doesn't always mean that they are resistant to changing the way they think and talk about women's mental health (in this team, it was quite the opposite as they were so ready for change), but the sessions were personally triggering for almost everyone.

To help professionals to see their clients differently, first, I have to help them to see themselves differently. Women, and professionals, have been taught to pathologise, self-diagnose and medicate themselves. They often believe they have disorders, or have been told they do by other professionals. My sessions can be heavy for everyone, especially when professionals have never been encouraged to be open about their own connections to their work and to their clients.

Further than this, we have created a curious dynamic in support services of all kinds where we pretend there is a difference between us, and our clients. The professionalisation of human support services has created a 'them and us' divide between the supporter and those seeking support. This means that professionals are expected to do two things:

1. Never admit or speak about their own traumas, or their own mental health
2. Never connect with their client on a personal level, or on common ground

This was something that came up for me whilst I was doing my PhD. I was advised to stop talking about my personal experiences, and my childhood, or risk being seen as one of the patients. I was taken to one side more than once, and warned that no one would take me seriously as an academic or as a psychologist if I admitted that I struggled too. The belief here is clear: we should never show 'weakness' as a professional, we should maintain the illusion that we have our shit together at all times. That we are infallible. That we are perfect. That we are the experts, and they are the clients.

And it's all a load of bollocks, really.

Professionals of all human disciplines are often traumatised, and dealing with their own lives and struggles. They are certainly not perfect, or objective, or infallible. It's all an illusion. A smokescreen.

Just as the image of the authoritative, perfect psychiatrist in a tweed suit, smoking a pipe, psychoanalysing his mentally ill patient who is lying on a leather chaise longue having a breakdown is an illusion of power created by patriarchy and psychiatry – so is the illusion that social workers, therapists, psychologists and mental health professionals are all perfect people with perfect lives, feeling healthy and content.

I often say that the most dangerous professionals working in this field are the ones who tell you that they are 'completely objective', 'only make decisions based on the facts' and can 'leave their personal stuff at the door'. In my view, any professional who says these things lacks basic self-awareness, and considers themself above human bias, and human error. Anyone who truly believes they can cut off their experiences, biases, socialisation and upbringings whilst they work with humans has no capacity (or desire) for self-reflection or humility.

Kellie-Anne and her team were unique in this sense, because they had developed an authentic working environment which meant that professionals could talk about their own triggers, their experiences of male violence and their own stressors. Part of the process then, was encouraging a trauma-informed environment for the professionals, so they could foster that with the women they worked with.

I think the entire team would agree that it was challenging, but valuable. They had many different layers of pathologisation to explore and consider, on their journey to becoming a trauma-informed and anti-pathologising service for women.

The work has challenged us to think critically about these labels and ask ourselves if our practice can really be trauma-informed if we as a service collude with a system that pathologises women's trauma. We now have a new lens with which to view women's distress and coping strategies – as perfectly normal responses to trauma. There is nothing 'mad' or 'bad' about the women, their responses make complete sense and are logical given what they have been subjected to. That's not to say that we minimise their struggles or diminish the distress they may be experiencing; we acknowledge that they may be finding it hard to cope, they may be feeling scared, angry, and sad and the feelings may be overwhelming. But by moving away from pathologisation, we are able to position these 'symptoms' outside of the woman, and send the message to her that there is nothing 'wrong' with her.

It's an incredible outcome, to see a service invest their time and compassion into centring the women they work with, and rejecting the psychiatric diagnosis of their traumas, poverty, exploitation, dependency, homelessness and distress. The team went on to change their charity ethos, and their internal language and processes. Further, they decided to become a beacon of trauma-informed practice for other services and professionals in the area, and invited all of their partners to a free training day with me, to learn about their journey and why they had decided to make the leap to a fully trauma-informed service.

One of the reasons they did this was because they recognised that even if Kairos adopted a fully trauma-informed approach to their work, they would still exist in a structure of local and national organisations and institutions that would pathologise, diagnose and medicate the women they were working with. They knew that they would be frequently in a position where they would be advocating for the rights of the women they work with, but would be told that the medication was necessary, or vital if they wanted to keep their accommodation, or even their children.

For this reason, they have chosen to take their activism further, and to work with as many statutory and third-sector partners as possible, to influence them to also adopt trauma-informed approaches in their own work. So far, they have started to influence legal professionals, NHS workers, police, social workers, and other local charitable organisations.

And they are not alone.

One of the most inspirational and influential organisations in the UK is 'Drop the Disorder', which recently celebrated its fifth birthday of activism and support. Founded by psychotherapist Jo Watson, I have seen Drop the Disorder go from strength to strength.

DTD is a grassroots, collaborative, activist, academic and survivor movement to challenge the pathologisation and psychiatric harm of people from all walks of life. They offer affordable and free events, discussions, social media networks, conferences, and books that anyone can access and understand. As I write this, their Facebook group (which I am a part of) has over 13,000 members.

Academics have been working to create trauma-informed alternatives to the medical model too, with Dr Lucy Johnstone and Professor Mary Boyle developing and publishing the Power Threat Meaning Framework. PTMF helps professionals to identify distress and trauma without using psychiatric diagnosis or medication, and has been published by the British Psychological Society.

Whilst I was finishing this book, fourteen more organisations and authorities contacted me to ask if I could help them to achieve the same thing. Meaning: change is possible.

Maybe, people are ready for it?

Let's cause change

I propose that there are ten direct ways to challenge, and then end, the pathologisation of women and girls. We have a responsibility to protect women and girls from this system of oppression, no matter how legitimised and protected it has become. Some of my proposals here may sound drastic, but it is my view that nothing less than drastic will work. We need urgent change, and we need to stop this lifelong cycle of oppressing women and girls by convincing them that they are mentally disordered.

1. Stop sharing and using psychiatric misinformation

The first and most crucial step is to immediately stop the sharing and utilisation of misinformation and myth from psychiatric theories such as the 'brain chemical imbalance' and that ECT poses no risk to patients, that medication 'rebalances chemicals in your brain', or that 'mental illness is genetic'. All of these narratives are contributing to a society which does not understand, or seek to understand, trauma. Children in school, students at university, professionals in training are still being taught myths and narratives that the APA and WHO themselves now publicly reject.

Despite this, millions of people still believe that mental health issues are caused by brain chemical imbalances and genetics from their parents. Neither of these theories is accurate and it is now time that genuine retractions and reparations are arranged.

GPs and nurses are still telling their patients every single day that they have brain chemical imbalances that don't exist, cannot be tested for, cannot be proven, and cannot be shown to have changed whilst on the medication which claims to correct them.

Doctors should not be able to give misleading or incorrect information about psychotropic drugs, and there should be clear pathways for accountability where this has occurred. I spoke to many women who were never told about the side effects or withdrawal impacts of their drugs. More interestingly, I have seen professionals deny that there are any side effects or withdrawal symptoms from commonly used medications. This has to change.

Labelling on medications, including descriptions and FDA announcements should be scrutinised and challenged until they are accurate. Advertisements for psychiatric medication should not be allowed to use sensationalist language, imagery or claims.

Informed consent and bodily autonomy should be prioritised at all times. Doctors and mental health professionals should have to have full conversations with their patients before prescribing drugs. They should have to explain how they work, why they are prescribing them, what side effects they might experience, how long they will be taking them for, and how it will feel when they stop taking them. Accurate, neutral information should be the gold standard – and the gold standard should be expected of everyone. They should also have lists of common questions and concerns that they can discuss with their patient, along with viable alternatives if their patient decides that they do not want to go ahead with the medication.

2. Commission an independent inquiry into the mass medication and psychiatric diagnosis of women and girls

Western countries that have bought into the psychiatric diagnosis of women and girls wholesale for decades, now need to commission independent inquiries and investigations to establish how many women and girls have been harmed by this practice, and how many of them have been medicated, undergone surgery, been subjected to ECT, been harmed by dosages of psychotropic medication and tranquillisers and how many have died.

Further, independent inquiries are now required to explore why the UK NHS (and health services around the world) are using such high levels of forced injection tranquillisers on girls under the age of eighteen in comparison to boys, and why the majority of all ECT patients in the UK are women over the age of sixty. This disparity must be accounted for, and explained. Having said this, I sincerely doubt there will be any scientific rationale for why the majority of all people forced to undergo ECT treatment are older women.

There needs to be transparency and dignity during this process, as women and girls of all ages have been impacted by psychiatric diagnosis and treatments. Independent inquiries and investigations (and academic research where possible) should focus on the links between women and girls who report male violence, and how many of them are then diagnosed with psychiatric disorders. Conversely, inquiries and investigations should explore the lack of criminal justice for women and girls who are considered or diagnosed with mental disorders; especially in rape, domestic abuse and sexual abuse trials.

For this to work, services need to stop acting like PR machines and corporate companies with marketing to think about. Human safety and human rights should come first. There needs to be less focus on reputation and brand management, and more focus on ethical practice. The public are losing trust in health systems, criminal justice systems, governments and professionals for one main reason: no one is being transparent with them. Statistics are fudged, buzzwords have replaced integrity, virtue-signalling campaigns are used instead of creating any systemic change, errors are covered up, professionals protect each other and organisations adopt policies that benefit themselves. The public might not know the ins and outs of all of this, but they do know it's happening, and they can feel when they are being lied to.

Interestingly, they are often called 'delusional', 'paranoid' and 'conspiracy theorists' when they attempt to hold institutions to account for malpractice. Now, where have we heard that before?

3. Ban the use of psychiatric accusations when women disclose, report, or give evidence about male violence or abuse

One of the most effective ways of stopping women and girls from getting justice or a fair process, is to accuse them of being mentally ill. Again, whilst the public campaigns claim that there is no stigma of 'mental health', all levels of justice systems rely upon this stigma to collapse trials and force withdrawals of statements and evidence.

There needs to be a clear ban on implying or accusing women and girls of being psychotic, delusional, mentally ill, crazy, emotionally unstable or any other psychiatric term to discredit their statements in a family or criminal court. To continue to do this should be seen as a breach of the Equality Act (2010) which protects against discrimination using mental health as a perceived or real characteristic.

To use mental health, disorder, diagnoses or any other accusation aimed at the mental well-being of someone in a court should be seen to be discrimination using protected characteristics like any other. This argument should be applied across disciplines, into the family court, safeguarding services and beyond. There should be no assumptions made about someone based on psychiatric labels.

To this end, there needs to be an investigation into forced or coerced psychiatric or psychological evaluations of women and girls in criminal and family courts. At present, no matter what the woman or girl says, she will be subjected to prejudice. She cannot freely refuse a psychiatric evaluation, even if she knows it will be used to discredit her, or oppress her. If she refuses the evaluation, she will be seen as refusing because she is mentally ill, non-compliant or deviant. If she accepts the psychiatric evaluation, there is a very high chance that she will be flippantly diagnosed by an unregulated court 'expert' as having a disorder after just one hour of meeting with them.

In this context, psychiatry is frequently used as a weapon against women and girls in justice processes, and this needs to stop immediately. Again, it would be useful if this could be contextualised within the Equality Act (2010), and for legislators to consider whether this amounts to discrimination.

Conversely, we need to stop the process of police officers, social workers, mental health professionals, lawyers and barristers from seeking psychiatric diagnoses of their own clients in order to 'prove psychological harm'. There is no need to use lifelong psychiatric labelling – which will prejudice their client, and subject their client to years of mind-altering drugs – in order to prove that serious crime causes trauma. Use research, use qualified expert witnesses – or – just ask your client for a statement. Use the victim impact statements properly, and not just as some bolt-on administrative task that you have to do because you're supposed to.

It might seem like a good idea at the time, to use psychiatric diagnoses as proof that rape, abuse or trafficking has harmed your client, but the acts are already illegal, and the risks to your client of medication and psychiatric diagnoses (that they may never be able to remove from their files) far outweigh the benefits.

If, as many people say, there is no stigma or pathologisation attached to diagnosis, and evaluation, treatment and medication is all a completely free and informed choice, there should be no problem with my proposals here.

4. Adopt a trauma-informed approach to mental health at every level of every system

We must now move past the era of medicalising and pathologising trauma, distress, emotion and suffering. Our systems don't work. We have created hundreds of psychiatric disorders and hundreds of psychiatric treatments, and yet, we have made no advances or improvements to the public mental health. We are not addressing poverty, oppression, inequality or trauma, we are simply naming distress with new medical labels, and then individualising it into the brains of the people.

This needs urgent reform. We must adopt a truly social model (looking at context, environment and social causes of distress) and a trauma-informed approach which rejects pathologisation and psychiatric diagnosis and theorises that trauma and distress is a normal, natural response to circumstances and experiences. We cannot continue to turn every negative emotion or behaviour into a medical disorder with a corresponding pill to take.

People must be allowed to feel emotions, recognise them, talk about them, process them, understand them and work through them. We cannot keep anaesthetising the general public, and then wondering what is going wrong. Statistically, our populations are filled with millions of traumatised humans, and none of them are being listened to or protected.

This change will require overhauling entire systems including health services, criminal justice services, prisons, governments, media and education. This is possible, as psychiatry has already proven.

We can shift the theories and narratives, and we can adopt humanistic, trauma-informed ways of supporting humans without pathologisation. As women and girls are the primary victims of these forms of oppression, they are likely to benefit from this shift immediately and immeasurably.

5. Challenge the misuse of ACEs

Across multiple countries in the world, there has been a growing interest in the concept of ACEs (Adverse Childhood Experiences), as discussed in Chapter 4. It is not a framework or theory as such, because it has been borrowed (stolen) from the original authors who recently published an article in a top medical journal to attempt to stop people from misusing their questionnaire (Anda et al., 2020).

Simply put, the ACEs questionnaire was a basic set of ten questions of possible adverse experiences that adults may have been subjected to when they were children. The questionnaire misses hundreds of possibilities such as bullying, poverty, racism, illness, homelessness, emigration, refugee status, drug and alcohol use and so on.

It has been used in social work practice, psychology, education, policing and health services. It is now considered to be a trauma-informed practice in which you can score yourself out of ten, give yourself an ACE score and then predict your chances of serious life events, illnesses and behaviours. This is not accurate, has never been proven and constitutes a gross misuse of the questionnaire, which has already been used to place unborn babies of abused women on risk registers, to refuse life and health insurance and to stop abused children seeking support.

To move forward, professionals must abandon the ACEs framework, and listen to the original authors, whose work has been misused and misappropriated.

Instead of ACEs, professionals and institutions can adopt specialist trauma-informed working, and focus on the human they are supporting instead of attempting to categorise and score their trauma out of ten. The ACEs framework has misled millions of people already, and whilst it might have some merit in considering population level statistical patterns and distributions, it has no place in individual practice, risk assessments, referral processes, predicting outcomes or therapeutic support.

Whilst this may come as a shock to governments and organisations who have bought into dodgy training, frameworks and programmes, it's time to bin ACEs before we all end up walking around with our 'score' being used for everything.

6. Retrain professionals

This is a simple one.

Change of this magnitude will require significant retraining of all professionals from nurses to judges. Professionals need to understand that the psychiatric diagnosis of women and girls seriously harms them, and prejudices them for the rest of their lives. They need to be taught different, safer ways of working with traumatised and distressed women and girls which do not involve medicating or sedating them.

This will take time, and will need to be regulated and controlled to ensure that the same issue that has occurred with ACEs, does not reoccur with trauma-informed approaches to mental health. It is of vital importance that this alternative, opposing approach to the medical model is not swallowed up, or watered down by dominant medical model institutions or professionals.

Trauma-informed approaches and theories should remain outside of the medical model, and never seek to medicalise, diagnose or medicate those we work to support.

In retraining professionals at every level, we also need to ensure that their workplaces and working environments become trauma-informed, too. There is no use trying to embed a trauma-informed approach into client-facing work when the staff team are burned out, traumatised and distressed by the work they do every day.

Similarly, there is no way to claim a trauma-informed working environment if professionals are discouraged or punished for talking about their own traumas, vicarious distress and personal connections to the work they are doing.

This means that every HR department in the world will need to consider retraining their officers and managers from a trauma-informed, anti-pathologising perspective which ensures their staff members are not disciplined or discriminated against for being distressed or traumatised.

7. Change the language and narratives being given to the general public

One of the most powerful ways that psychiatry became mainstream was by writers, philosophers, publishers, charities, governments, celebrities and media giving thousands of incorrect and misleading messages about mental health, trauma, disorders, medication and treatments across several decades.

We now need to collectively retract and correct these messages, and launch humanistic, compassionate and trauma-informed messages to the millions of people who have been told that they have a mental disorder.

This again is probably going to take a long time; however, with the power of modern social media, this should be a quicker process than the one which caused the medical model to become so dominant. Social media means we have the power to reach millions of people in minutes, and if these messages come from powerful companies, influential people and leaders of countries and institutions, we can make serious change very quickly.

8. Challenge and disrupt misogyny

Probably the hardest challenge on this list, misogyny is the root cause of this issue, and is the consistent thread which runs throughout every chapter, every sentence and every issue I have written about in this book. The hatred for women is palpable – psychiatry merely provided a legitimate medical vehicle for it.

Misogyny is one of the last forms of oppression to receive any acknowledgement. When women talk about it, they are positioned as crazy, hysterical, overexaggerating feminists and, therefore, misogyny is able to continue unending. I regularly consult with police forces, the NHS, local authorities and private companies that have leaders or directors who say they have a misogyny problem, but nine times out of ten, they cannot get their decision makers, budget holders or boards to acknowledge or believe that misogyny exists. In 2020, I met with several national institution leaders who all wanted to address the blatant misogyny in their services, and only one of them managed to convince their board and secure funding in order to address it. In the rest of the cases, they were blocked by seniors who told them either that misogyny didn't exist, or that addressing the way women were being treated on their caseloads or in their workplaces was 'unfair to men'.

There need to be strategic, systemic, global approaches to addressing misogyny, which impacts and harms 51 per cent of the global population.

The main issue with tackling misogyny is that it requires the other 49 per cent of the population to acknowledge that it exists, and the reason why it exists is because women are positioned, portrayed and believed to be inferior to men. And as many other feminists and scholars have said before me, when people have been accustomed to privilege, equality feels like oppression. Arguably, addressing misogyny on any level appears to make many men very uncomfortable. Despite this inevitable opposition, this change is imperative.

Whilst misogyny continues to be supported, psychiatry and the pathologisation of women and girls will remain legitimised.

9. Remove funding from pharmaceutical companies and invest in accessible and free trauma therapy

Pharmaceutical companies profit billions of dollars per year through inventing, repurposing, marketing, making and selling psychotropic drugs which are now prescribed to millions of adults in the UK alone.

Globally, hundreds of millions of people are taking antipsychotics, antidepressants and sedative drugs to 'manage' their diagnoses.

This is clear evidence that there is a substantial budget available for tackling distress, trauma and emotional harm.

This could be used to create free trauma-informed services – and free trauma centres where people who felt suicidal or in crisis could go and seek help without the fear of being sectioned, diagnosed, medicated or sedated. The money is there.

I am no longer accepting the excuse that there is no funding for trauma therapies, trauma support and information for people who need it. The funding exists, it's just being spent incorrectly.

10. Ban the use of ECT and psychiatric euthanasia for everyone, and provide compensation for everyone harmed by psychiatric drugs

The use of ECT is dangerous, archaic and based on misinformation about its efficacy and risks. Most people in the UK are not even aware that it is used on over 2,500 people per year to treat 'mental disorders'. In the majority of cases, statistics show that people are given ECT against their will, and without informed consent. There is no place for this treatment in a trauma-informed future. No human requires electric shocks to the brain until they have a series of convulsions as a 'treatment' for depression.

Further, whilst it is still only confined to a handful of countries, we must stop the use of psychiatric euthanasia and the concept of humans being beyond help with no prospect of improvement. Death cannot possibly be considered a treatment for human distress, and professionals who have been unanimously agreeing and then sanctioning the deaths of young women and girls who have been raped and abused should be subjected to investigation and suitable action.

There is no evidence to prove that their mental health was so damaged and irreversible that they would be better off dead. This is a gross and tragic use of medical and psychiatric diagnosis.

Whilst voluntary euthanasia might be suitable for some people with painful, debilitating diseases and medical conditions, these have long and sophisticated evidence bases, clear tests and result protocols which mean that they can be identified, proven, monitored and managed.

The same cannot be said for psychiatric disorders, for most of which there is significant debate as to whether they even exist, and there are no tests, scans or investigations which can prove their presence, or their treatment.

On that basis, and because of the cultural, historical and contextual positioning of mental disorders which changes regularly, there should not be such final and irreversible 'treatments'. Death is not a legitimate medical treatment for, or solution to, trauma and distress.

Divorcing feminism from psychiatry

I cannot emphasise how important this point is. Feminism must reject psychiatry. Totally.

I hope to have successfully demonstrated in this book that psychiatry is no ally to feminism, women's rights, women's liberation or empowerment. The diagnosis of women and girls as mentally disordered is not empowering, and has instead contributed to the torture, control, gaslighting, injustice and deaths of women and girls for centuries. It is pivotal that feminists from every approach and wave understand the systemic and institutional power psychiatry has had over women and girls of every background, culture, sexuality and ethnicity for as long as it has been a discipline.

Psychiatry is the patriarchy with a prescription pad and a pen full of ink.

The father of pathologisation.

Psychiatry has aimed and succeeded to control women for so long, that no one even notices anymore. Women have bought into it and trust it. We must shake ourselves awake, immediately, and protect women and girls from psychiatric diagnosis.

This system of gaslighting has been built on the belief that women are defective, evil, psychotic, inferior baby-making machines who should submit to their husbands and nothing more. Whether the feminism is radical, liberal, intersectional or otherwise – psychiatry must be rejected in order for women to be protected and liberated.

Feminism is not compatible with psychiatric diagnosis of any kind.

In the same vein, we must educate and raise awareness of the ways psychiatric language and insults harm women and girls and excuse offenders of male violence and misogyny. I have witnessed the rise in psychiatric terms being used by women and towards women to discredit or harm. This must end.

Calling each other 'narcissistic', 'hysterical', 'borderline', 'histrionic', 'unstable', 'mental', 'crazy' and 'bipolar' is playing right into the hands of the patriarchy and the psychiatric tradition. Accusing women you dislike of having personality disorders is of the same approach – we must eradicate psychiatric language in feminism, so we can protect women and girls from normalising and demonising women's trauma.

The same can be said about abusers and perpetrators of male violence – but for a different reason. I have seen more and more feminist writing which seeks to position violent offenders, abusers and misogynists as having personality disorders, being 'narcissistic', 'psychopaths' or 'sociopaths'. This is an own goal. We must not engage in any kind of psychiatric diagnosis of the oppressors.

They are not mentally ill, they are making an active choice to harm women and girls. Rapists, traffickers, exploiters, abusers, stalkers and harassers are not suffering from a mental disorder which requires treatment and therapy, they are grown adult men making active decisions based on their own motivations and desires to harm and kill women and girls.

We must see a new wave of feminism and women's rights movements which proudly reject the diagnosis of women and girls as mentally disordered liars and exaggerators.

Trauma-informed feminism must begin today.

I propose the development of feminism which builds on radical approaches, and the evidence and arguments I have set out in this book. A form of feminism which rejects psychiatry, stops colluding with the oppression of women and girls, refuses to use mental health and trauma as a slur, and seeks to deconstruct patriarchy in mental health and medicine. This will be my life's mission.

Introducing independent advocates in mental health and psychiatry

I also want to propose a way of protecting people whilst these long-term challenges, investigations and changes are under way: Independent Trauma-Informed Advocates.

This is an idea I have had for some time. Women and girls write to me and ask for help, representation and support when trying to challenge psychiatric diagnosis, mistreatment, discrimination and dismissal of them in different settings across the world. They need lawyers, of course, but they could also benefit from having a recognised independent advocate who was able to hold professionals to account.

Imagine a national team of independent trauma-informed advocates who could attend appointments, review cases, review psychiatric records and decision making, and advocate for women and girls who had been pathologised and harmed. Imagine women having someone with them at appointments where they are being told that they are mentally ill, delusional or exaggerating their abuse and trauma. Imagine having a trained, independent advocate who can intervene in the treatment of a woman who is having her medication increased, or is being blackmailed into accepting diagnoses and treatments she doesn't want.

Imagine having the:

- ◆ Right to have an Independent Trauma-Informed Advocate
- ◆ Right to the review of your psychiatric records and treatments by an independent specialist
- ◆ Right to withdraw from medication at any time, with adequate support and advice
- ◆ Right to refuse a psychiatric diagnosis
- ◆ Right to have your previous psychiatric diagnoses removed
- ◆ Right to have erroneous and discriminatory information removed from your records
- ◆ Right to check whether your mental health appears on any other records
- ◆ Right to have an advocate present for scrutiny and representation

I have thought about this a lot for the past couple of years. Women and girls are attending appointments in which their traumas are not being recorded. Their concerns are being selectively ignored. Their requests to stop taking medication are being ignored. They are being given incorrect information and medication. They are being threatened or coerced into taking medication and treatments that are not in their best interests.

Why not introduce an independent advocate scheme?

This is something I would endorse and work hard to achieve, especially as overhauling pathologising systems is going to take decades. There needs to be something of a protective buffer for women and girls until significant changes are made.

Conclusion

Writing this book has been one of the most important, exhausting, and heartbreaking experiences of my life so far. I am immensely privileged to have spoken, and written, to so many women who have been subjected to life-changing harm by psychiatric narratives, diagnosis and treatments. I would like to take this opportunity to thank them all, once again. Many of them chose to use pseudonyms, but they each know who they are and were able to read this book before it was published. They also gave me feedback on their sections and my use of their experiences before it was finalised.

To each and every one of you, thank you so much for trusting me to tell your stories and to push for change for thousands of other women who cannot speak or tell their stories.

Women have been pathologised since Eve, and I hope that I have gone some way towards demonstrating the tragic path this journey has taken, through the control of women, the witch trials, the religious oppression of women, the framing of us all as evil, hysterical, defective versions of men, towards mentally unstable, borderline, psychotic sex objects for men to fuck and then discredit as mentally ill.

We are framed like this, so we do not realise our true power.

We do not exist in this world to be sexy but psycho. Hot but crazy. Cute but borderline.

No longer will we be defined and diagnosed by men who seek to harm and control us. No longer will we accept our traumas and mental health being used against us, and to prevent us seeking justice.

Women and girls, take a deep breath and take your first step towards breaking free from the centuries of bullshit psychiatric diagnoses and psychotropic pills you have been fed, and prepare to dig deep.

What is hurting you? What did someone do to you? What is scaring you? What is enraging you? What is making you feel trapped? Who is oppressing you? What are you trying to cope with? What are you responding to? What is overwhelming you? Who made you feel guilty? Shamed? Blamed?

It's not in your head, I promise.

Know thyself.

Final thoughts

I started this book by telling you a story about my own experiences of swerving pathologisation more than once. I still look back on those experiences as near misses.

That's all they were, you know, near misses.

I am not stronger than you. I am not more 'resilient'. I am not special or different in some way. I simply avoided a system that would no doubt have taught me that I was a problem. I avoided medication and diagnosis. I kept away from systems that I knew would harm me.

I wonder where I would be today, if I had believed that I was mentally ill and disordered?

I wonder if I would have even thought I was capable of writing books and changing the world if I had believed the police that day? Or if the academics were successful in having me thrown off my PhD programme?

I wonder if I would have just eventually started to believe that I was damaged for life?

What I have learned is that pretty much everyone I know hits enough criteria for several psychiatric diagnoses at once, including myself.

There have been plenty of times when I've questioned myself, doubted myself, and wondered if I am 'normal'.

There have been times when I have asked myself if my journey through my trauma is normal, healthy and progressive. I've wondered if my health issues are related. I've wondered if my thoughts are normal. I've wondered if I would keep reprocessing the same events over and over again. I've worked through traumatic flashbacks, terrifying nightmares and debilitating phobias.

I spent years learning that I was actually completely normal. I was rational. I was experiencing common trauma responses. I learned about my coping mechanisms. I started to understand my brain and body.

It is possible to do all of this without medication, or psychiatric diagnosis.

Whenever someone challenges me about the necessity of medication and psychiatric intervention, I always think about the years I have spent working in rape centres, victim support services and with child trafficking victims. In all of those services, there were volunteer and paid therapists, support workers and group facilitators, but there were no doctors, no nurses, no psychiatrists and no medication. None of us could prescribe anything other than compassion, time, love, patience, respect and space.

If none of us could provide a medical intervention, why did all of our clients make such immense progress? How were we able to talk someone down from suicide? How were we able to talk a woman through her nightmares, disassociation and panic attacks? Why did we all have the skill to keep someone grounded whilst they recalled the times they were raped?

We weren't miracle workers. We weren't mind readers. We weren't healers.

We were a group of average people who had given up our time, and learned to help people process their traumas with nothing more than our body language, commitment and voices. We saw incredible changes in our clients. We restored their self-belief and confidence. We worked with them on their self-blame, shame and guilt. We were there whilst they raged, cried and swore. We were there whilst they told us that they didn't want to live anymore.

What if, instead of seeing these skills as soft, hippy, nice things to do, these skills became front and centre of everything we do?

Isn't the fact that hundreds of women's centres are capable of successfully supporting women and girls with multiple traumas without any psychiatric input, proof that it is not required?

It never ceases to amaze me how much of women's work, research and activism is dismissed and ignored as too basic, or not scientific enough to qualify as a real solution. And yet, every woman I have ever worked with or spoken to has needed broadly the same thing: to be listened to, to be believed, to be supported, to be protected from harm and to be helped in practical difficulties.

I want to finish this book by talking about how a trauma-informed approach to women and girls could change the way we work forever. A system has been in place for hundreds of years that has sought to control, medicate, torture, gaslight and abuse women and girls – but we are now in a position to change this.

You can finish reading this book and feel utterly exhausted by the evidence I have laid out, or you can finish reading this book and feel angry and empowered to make a change that could protect yourself, women you love – and even thousands of women and girls in our communities.

Just like I have done, you can use your voice, your knowledge, influence, power and compassion to support women and girls without suggesting they are mentally ill or disordered.

We can build organisations, relationships, systems and responses that deliberately oppose psychiatric diagnosis and pathologisation. They are possible. Just this week, I have met with three large national services who have asked me to help them to rebuild their mental health services to be trauma-informed, and anti-pathologising. Systemic change is possible, and it's exciting.

I am just one voice, but imagine if thousands of us, or millions of us, were all saying the same thing:

> *We've had enough. Women are not crazy, hysterical, borderline, bipolar, psychotic or depressed – they've just had enough of your misogynistic shit.*

We can help women to taper off dangerous drugs. We can protect their bodies and minds from drugs that have never even been tested on female bodies.

We can listen to women when they tell us they are being harmed and abused. We can advocate for them, and stand up for them. We can centre their voices and we can help them to demand change.

Take my book, and cause a revolution with me.

A revolution in your home, your mind, your workplace, your university, your community or your government. Reject the medical model of mental health for its blatant brand of woman-hating. Embrace true compassion for traumatised women and girls who do not need more pills, and more labels. Create support groups. Book clubs. Consciousness-raising sessions.

Go and talk to your friends, partners, colleagues, family members and children about their emotions, their fears, their dreams, their experiences and their traumas. Stop hiding from the complexity of human trauma.

Stop saying you're okay when you're not. Stop asking people how they are and then hoping they don't answer you in any detail.

We will only get one real shot at transforming our world into a trauma-informed, ethical, safe, anti-oppressive, anti-pathologising place to live. If we fail, we will surely see the continuation of what we have now: a sophisticated system of harmful beliefs, narratives, interventions, treatments and medications that position women and girls as damaged and mentally ill.

I say we only get one real shot at this, because the medical model and the vast industry which sits behind it have become exceptionally talented at pulling alternative and opposing models under their own umbrella, to pretend they're making progress and kill off any competition. We must do everything we can to resist this, because it will happen.

I truly believe we can do this.

We are 51 per cent of the population on this rock, and it's about time we were respected and treated like it.

Now, take this book, and share it with another woman who needs to read it. Talk about it. Post about it. Write about it. Teach about it. Think about it.

We don't need to wait for psychiatry and the mental health movement to change, modernise or correct their misogyny. We don't need to ask them to reform, or work within them.

We can simply leave them in the dust, and move forward without them. Radical change means dismantling oppressive systems, not trying to work within them.

End the pathologisation of women and girls, and step forward into a trauma-informed, compassionate, ethical world.

References

ADAA (2019) https://adaa.org/living-with-anxiety/women/facts

APA (2007) Report of the APA Task Force on the Sexualization of Girls, American Psychological Association https://www.apa.org/pi/women/programs/girls/report-full.pdf

APA (2021) What is gender dysphoria? https://www.psychiatry.org/patients-families/gender-dysphoria/what-is-gender-dysphoria

All Party Parliamentary Group on Endometriosis (2020) Endometriosis in the UK: time for change. Retrieved from https://www.endometriosis-uk.org/sites/endometriosis-uk.org/files/files/Endometriosis%20APPG%20Report%20Oct%202020.pdf

Anda, R., Porter, L. & Brown, D. (2020) 'Inside the Adverse Childhood Experience Score: Strengths, Limitations, and Misapplications', *American Journal of Preventative Medicine*, Volume 59, Issue 2, p293-295

Bentall, R. (2013) *Doctoring the mind: Why psychiatric treatments fail*, Penguin, UK

Blanchard, A., Dunn, T. & Sumich, A. (2020) 'Testing the "Hot Crazy Matrix": Borderline personality traits in attractive women and wealthy low attractive men are relatively favoured by the opposite sex'. *Personality and Individual Differences*. 169. 109964. 10.1016/j.paid.2020.109964.

BBC (2018) 'Everybody was telling me there was nothing wrong' The Health Gap, BBC https://www.bbc.com/future/article/20180523-how-gender-bias-affects-your-healthcare

BMA (2021) Sexism in Medicine, British Medical Association

BMJ (2020) Letter to the president of the Royal College of Psychiatrists (370:m2657)

Bowlby, J. (1969) *Attachment and Loss: Volume 1. Attachment*, New York, Basic Books.

Bowlby, J. (1988) *A Secure Base: Parent-Child Attachment and Healthy Human Development*, New York, Basic Books.

Brietbart et al., (1996) 'The undertreatment of pain in ambulatory AIDS patients', *Pain*, 65 (1996) 243-249

Brown, R. & Ward, H. (2013) 'Decision-making within a child's timeframe: An overview of current research evidence for family justice professionals

concerning child development and the impact of maltreatment'. Childhood Well-being Research Centre. Available online at:
https://www.gov.uk/government/uploads/system/uploads/attachment_data/file/200471/ Decision-making_within_a_child_s_timeframe.pdf

Bullock, H. E. (1995) 'Class acts: Middle-class responses to the poor'. In B. Lott & D. Maluso (Eds.), *The Social Psychology of Interpersonal Discrimination* (pp. 118–159). Guilford Press.

Carr, S. & Spandler, H. (2019) 'Hidden from history? A brief modern history of the psychiatric "treatment" of lesbian and bisexual women in England'. *The Lancet Psychiatry*, 6(4), 289–290.

CDC (2020) https://www.cdc.gov/nchs/products/databriefs/db388.htm

Chen, E. H., Shofer, F. S., Dean, A. J., Hollander, J. E., Baxt, W. G., Robey, J. L., Sease, K. L. & Mills, A. M. (2008) 'Gender disparity in analgesic treatment of emergency department patients with acute abdominal pain'. *The Lancet Psychiatry. Academic emergency medicine: official journal of the Society for Academic Emergency Medicine*, 15(5), 414–418. https://doi.org/10.1111/j.1553-2712.2008.00100.x

Cleeland et al., (1994) 'Pain and Its Treatment in Outpatients with Metastatic Cancer', *N Engl J Med* 1994; 330:592-596
DOI: 10.1056/NEJM199403033300902

CWIG (2009) Child Welfare Information Gateway, Child Maltreatment. Children's Bureau.

Davies, J. (2014) *Cracked: Why psychiatry is doing more harm than good*, Icon Books, UK

Davies J. (2017) 'How Voting and Consensus Created the Diagnostic and Statistical Manual of Mental Disorders (DSM-III)'. *Anthropology & Medicine*, 24(1), 32–46. https://doi.org/10.1080/13648470.2016.1226684

De Wit A.E., Booij S.H., Giltay E.J., Joffe H., Schoevers R.A. & Oldehinkel A.J. (2020) 'Association of Use of Oral Contraceptives With Depressive Symptoms Among Adolescents and Young Women'. *JAMA Psychiatry.* 2020;77(1):52–59. doi:10.1001/jamapsychiatry.2019.2838

Deacon B. J. (2013) 'The biomedical model of mental disorder: a critical analysis of its validity, utility, and effects on psychotherapy research'. *Clinical Psychology Review*, 33(7), 846–861. https://doi.org/10.1016/j.cpr.2012.09.007

Demand Chemical Imbalance Retraction (2021) http://demandcir.blogspot.com

DSM-V (2013) *American Psychiatric Association Diagnostic and statistical manual of mental disorders: DSM-5*. 5th edn. Washington, D.C.: American Psychiatric Publishing.

Eaton J. (2019) 'Logically, I know I'm not to blame, but I still feel to blame: Exploring and measuring victim blaming of women subjected to violence and abuse', University of Birmingham

Fairchild, K. & Rudman, L. A. (2008) 'Everyday stranger harassment and women's objectification'. *Social Justice Research*, 21(3), 338–357. https://doi.org/10.1007/s11211-008-0073-0

Felitti, V. J., Anda, R. F., Nordenberg, D., Williamson, D. F., Spitz, A. M., Edwards, V., Koss, M. P. & Marks, J. S. (1998) 'Relationship of childhood abuse and household dysfunction to many of the leading causes of death in adults. The Adverse Childhood Experiences (ACE) Study'. *American Journal of Preventive Medicine*, 14(4), 245–258. https://doi.org/10.1016/s0749-3797(98)00017-8

Fertility and Sterility, (2020) Vercellini, P., Buggio, L., Somigliana, E., Barbara, G., Viganò, P. & Fedele, L. (2013). RETRACTED: 'Attractiveness of women with rectovaginal endometriosis: a case-control study'. *Fertility And Sterility*, 99(1), 212-218. doi: 10.1016/j.fertnstert.2012.08.039

Fredrickson, B. L. & Roberts, T.A. (1997) 'Objectification Theory: Toward Understanding Women's Lived Experiences and Mental Health Risks'. *Psychology of Women Quarterly*, 21(2), 173–206. https://doi.org/10.1111/j.1471-6402.1997.tb00108.x

Freud, S. (1913) 'The claims of psycho-analysis to scientific interest' *S.E.* 13 165–190

Garcia, L. (1998) 'Perceptions of Resistance to Unwanted Sexual Advances', *Journal of Psychology & Human Sexuality*, 10:1, 43-52, DOI: 10.1300/J056v10n01_03

Gottlieb A. (2020) 'Menstrual Taboos: Moving Beyond the Curse'. In: Bobel C., Winkler I.T., Fahs B., Hasson K.A., Kissling E.A., Roberts T.A. (eds) *The Palgrave Handbook of Critical Menstruation Studies*, Palgrave Macmillan, Singapore. https://doi.org/10.1007/978-981-15-0614-7_14

Guardian (2019) Revealed: Pill still most popular prescribed contraceptive in UK https://www.theguardian.com/uk-news/2019/mar/07/revealed-pill-still-most-popular-prescribed-contraceptive-in-england

Guardian (2020) Denial of women's concerns contributed to decades of medical scandal, *Guardian*, https://www.theguardian.com/society/2020/jul/08/denial-of-womens-concerns-contributed-to-medical-scandals-says-inquiry

Gunderson, J. G., Stout, R. L., McGlashan, T. H., Shea, M. T., Morey, L. C., Grilo, C. M., Zanarini, M. C., Yen, S., Markowitz, J. C., Sanislow, C., Ansell, E., Pinto, A. & Skodol, A. E. (2011) 'Ten-year course of borderline personality disorder: psychopathology and function from the Collaborative Longitudinal Personality Disorders study'. *Archives of General Psychiatry*, 68(8), 827–837. https://doi.org/10.1001/archgenpsychiatry.2011.37

Hämmerli, S., Kohl Schwartz, A. S., Geraedts, K., Imesch, P., Rauchfuss, M., Wölfler, M. M., Haeberlin, F. von Orelli, S., Eberhard, M., Imthurn, B. & Leeners, B. (2018) 'Does Endometriosis Affect Sexual Activity and Satisfaction of the Man Partner? A Comparison of Partners From Women Diagnosed With Endometriosis and Controls', *The Journal of Sexual Medicine*, 15(6), 853–865. https://doi.org/10.1016/j.jsxm.2018.03.087

Harrison, J. N., Cluxton-Keller, F. & Gross, D. (2012) 'Antipsychotic medication prescribing trends in children and adolescents'. *Journal of Pediatric Health Care: official publication of National Association of Pediatric Nurse Associates & Practitioners*, 26(2), 139–145. https://doi.org/10.1016/j.pedhc.2011.10.009

Harrop, C., Read, J., Geekie, J. & Renton, J. (2021) 'How Accurate are ECT Patient Information Leaflets Provided by Mental Health Services in England and the Royal College of Psychiatrists? An Independent Audit'. *Ethical Human Psychology and Psychiatry*. https://doi.org/10.1891/EHPP-D-21-00003

Hoffmann, Diane E. & Tarzian, Anita J. (2001) 'The Girl Who Cried Pain: A Bias Against Women in the Treatment of Pain'. Available at SSRN: https://ssrn.com/abstract=383803 or http://dx.doi.org/10.2139/ssrn.383803

Holland, J. (2006) *A Brief History of Misogyny: The World's Oldest Prejudice*

Howard et al. (2013) 'Domestic Violence and Perinatal Mental Disorders: A Systematic Review and Meta-Analysis', *PLOS Medicine*, https://doi.org/10.1371/journal.pmed.1001452

Jackson, G. (2015) *Pain and Prejudice: A call to arms for women and their bodies*, Piatkus

Jenell Johnson (2014) *American Lobotomy: A Rhetorical History*, University of Michigan Press

Khan et al. (2018) 'Differences in management and outcomes for men and women with ST-elevation myocardial infarction', *Med J Aust* 2018; 209 (3): 118-123. || doi: 10.5694/mja17.01109

Kunkel, Dale, Farrar, Kirstie & Biely, Erica. (1999) 'Sexual messages on television: Comparing findings from three studies', *Journal of Sex Research* – J SEX RES. 36. 230-236. 10.1080/00224499909551993.

Lancet (2016) 'Sex and gender differences in mental disorder', VOLUME 4, ISSUE 1, P8-9

Le Bon, G. (1895) *Crowd Behaviour*

Lister, K. (2014) 'The Victorian Period: Menstrual Madness in the Nineteenth Century'. In F. A. Papps (Ed.), '*And Then the Monsters Come Out': Madness, Language and Power* (pp. 74-86), [8] Inter-Disciplinary Press.

Long, J. (2012) *Anti-porn: The Resurgence of Anti-pornography Feminism*, Zed Books, London

Loughnan, S., Pina, A., Vasquez, E. & Puvia, E. (2013) 'Sexual Objectification Increases Rape Victim Blame and Decreases Perceived Suffering', *Psychology of Women Quarterly* DOI: 10.1177/0361684313485718

Main, M., & Solomon, J. (1986) 'Discovery of an insecure-disorganized/disoriented attachment pattern'. In T. B. Brazelton & M. W. Yogman (Eds.), *Affective Development in Infancy* (pp. 95–124). Ablex Publishing.

NCBI (2021) Diagnostic criteria for premenstrual dysphoric disorder https://www.ncbi.nlm.nih.gov/books/NBK279045/table/premenstrual-syndrom.table1diag/

MGH (2015) Postpartum Psychiatric Disorders – MGH Center for Women's

Mental Health. (2015). Retrieved 18 September 2021, from https://womensmentalhealth.org/specialty-clinics/postpartum-psychiatric-disorders/

MGH (2021) Psychiatric disorders during pregnancy: Weighing the risks and benefits of pharmacological treatment during pregnancy. Retrieved from https://womensmentalhealth.org/specialty-clinics/psychiatric-disorders-during-pregnancy/

Mind (2021) https://www.mind.org.uk/information-support/types-of-mental-health-problems/statistics-and-facts-about-mental-health/how-common-are-mental-health-problems/

Moller, A., Sondergaard, H.P., Helstrom L. (2017) 'Tonic immobility during sexual assault – a common reaction predicting post-traumatic stress disorder and severe depression', *Acta Obstet Gynecol Scand* 2017; DOI: 10.1111/aogs.13174

Moncrieff J, Cohen D (2006) 'Do Antidepressants Cure or Create Abnormal Brain States?' *PLoS Med* 3(7): e240. https://doi.org/10.1371/journal.pmed.0030240

Moshman D. (2013) 'Adolescent rationality', *Advances in Child Development and Behavior*, 45, 155–183. https://doi.org/10.1016/b978-0-12-397946-9.00007-5

Moulin et al. (2014) *Baby Bonds: Parenting, Attachment, and a Secure Base for Children*, University of Bristol

Pew Research Centre (2015) Future of World Religions: Population Growth Projections, 2010-2050. Retrieved 11 August 2021, from https://www.pewforum.org/2015/04/02/religious-projections-2010-2050/

Read J, Cunliffe S, Jauhar S, McLoughlin D M. (2019) 'Should we stop using electroconvulsive therapy?' *BMJ* 2019; 364 :k5233 doi:10.1136/bmj.k5233

Read, J. & Dillon, J. (2014) *Models of Madness: Psychological, Social and Biological Approaches to Psychosis*, 2nd (revised) edition. ISPS series Published by Routledge, Hove, UK

Reich, D. B., & Zanarini, M. C. (2008) 'Sexual orientation and relationship choice in borderline personality disorder over ten years of prospective follow-up', *Journal of Personality Disorders*, 22(6), 564–572. https://doi.org/10.1521/pedi.2008.22.6.564

Robertson, J. (2014) *Waiting Time at the Emergency Department from a Gender Equality Perspective*, Institute of Medicine at the Sahlgrenska Academy University of Gothenburg

Romer D (2010) 'Adolescent Risk Taking, Impulsivity, and Brain Development: Implications for Prevention', *Developmental Psychobiology*, 52(3), 263–276.

Salter, M. (2012) 'The Role of Ritual in the Organised Abuse of Children', *Child Abuse Review* https://doi.org/10.1002/car.2215

Schooler, D., Ward, L. M., Merriwether, A., & Caruthers, A. S. (2005) 'Cycles of Shame: Menstrual Shame, Body Shame, and Sexual Decision-Making', *The Journal of Sex Research*, 42(4), 324–334. http://www.jstor.org/stable/3813785

Segrest, M. (2020) *Administrations of Lunacy: Racism and the Haunting of American Psychiatry at the Milledgeville Asylum*, New Press

Sollée, K. (2017) *Witches, Sluts, Feminists*, ThreeL Media

Somasundaram, O. (1985) 'The Malleus Malifcarium and the psychopathology of sex', *Indian Journal of Psychiatry*

Stetka & Watson, (2016) 'Odd and outlandish psychiatric treatments through history', *Medscape*, https://www.medscape.com/features/slideshow/odd-psychiatric-treatments

Strange, J. (2000) 'Menstrual fictions: languages of medicine and menstruation, c. 1850–1930', *Women's History Review*, 9:3, 607-628, DOI: 10.1080/09612020000200260

Taylor, J. (2020) *Why Women are Blamed for Everything: Exposing victim blaming*, Little Brown, Hachette, UK

Taylor, D., Barnes, T. & Young, A. (2018) *The Maudsley: Prescribing Guidelines in Psychiatry* 13th Edition, Wiley Blackwell

Timimi, S. (2021) Insane Medicine: How the Mental Health Industry Creates Damaging Treatment Traps and How you can Escape Them

Timoclea, R. (2020) *'Demonic Little Mini-skirted Machiavelli': Expert conceptualisations of complex post traumatic stress disorder (CPTSD) and borderline personality disorder (BPD) in female forensic populations*, VictimFocus, UK

UCSF, (2021) Domestic violence and pregnancy, University California San Francisco, https://www.ucsfhealth.org/education/domestic-violence-and-pregnancy

Ullman, S. (2010) *Talking About Sexual Assault: Society's response to survivors*, American Psychological Association

Umeh (2019) *Mental Illness in Black Community 1700-2019: A short history*, Black Past, https://www.blackpast.org/african-american-history/mental-illness-in-black-community-1700-2019-a-short-history/

Ussher, J. (2013). 'Diagnosing difficult women and pathologising femininity: Gender bias in psychiatric nosology', *Feminism & Psychology*, 23(1), 63-69. doi: 10.1177/0959353512467968

Vercellini, P., Buggio, L., Somigliana, E., Barbara, G., Viganò, P., & Fedele, L. (2013). RETRACTED: 'Attractiveness of women with rectovaginal endometriosis: a case-control study', *Fertility And Sterility*, 99(1), 212-218. doi: 10.1016/j.fertnstert.2012.08.039

Woods, T.A., Kurtz-Costes, B. & Rowley, S.J. 'The Development of Stereotypes About the Rich and Poor: Age, Race, and Family Income Differences in Beliefs', J *Youth Adolescence* 34, 437–445 (2005). https://doi.org/10.1007/s10964-005-7261-0

WHO, (2021) Gender and women's health, https://www.who.int/teams/mental-health-and-substance-use/promotion-prevention/gender-and-women-s-mental-health

Index